A Teaching Assistant's Guide to Completing NVQ Level 2

Based on the updated National Occupational Standards for Supporting Teaching and Learning in Schools, this new edition of *A Teaching Assistant's Guide to Completing NVQ Level 2* caters directly to the criteria of the course, providing the necessary 'Knowledge and Understanding' required as well as invaluable information regarding evidence collection.

Incorporating the changed guidelines regarding evidence collection, this comprehensive guide demonstrates the role of the assessor in observing and questioning the candidate and that of the candidate asking colleagues to provide witness statements.

As well as providing in-depth underpinning knowledge for all mandatory units and a vast array of optional units, this book offers a range of tried-and-tested materials and practical advice for NVQ Level 2 candidates. The authors have included numerous self-assessment activities, case studies and quizzes to enable candidates to check their understanding of key concepts, to make connections from theory to practice and to assist them in their observation and assessment sessions.

Written in an engaging and approachable manner and illustrated with many cartoons, this book aims to give the candidate the knowledge necessary to embark on this qualification with confidence.

A wide range of chapters provides essential advice for NVQ Level 2 candidates, including how to:

- support children's development;
- provide effective support for colleagues;
- observe and report on pupil performance;
- provide support for learning activities;
- support a child with disabilities or special educational needs.

Highly practical and rooted in everyday classroom practice, this book is specifically aimed at teaching assistants enrolled on, or embarking upon, NVQ courses that support the government's National Occupational Standards. In addition, this book will be of benefit to schools and teachers who are supporting teaching assistants taking this course.

Susan Bentham is a Senior Lecturer in the School of Education at the University of Chichester.

Roger Hutchins is a Special Educational Needs Co-ordinator in two primary schools in Portsmouth.

A Teaching Assistant's Guide to Completing NVQ Level 2

Supporting teaching and learning
in schools

Second edition

Susan Bentham and Roger Hutchins

Routledge
Taylor & Francis Group

LONDON AND NEW YORK

First edition published 2007
Second edition published 2010
by Routledge
2 Park Square, Milton Park, Abingdon, Oxon OX14 4RN

Simultaneously published in the USA and Canada
by Routledge
270 Madison Avenue, New York, NY 10016

Routledge is an imprint of the Taylor & Francis Group, an informa business

Typeset in Sabon and Gill Sans by
Florence Production Ltd, Stoodleigh, Devon
Printed and bound in Great Britain by
TJ International Ltd, Padstow, Cornwall

British Library Cataloguing in Publication Data
A catalogue record for this book is available from the British Library

Library of Congress Cataloging-in-Publication Data
Bentham, Susan, 1958–
   A teaching assistant's guide to completing NVQ level 2: supporting, teaching
   and learning in schools/Susan Bentham and Roger Hutchins. – 2nd ed.
        p. cm.
      Includes bibliographical references and index.
   1. Teachers' assistants – Vocational guidance – Great Britain.   2. National Vocational
   Qualifications (Great Britain)   I. Hutchins, Roger, 1953–   II. Title.
   LB2844.1.A8B455 2010
   371.14'124–dc22   2009017573

ISBN 10: 0–415–49017–0 (hbk)
ISBN 10: 0–415–49018–9 (pbk)
ISBN 10: 0–203–86756–4 (ebk)

ISBN 13: 978–0–415–49017–7 (hbk)
ISBN 13: 978–0–415–49018–4 (pbk)
ISBN 13: 978–0–203–86756–3 (ebk)

Contents

Figures

Tables

Acknowledgements

Susan Bentham says: 'Thank you' to Michael and Bobby, colleagues, especially Jackie and to my many students for their support and a very special thank you to my son, Matthew – for his great artwork.

Roger Hutchins says: 'Thank you' to Anne and to the staff at both schools for their continuing support, hard work and dedication.

Glossary

Active learning/active learners   The process when learners take responsibility for their learning and are given the opportunity to participate and be actively engaged in their own learning.

Active listening   Communicating to the person we are talking with that we have indeed heard and understood them, accomplished by techniques such as rewording and reflecting.

Amanuensis   A person who scribes for another who dictates both the text and the punctuation, e.g. 'capital letter, full stop, new paragraph'.

Annual reviews   Legal reviews to be held at least once a year for pupils who have a statement of special educational need.

Asperger's Syndrome (AS)   A disability affecting social communication, building and maintaining friendships and giving expression to imaginative ideas.

Assessment for Learning (AfL)   Assessment *for* Learning (formative assessment) as opposed to assessment *of* learning (summative assessment) has been defined as: 'the process of seeking and interpreting evidence for use by learners and their teachers to decide where the learners are in their learning, where they need to go and how best to get there.' (Assessment Reform Group (ARG) 2002)

Assessment (formative)   Ongoing, continuous assessment that measures progress in small stages and informs planning for future teaching.

Assessment (summative)   Testing (either formal or informal) that assesses how much pupils have learned in a particular subject or over a specific time period.

Attainment levels/targets – see National Curriculum.

Attention Deficit (Hyperactivity) Disorder (ADD/ADHD)   A medical diagnosis that describes a range of emotional and/or behavioural difficulties, such as extreme impulsivity, inattentiveness and continuous activity.

Auditory learners – see Learning styles.

Autism/Autistic Spectrum Conditions (ASC)   A disability severely impairing a person's ability to maintain normal contact with the world; appears before the age of 3.

Board of Governors   A body of volunteers who have the legal responsibility of ensuring that the school is following correct national and local procedures; governors act as 'critical friends' to schools.

Children in Care (Looked After Children)   All children and young people who are on Care Orders or who are accommodated under The Children Act (1989) or who are remanded into the care of the local authority.

Common Assessment Framework (CAF) The CAF is an essential part of *Every Child Matters*. It is a means whereby all children's services assess the needs of children and their families using the same procedures. The aim is that information can be shared easily and readily between agencies.

Designated Officer for Safeguarding Children (DOSC) The designated member of staff who is responsible for overseeing and administering issues relating to child protection.

Differentiation A means by which teachers offer a common curriculum to all pupils in their classes, but tailored to meet the needs of individuals.

Disability A condition which is substantial and long-term, i.e. lasting longer that 12 months, which impairs learning and normal living.

Dyscalculia A specific learning difficulty relating to problems in developing an understanding of mathematics.

Dyslexia Primarily a specific difficulty with learning to read, write and/or spell, often accompanied by poor organisational skills; this despite being taught in ways proven to be effective with other children.

Dyspraxia (Developmental Co-ordination Disorder) Impairment of the organisation of movement that is often accompanied by problems with language, perception and thought; symptoms are evident from an early age, often from birth.

Educational Psychologists (EPs) Qualified teachers who have trained further in psychology; support pupils and adults working with pupils who are experiencing sustained difficulties in learning or behaviour; not to be confused with medical psychiatrists.

Education Welfare Service (EWS) Local authority staff working with students and families who have social difficulties with school such as poor attendance.

Ethnic minority A pupil who is identified by parents/carers as belonging to any ethnic group other than 'white British'; parents/carers have the right not to state an ethnic identity.

'Every Child Matters' A government initiative seeking to ensure that every organisation involved with providing services for children works together, shares information and develops networks so that every child, whatever their background or their circumstances benefits from the stated 'five outcomes':
- be healthy
- stay safe
- enjoy and achieve
- make a positive contribution
- achieve economic well-being.

Foundation Stage Pre-National Curriculum schooling – the Reception and Early Years of infant or primary schools.

Framework for Teaching English and Mathematics The equivalent of the Primary Framework for secondary schools.

Gifted and talented pupils Those pupils identified in school as being the most able in academic subjects or the most talented in areas such as art, sport or music.

Higher Level Teaching Assistant (HLTA) A status given to TAs who reach certain standards of education and performance which enables them to be given greater spheres of responsibility in schools.

Ideal self How an individual would like to be.

Inclusion   The process whereby, so far as possible and in compliance with parental preference, all pupils regardless of ability or disability are educated in their local mainstream schools.

Individual Behaviour Plans/Behaviour Support Plans   A tool to plan intervention to modify pupil behaviour – sets out what is expected from the pupil and states how the school and home will support the pupil in reaching these targets.

Individual Education Plan (IEP)   A tool to plan intervention for pupils with special educational needs – sets out what should be taught that is *additional to* or *different from* what would normally be delivered in the class, focusing on three or four short-term targets that are SMART (Specific, Measurable, Attainable, Relevant and Timed).

Interactive whiteboard   An ICT tool that enables programs to be displayed in front of the whole class and which enables pupils and teachers to write their own comments and notations.

Kinaesthetic learners – see Learning styles.

Lead professional   The person identified via a Common Assessment Framework (CAF) who has the responsibility for co-ordinating provision for a child or young person identified as requiring support.

Learning objectives   The focus of any one particular lesson that should be understood by all pupils and their work assessed in relation to that learning objective.

Learning styles   An individual's unconscious preference in regard to how they process and learn new information: some learn better through hearing (auditory learners), others through what they see (visual learners) and others through what they touch or handle (kinaesthetic learners). Most employ a combination of all three learning styles which is why schools seek to teach using 'VAK' techniques (visual, auditory and kinaesthetic).

Local authority   The body comprised of elected members (councillors) and employed officers who, together, are responsible for a range of services in a given local area, including all services for children. There are 150 local authorities in England and Wales.

Medical protocol   A simple text setting out the nature of a pupil's medical condition, the likely symptoms, the response required and people to contact.

Multiple intelligences   The view that children and adults are skilled and able in a wider range of activities than 'reading, writing and arithmetic'.

Multi-sensory   Materials that seek to employ as many senses as possible in the learning process.

National Curriculum (Curriculum 2000)   The National Curriculum sets out the minimum that has to be taught in schools, and a framework against which attainment can be measured. For each subject there are *programmes of study* that set out what pupils should be taught, and *attainment targets* which set the level of performance pupils are expected to achieve.

National Curriculum Level Descriptors   These are statements about what pupils should be achieving at any of the 'levels' within the National Curriculum. Beginning at Level 1, they go up to Level 10. Each level is subdivided into A, B or C, where A is the highest (e.g. a 2A is higher than a 2B, which is itself higher than a 2C). This terminology is being replaced with the terms 'high, secure and low levels'.

At the end of Key Stage 1 (7 year olds) the expectation is that the majority of pupils will have achieved a Level 2 and be solid in their knowledge and skills relating to this level. By the end of Key Stage 2 the majority of pupils are expected to achieve a solid level 4 and so on. The Level Descriptors provide an outline of what children at various ages are expected to be able to do, particularly in maths and literacy.

National Literacy Strategy (NLS)   Introduced in 1998 to provide teaching plans for literacy to put the National Curriculum into practice in primary schools, it gave teaching objectives for each term.

National Numeracy Strategy (NNS)   Introduced in 1999, it illustrated how maths can be taught from Reception to Year 6. 'Key objectives' were set out for each year group.

Occupational therapist   Occupational therapists are medical professionals who seek to treat both physical and psychiatric conditions through activity. They often work with families and schools providing therapy programmes.

Pastoral Support Plan   This is similar to an Individual Behaviour Plan but is more detailed and is put into place when a pupil is at risk of being excluded from school.

Personal Education Plans (PEPs)   Plans drawn up by social services in conjunction with other services such as education for children who are being looked after by the local authority.

Personalised learning   A government agenda seeking to ensure that learning is adapted to the needs of each individual pupil.

Phonics   The 'building blocks' of written language allowing the 'decoding' of written words into sounds or the construction of written sounds into words.

Phonological awareness/phonology   Awareness of sounds within words – e.g. ability to generate rhyme and alliteration, or to segment and blend sounds.

Programmes of study – see National Curriculum.

QCAs   National tests published by the Qualification and Curriculum Authority (QCA) used voluntarily by schools at the end of Years 3, 4 and 5.

Renewed Primary Framework   The renewed Framework for Literacy and Mathematics was introduced to primary schools during 2007. It is an electronic resource, building on and replacing the National Literacy and Numeracy Strategies.

Rose Report (2006)   A government-commissioned report into the early development of reading skills chaired by Jim Rose; this report informed the renewed Primary Framework for Literacy.

SATs (Standard Attainment Tasks)   National tests, published by QCA, that schools must use at the end of Key Stages 1 and 2 to measure pupil progress and the effectiveness of teaching.

Scheme of work   What schools decide to teach in a particular subject or topic taken from the National Curriculum within a limited time-frame.

Self-image   How individuals see themselves.

Semantic-pragmatic language disorder   Problems with semantics (the meaning of words) and pragmatics (the way language, both verbal and non-verbal, is used in social interactions).

Sensory or physical impairment   Visual, hearing or physical processes which to a greater or lesser extent restrict a person's ability to access what would normally be available. People with such impairments may or may not be registered as disabled.

Special educational needs (SEN)   'A child has special educational needs if he or she has a learning difficulty which may be the result of a physical or sensory disability, an emotional or behavioural problem or developmental delay' (Education Act, 1981). 'Children have special educational needs if they have a *learning difficulty* which calls for *special educational provision* to be made for them' (Education Act, 1996, Section 312).

Special Educational Needs Co-ordinator (SENCO)   The person or persons in school responsible for overseeing the day-to-day operation of special needs provision.

Speech and language therapists   Health professionals, who assess and review individual children, provide resources and give advice where there is a concern over language.

Statements of Special Educational Need   Documents regulated by law setting out the educational and non-educational needs of individuals and the provision to be put in place to meet those needs.

Teaching styles   The way in which a teacher approaches the teaching process: often an individual's teaching style is based on their own preferred learning styles and their experience of being taught themselves.

Visual learners – see Learning styles.

Overview of NVQ course – what you need to know before you begin

Getting started

Congratulations! Starting an NVQ (National Vocational Qualification) course in supporting teaching and learning is both challenging and exciting. NVQs are designed to provide valid and relevant vocational qualifications that are valued by the workforce. Gaining an NVQ can provide progression routes to further training and career opportunities. Whatever level you wish to aspire to, enrolling on an NVQ course will give you the opportunity to study and discover more about supporting the students you are working with. An NVQ gives you the opportunity to reflect or think about what you are doing in the classroom and to think about how you can improve on your practice.

NVQs in supporting teaching and learning are worthwhile but they are also hard work. This book aims to help you through the process.

Individuals who choose to do this course are often referred to as candidates. One of the first questions candidates enrolling on an NVQ course ask is: what does an NVQ involve? What do I have to do?

NVQs are about demonstrating that you are competent at a particular task or skill, for example being able to give feedback to the teacher on the pupil's response to a certain activity. **Competence** is about demonstrating that you are able to do a task and demonstrating that you understand why that task is important.

Therefore, an NVQ requires you to:

- Show that you are able to do the task. Evidence of **performance** will be required.
- Show that you understand why that task is important. This requires you to provide evidence of underpinning **knowledge**.

Let's look at an example from Unit 1 (performance indicator 5) where candidates are asked to provide evidence in relation to *using praise, commentary and assistance to encourage pupils to stay on task*. In regard to **evidence of performance**, it is most likely that your assessor will observe you doing this while you are engaged in real work activities. After all, in terms of supporting teaching and learning, offering praise ('Well done Sally'), commentary ('You remembered to use a question mark') and assistance ('I see you are still having difficulties spelling Tyrannosaurus Rex, shall I help you look it up in the dictionary?') is something you do on a day-to-day basis. In regard to providing **evidence of knowledge,** your assessor might ask you for details regarding your school's policy on the use of praise, assistance and rewards, and how exactly does offering praise, commentary and assistance promote effective learning.

Structure of the course

The NVQ 2 in supporting teaching and learning in schools is divided into units of competence. To achieve the NVQ 2 a teaching assistant (TA) needs to complete **seven units of competence.**

There are **five mandatory units of competence.** You must complete these units:

- Provide support for learning activities.
- Support children's development.
- Help to keep children safe.
- Contribute to positive relationships.
- Provide effective support for your colleagues.

In addition, an NVQ2 candidate will be required to achieve **two optional units.** The optional units include the following:

- Support literacy and numeracy activities.
- Support the use of information and communication technology for teaching and learning.
- Use information and communication technology to support pupils' learning.
- Observe and report on pupil performance.*
- Support children's play and learning.*
- Contribute to supporting bilingual/multilingual pupils.
- Support a child with disabilities or special educational needs.
- Support individuals during therapy sessions.
- Support children and young people's play.*
- Provide displays.*
- Invigilate tests and examinations.*

Units marked with an asterisk will be presented as mini-chapters that will focus on key aspects of the unit.

I want that one!

Figure 0.1
TAs come in all
shapes and sizes

Which units you choose to complete very much depends on your role within the school. Candidates who enrol on this course will come from a variety of backgrounds and could be working in primary, secondary or special schools. In addition, the revised NVQ for supporting teaching and learning acknowledges that many candidates enrolled on the course will have a range of roles within schools. Many candidates will be working as teaching assistants in either a paid capacity or as a volunteer within the classroom. Further, some students might be working as midday meal supervisors, after-school supervisors and cover supervisors, and be involved in study support or helping invigilate exams. As such, the optional units you choose very much depend on your role within the school.

Let's get complicated

Once you have settled on what units you are going to cover you will need to start the lengthy process of collecting evidence. Each unit is subdivided into elements or smaller units and each of these requires you to demonstrate evidence regarding both performance and knowledge.

Some candidates who enrol on this course will do so through colleges while others might be working towards the qualification within their school as a form of in-house training. Regardless of how you are doing the course, all candidates will have an assessor. An assessor will guide candidates through the process, help them collect the required evidence and give feedback on evidence.

Once you have enrolled on this course you will receive a copy of all the standards, that is performance indicators and knowledge base criteria that you will need to provide evidence for. Do not panic. Your assessor is there to guide you.

What is evidence?

In NVQ-speak, evidence needs to have the following qualities to be accepted as evidence.

Valid

To be valid, the way assessment is carried out and the nature of the evidence collected must be appropriate, that is, it really must demonstrate the competence of a candidate. For example, to demonstrate competence in giving teachers feedback on pupil perform-ance it is not enough for the candidate to write a statement saying that they do this on a day-to-day basis. The candidate will need to present evidence in regard to how they do this. For example, the candidate may:

* include reading and spelling records that they have filled in;
* have the teacher write a statement regarding how they report on pupil performance.

Reliable

Reliability refers to consistency. On the one hand, does the candidate provide evidence of performing this behaviour on more than one occasion and in a variety of situations? On the other hand, reliability refers to consistency between assessors. If the evidence is reliable then all assessors should judge it as valid evidence.

Sufficient

Sufficient means that the evidence presented by the candidate is enough to prove competence. If the evidence is not sufficient it may mean that the candidate needs to write or say more. For example, a photocopy of the school's behaviour policy is not sufficient evidence that the candidate understands the school's behaviour policy. A candidate may be questioned by an assessor on their understanding of the behaviour policy.

Authentic

This relates to whether the evidence produced is genuine and is a true account of what the candidate can do.

Current

The evidence produced must reflect current understanding and practices.

All evidence that is presented must be valid, reliable, sufficient, authentic and current to count as appropriate evidence. All the above points may seem complicated but they are essential to ensure the integrity and quality of the qualification. When you compile your evidence, an assessor will be judging your evidence on the above points and give you any necessary advice.

Ways of gathering evidence

Observation

Observation is a required assessment method for all units. For each unit your **assessor** will observe you in real work-related activities and write up their observations to provide you with evidence of performance. In addition, your assessor, on the basis of observing you in the workplace, will decide what evidence of knowledge and understanding you have demonstrated. Often, to clarify aspects of your knowledge and understanding, they will ask you questions.

Expert witness and witness testimony

Colleagues (teachers, Higher Level Teaching Assistants (HLTAs) and Special Educational Needs Co-ordinators (SENCOs)) in the workplace can write a short statement describing your practice. Their statement can provide evidence of your performance to supplement assessor observation. Expert witnesses need to be familiar with the work of candidates. Your assessor will give you more details with regard to who can be a witness/expert witness and the relevant forms that witnesses will need to fill in.

Products of performance

These will often support your workplace accounts. These could be individual or session plans, feedback forms and reading records. Confidentiality is important. It is essential that when writing accounts or case studies you do not use the full names of pupils who you are working with. Some candidates will refer to the pupils by their initials. When including copies of reading records or feedback forms as supporting evidence it is important to block out names.

Questioning

Your assessor may ask for more details regarding what they have observed, what you have written in an account or on issues relating to underpinning knowledge.

Professional discussion

This will involve having a discussion with your assessor on aspects of your role. This conversation will be recorded and used as evidence. A professional discussion is more than just answering a set of questions, but allows the candidate to demonstrate their understanding of their role.

Personal accounts and case studies

Personal accounts and case studies evidence will be used to supplement observational evidence provided by your assessor and will be used where evidence required for a unit rarely occurs or is difficult to observe.

A personal account can be compared to a diary in which you describe 'what you did' during a particular period of time at school. What you write will need to be matched to performance indicators, that is, the type of behaviour you need to demonstrate that you can do. Personal accounts, in order to be considered as appropriate and authentic, will need to be countersigned by someone who has observed what you have done; usually this will be the teacher.

Accreditation of prior learning

Your past experience relating to courses attended and qualifications gained may provide evidence. You will need to talk to your assessor regarding this as evidence, to be considered valid, will need to be judged as current.

Figure 0.2
Where to start?

Written knowledge

Certain elements require you to demonstrate knowledge and understanding; this can be shown by writing answers to various questions.

What you need to do

As a candidate enrolling on an NVQ 2 course for those involved in supporting teaching and learning, your responsibilities are to:

* identify and collect evidence to meet the required indicators for knowledge and performance;
* present the evidence in a structured format called a portfolio.

This might seem overwhelming to begin with but there are many people you will meet who will help you in this process.

Who will help you

The course tutor

If you enrol for a course run through a college the course tutor will be responsible in part for delivering the course. They will give you valuable advice regarding how to collect evidence and set up your portfolio as well as discussing issues relating to underpinning knowledge.

The assessor

The role of an assessor is to look at the evidence presented and to make judgements regarding whether the evidence meets the required indicators or not. They are there to help you collect the necessary evidence. Your assessor will discuss with you issues regarding confidentiality, in regard to what records can and cannot be presented within your portfolio.

The mentor

Candidates may have a special person within the school to whom they can go and ask for help and advice.

Internal verifier

An internal verifier may be based in a college. They are responsible for ensuring that the quality and the integrity of the course are maintained. In particular they need to ensure that all assessors are marking to the same standard.

External verifier

All NVQ 2 courses for those involved in supporting teaching and learning are accredited through exam boards. An external verifier is employed by the exam board to visit various colleges and centres who are offering the course to ensure that all centres are maintaining the appropriate standards.

How this book will help you

This book aims to help you complete the process of an NVQ by:

- providing you with examples of how to present the required evidence through records of observations and witness testimony, notes of professional discussions, personal accounts and products of performance;
- covering relevant underpinning knowledge. To help you understand the knowledge required numerous activities, self-assessment questions and quizzes are included;
- giving examples of how to use feedback from assessors to improve your work;
- providing photocopiable resources;
- outlining summaries of important government documents plus website references;
- presenting a Glossary of important terms. Words highlighted in bold within each chapter will be defined in the Glossary.

Who are Miranda, Nicki, Sadie, Nazreen and friends?

One request often heard by candidates just starting an NVQ 2 is to have a look at someone else's completed portfolio – just to get an idea about what is expected. In this book we have presented examples of ongoing work submitted by imaginary candidates. Miranda works in a primary school, Nicki works in a secondary school and Nazreen and Sadie work in a junior school. In a sense this book tells the story of their struggles to put forward a portfolio of evidence. As you will see some of their evidence is better presented than others. At all points both their teacher and assessor will give comments about their work. The assessor will explain terminology and give ideas about how to collect further evidence. It is hoped that through this ongoing dialogue between the assessor and the candidates, you will acquire a real sense of what is needed to gain this qualification.

All names of characters used in this book are fictitious and any relationship to real persons is purely coincidental.

Examples of the required performance evidence will be presented at various sections within this book (see Chapters 6, 8, 10, 11, 16). The evidence produced will illustrate the holistic nature of assessment whereby one piece of evidence can be used to meet the criteria for a number of units.

Advice on starting out from an assessor

- Get organised!
- Some candidates find it easier to separate evidence for Knowledge Base and Performance Indicator standards into separate binders.
- Use your time wisely.

Tips for collecting evidence

- Always look out for opportunities to cross-reference your evidence to other units. This will cut down on the work you have to do.

- Remember it is better practice to collect evidence from a variety of sources. For example:
  - copies of pupils' work;
  - copies of memos you have written;
  - copies of reading records/student records;
  - a record of a conversation you may have had, however brief, with a member of staff regarding a pupil;
  - a note received from a parent or guardian;
  - copies of differentiated work you have provided;
  - minutes of meetings you have attended.

However, all these sources of evidence will need to be **annotated**. Annotation requires that you write a few lines explaining what the evidence means and how it meets the standard. All evidence presented will need to **comply with requirements regarding confidentiality**.

Starting an NVQ course can be daunting – let's look at the first session for our imaginary students.

So what's it all about?

It was the first day of college and the NVQ 2 candidates filed eagerly and perhaps apprehensively into Room 101. For many of them it had been a long time since they had been at school, that is, at school as a pupil. Terrie, NVQ 2 assessor and tutor, had also arrived early to welcome the candidates to the class and to make sure that she had everything in order.

There was quite a crowd. As Terrie entered the room she noticed a group of candidates having an animated conversation. One woman was commenting that she was so worried about coming today that she had got lost on her way to college and that was something considering she had lived all her life in this town. A rather confident woman, Nicki, assured her that there was nothing to this course and stated: 'My mate says that this is a doddle! And as far as having to provide evidence – it's all about writing a good story – you know what I mean. Everyone does it! It's just a game!'

Of course Terrie heard these comments and the candidates did look somewhat taken back when they realised that this woman was not just another candidate but the course tutor.

Terrie, for her part, decided to bide her time and to come back to this important issue.

Nicki said quietly to those around her: 'That's just my luck – I just don't know when to shut up, Stan said to me only this morning that he bet that I would get a detention!'

After the introductions, Terrie asked the candidates what their expectations were for the course. The replies consisted of gaining new qualification and skills – but Terrie asked what else? Then Terrie explained: 'In my first year of teaching this course one of the teaching assistants I worked with told me that she never thought about what she did – she just did things – can anyone relate to that?'

Sadie, the woman who had managed to get lost driving to college, stated that often she felt like that. Terrie then added: 'What this course is about is making you think, really think and question what you do in order to improve what you do – now when I entered the room I couldn't help hearing someone say that their mate thought this course was a doddle.'

Nicki gulped and replied: 'That was me – my mate did this course a few years ago and she said – well she said that it was just a matter of coming up with a good story!'

Terrie replied: 'Well, this course is like anything in life – you'll get out of it what you put in. Now I was reading a piece of research that asked students who had taken NVQ courses what they thought about it. These candidates said that in order to achieve the NVQ 2 they had to write stories about things that had happened to them at work, routine, everyday things. These candidates then said that the trick was to write the story in such a way, using the right words that it matched the required performance standards. So in effect these candidates said that you needed to present the information in such a way that it seemed like you had done the right thing and of course you probably had.'

'So Miss – you could make it all up – and if you did how would you know? – Not that I would,' blurted Nicki.

Terrie quickly replied: 'Now Nicki – first my name is Terrie. How would I know – well, in terms of evidence we are now relying more on observations and witness testimony. Either, I will come and assess you or the teacher will write a statement about what you do and of course I will question you about what you do and why you do it. But the important point is not whether I will find out if you are telling the truth about what happened but rather what do you want to get out of the course. This course is a great opportunity for you to gain new skills.'

'That's another thing my mate said – that there were some bits that seemed pointless in that you had to have evidence of silly things like setting out tables, or how to talk to parents – I don't mean to be all negative – but what was that all about?' said Nicki.

'You've raised a good point – some say that as NVQs require you to collect evidence about what you do day to day, that they are just giving you credit, accrediting skills that you already have and that you are not actually learning anything new. But again I come back to what I said about only getting from this course in terms of what you put in. Let's look at the example you mentioned about talking to parents. Now one teaching assistant I worked with sometimes filled in at reception during the lunch hours and sometimes would be asked by the teachers to contact parents. This teaching assistant told me that when she thought about phoning and talking to parents she would always make a point of asking the parents how they wished to be called. Some parents wanted to be addressed as Mrs, some preferred to be called by their first name. Now this may seem like a small issue about a routine activity such as phoning parents – but is it important?'

'How people address you and if they have taken the time to ask makes you feel special and valued,' volunteered Miranda.

'Good,' so Terrie continued: 'We see that thinking about routine everyday activities are important . . So what can we take from all of this?'

'That the course is not a doddle and that we need to think,' said Nicki.

'But thinking is hard,' said Sadie, 'Well – I haven't been in a classroom, learning that is, in decades. I left school at 15. I'm worried about this. Do I have to think?'

'Don't worry – your assessor, that's me, your teacher and your fellow candidates are here to help each other. You can do this!' said Terrie.

'Yeah you can do this – you go girl!' said Nicki.

'Now, moving on, I think coffee is in order. I hear that they serve some really wicked home-made sticky toffee buns at the canteen,' said Terrie.

'What are we waiting for,' said Nicki, 'I can do anything after a sticky bun!'

Figure 0.3 I can do anything after a sticky bun!

Chapter 1

Unit 1: Provide support for learning activities

In this chapter we will look at three elements:

1   Support the teacher in planning learning activities.
2   Support the delivery of learning activities.
3   Support the teacher in the evaluation of learning activities.

The relationship between your own role and the role of the teacher within the learning environment, and your role and responsibilities for supporting pupils' learning and the implications of this for the sort of support you can provide

As a teaching assistant you are a valued member of the school community. All schools advocate a collegiate approach to working; that is, for a school to run smoothly and effectively everyone has a role to play. A TA's role in supporting pupils will be summarised in your job description. Most job descriptions will state that:

- You will assist the teacher in implementing the lesson plans. Specifically you will work with the pupils assigned to you and help them to meet the **learning objectives** as outlined by the teacher.
- Schools are not just about learning academic facts; they are also about developing social and emotional skills. As a TA you need to develop a good relationship with the pupils you support, as well as helping and encouraging them to develop positive relationships with each other. In doing this you will teach pupils how to manage conflicts and how to deal with their emotions positively.
- As a TA you will have high expectations in regard to pupil achievement and behaviour. You can help a pupil by reminding them of what they are supposed to be doing and encouraging and praising them for their efforts.
- As a TA you are not there to do the work for the pupil, rather you are there to help them to learn to do the work for themselves. You can help pupils set clear goals for themselves. In order to do this you need to be able to talk to the pupil in a way that they can understand.
- As a TA you will give feedback to the teacher regarding how the session went. For example, you will need to make comments on: who could do the work; who found the work difficult; who would benefit from extra time or help in that area; who was disruptive and who was very supportive and encouraging.

Self-assessment activity 1.1

To encourage you to think about how your role relates to the role of the teacher fill in the following diary for one day.

Time	Activity	My role within the activity (Hint: what was I asked to do?)	The teacher's role within the activity. (Hint: what was the teacher responsible for?)

The school policies for inclusion and equality of opportunity, and the implication of these for how you work with pupils

School policies for inclusion

Those involved in the field of education often talk about **inclusion**. The aim of inclusion is that all children or pupils, regardless of abilities, **disabilities** or **special educational needs** (SEN), are educated together in age-appropriate mainstream local schools. In the past the emphasis has been on difference or deficit. The problem with this approach is that differences between children can be attributed to 'within child factors'. So, if student A is doing better than student B; is this because Student A is simply more able than Student B? Explanations regarding the variation between pupils in regard to academic achievement could be due to individual differences in the ability to learn or differences in opportunities to learn. An inclusive approach focuses on how the school environment can be changed to enhance learning for all.

Inclusion involves changing the educational environment to match the individual needs of the pupil. As a TA you need to consider:

- How do the students I support learn?
- What range of teaching strategies do I use?
- How do the teaching strategies I use match how the students learn?

Inclusion means that all pupils are involved in all aspects of school life. Inclusion is about creating relationships and valuing differences. Inclusion is not a place or a specific policy but rather a journey that all involved in supporting teaching and learning embark on. Inclusion is a feeling and a school is inclusive to the extent that all pupils feel valued, included and engaged in learning.

In working to create an inclusive school, particular attention needs to be given to those students who are considered vulnerable. Vulnerable children could include young people:

- in **care**;
- who have English has an additional language;
- who frequently move from place to place;
- who present with emotional or behavioural issues;
- who have medical conditions, **sensory or physical impairments**;
- who experience difficulties with learning;
- a combination of the above.

Legislation regarding inclusion

Inclusive education is enshrined in law, notably by the Children Act (1989), various education acts, the Special Education Needs and Disability Act (2001), the Children Act (2004) and the Disability Discrimination Act (2005). More details on these and other pieces of legislation are given in Chapters 17 and 18. Schools have a legal requirement not to discriminate against pupils with disabilities and are required to make provision for them. Plans must be put in place to make every school accessible to persons with disabilities. No school can refuse to admit a pupil on the grounds that they feel unable to meet their needs.

Schools will state how they promote equal opportunities and disability awareness in school policy documents. As a TA enrolled on an NVQ 2 course it is important that you obtain a copy of these policies and that you read them.

Individual Education Plans (IEPs)

In meeting the needs of pupils, schools will follow the Special Educational Needs Code of Practice (DfEE 2001). The Code of Practice is a government document that outlines levels of intervention that the school will follow.

Monitoring (early identification)

This is an unofficial first step. This is where the school will keep an eye on a specific pupil. It could be that the pupil is having problems with reading, writing or maths. At this stage the child will receive **differentiated** work, which is work that is set for the pupil's specific ability.

School Action

If there is still concern for the pupil, after receiving differentiated learning opportunities, the pupil is put on the school's SEN register. This concern could be that the:

- pupil is making little or no progress, even with differentiated work;
- pupil shows signs of difficulty in literacy or maths that could affect their work in other subject areas;
- pupil presents with ongoing emotional and behavioural problems that are not being dealt with by existing school behaviour management techniques;
- pupil has sensory, or physical difficulties and even with specialist equipment is making little or no progress;
- pupil has communication and/or interaction difficulties and makes little or no progress despite differentiated learning opportunities.

Once the pupil is on the SEN Register, at the School Action Stage, the **SENCO** will collect all available information, seek new information and carry out further assessment. The result of this will be the formulation of an IEP. An IEP will outline the support the pupil will be given. Specifically an IEP will outline:

- short-term targets;
- teaching strategies;
- provisions to be put into place;
- when the plan should be reviewed;
- what the pupil needs to do to meet the targets. This has been called the success or exit criteria;
- a review of the IEP, that is, whether the pupil has met the targets.

School Action Plus

If, after receiving an individualised programme of support, which is described in the IEP, the pupil is still making little or no progress, the pupil can move to the next level of intervention. At this point the school will ask for help and support from outside agencies. This could include a behaviour support team, **speech and language therapists** or **educational psychologists**.

Statement of Special Educational Need

If, after receiving help from outside agencies, it is felt that the pupil is not making adequate progress then the school, in discussion with the parents and external agencies, can ask the **local authority** to implement a statutory assessment. The educational psychologist will be involved and if it is felt that the pupil is still not making progress a **Statement of Special Educational Need** is written.

The Code of Practice is said to be key in ensuring that inclusion happens in schools as it is committed to responding to pupils' diverse needs and to setting suitable learning challenges for all pupils. Within the present educational climate, with its emphasis on **assessment for learning** (see pages 22 and 176) and **personalised learning**, all pupils will have targets and be involved in the target-setting process. As such, IEP targets will often deal with pupils who have more complex and diverse needs.

TAs will be involved on a day-to-day basis in helping pupils meet their targets.

Role of the TA required in promoting inclusion

- TAs can encourage all children, especially children with special educational needs, to have a sense of pride in who they are.
- TAs can encourage friendships between all children.
- TAs can help pupils meet their targets as stated on their IEPs.
- TAs can challenge negative attitudes and low expectations. TAs can use strategies that help all pupils to develop their potential. Some specific strategies you can use include encouraging co-operation, helping pupils to recognise theirs and others' strengths, promoting independence and matching teaching styles to **learning styles** (see pages 25–8).

Individual Education Plan

Area of concern: behaviour, extreme incidents of inappropriate language

Name:	Jody Smith		*Stage:*	School Action	
			Year group:	Year 3	
			Start date:	Sept. 2009	
			Review date:	Jan. 2010	
			Support began:	Sept. 2008	
Class teacher:	Mrs Gardner				
Support by:	Miranda Marshall TA				

Targets to be achieved	Achievement criteria	Possible resources/ techniques	Possible class strategies	Ideas for teaching assistant	Outcome
To speak politely to other pupils and adults	No incidents or rudeness for 3 days out of 5	• Clear expectations • All incidents of talking politely praised	• Discuss what is meant by being polite • Ignore minor episodes of rudeness	• Discuss what is polite behaviour in the classroom • Praise efforts • Use star chart	Incidents of rudeness down from 5 a week to 2

Strategies to promote inclusion: encouraging co-operation

Co-operative learning techniques describe specific ways to encourage pupils to work together. A well-known co-operative learning technique has been referred to as the jigsaw technique or jigsaw classroom (Aronson and Patnoe 1997). The jigsaw technique is as follows:

- Pupils are divided into groups. Groups should be diverse in terms of bringing together pupils from different cultural backgrounds and different levels of ability.
- The task is divided into segments. Each pupil is given responsibility for one segment. For example, if the group task was to write about the life of the Victorians, the segments could include: family life, work life, the government, the royal family and transport. Each pupil would be responsible for one segment or one piece of the puzzle.
- The pupils are then are asked to form expert groups with other pupils who are working on the same segment or piece of the puzzle. For example, all those pupils who are working on the royal family would come together to research the topic.
- After the pupils have worked with their expert groups they are then asked to come back to the main group and present their findings. The other group members are encouraged to ask questions.

The jigsaw strategy is just one technique that can be used in a classroom. The advantage is that it encourages children of varying abilities to work and co-operate with each other. In these group tasks pupils are required to:

- contribute their ideas to the discussion;
- listen to others' ideas;
- give every member of the group an opportunity to speak;
- value each others' contributions;
- ask each other for help before asking the teacher or teaching assistant to intervene;
- try and settle arguments among themselves.

These group requirements can be presented to the pupils as guidelines or rules for helping them work together. For groups to work effectively, they will need guidance and help from teachers and teaching assistants. In groups, you can have difficulties with the following kinds of pupils:

- pupils who like to dominate the group;
- pupils who are free-riders – these pupils do not contribute and let others do the work for them;
- less able pupils who struggle to keep up;
- able pupils who may get bored;
- needy pupils who are making constant demands on your attention.

TAs can help by reminding pupils of what they need to do to work together. TAs can praise pupils for doing this. Remember, praise encourages co-operation and effective interactions. In relation to less able pupils it is important to give them a task that they can do. Perhaps you could ask a more able pupil to assist a less able pupil. In helping a less able pupil, the more able pupil also benefits as the skills involved in explaining work to others helps to consolidate their own understanding.

Helping to find value in everyone: multiple intelligence

Encouraging pupils to notice and value what other pupils can do well encourages positive interactions and co-operation between pupils. Traditionally pupils in schools have been valued for academic successes. This can result in competition between some pupils for the highest marks. It is possible that pupils who think that they cannot compete and that they never will get the highest marks could label themselves as 'thick' and just give up.

Gardner's (1993) theory of multiple intelligence criticises the notion that intelligence is just about academic success. This theory states that there are different types of intelligence and that society needs individuals with different types of intelligence.

Figure 1.1 TAs need to look for talent in all pupils

Types of intelligence	Pupils who have these skills are good at
Logical-mathematical	This pupil has a flair for maths. Pupils with this type of intelligence are good at performing calculations and analysing how things work. Future careers could include engineers, computer scientists, accountants and analysts.
Linguistic	This pupil excels at written work. This pupil is naturally good with words and the use of language. They enjoy writing stories and commenting on others' work. Future careers could include journalists, linguists, writers and lawyers.
Musical	This pupil has a flair for music, sound and rhythm. This pupil could be good at singing or playing a musical instrument or teaching another pupil how to sing or play a musical instrument. Future careers could include musicians, singers, composers and DJs.
Bodily-kinaesthetic	This pupil has good body movement control. This pupil is physically agile and has good co-ordination. This pupil could be good at sports and they could be good at demonstrating physical skills to others. Future careers include dancers, athletes, soldiers, fire-fighters and divers.
Spatial-visual	This pupil is good at creating and understanding visual images and shapes. This pupil could be good at painting, designing logos and drawing maps. Future careers include artists, designers, architects, photographers and town planners.
Interpersonal	This pupil is good with people. This pupil can easily understand other people's feelings. Future careers could include counsellors, psychologists, clergy and sales people.
Intrapersonal	This pupil is good at self-awareness, that is, they are good at understanding why they do what they do. Self-awareness is an essential part of what is now termed emotional intelligence.

The objectives of the learning activities to be supported

Objectives of the learning activities

The day-to-day life of a school can seem incredibly busy and even chaotic at times. But in order for schools to function they rely on careful and detailed planning. These plans are not made in isolation but will follow a **scheme of work** as detailed in the **National Curriculum**.

From the scheme of work the teacher will write up plans that would cover what the class will do during a term or half term. From these long-term plans, weekly and daily plans are drawn up. Some pupils will need to have their work differentiated, that is, adapted to their ability level; this will include pupils who have individual learning targets as identified on IEPs.

Each day a pupil will participate in a variety of learning activities, such as maths, science, English and PE, as specified on the daily plan and each of these activities will have **learning objectives** or targets. See for example the literacy plan on p. 18. A learning objective describes what a learner should know, understand and/or be able to do after participating in a lesson.

While it is useful for the TA and the teacher to discuss the weekly plans in advance, it is essential that when working with an individual or a group the TA knows the learning objectives for that session.

Anywhere Primary School

Literacy planning

Date: Tues 28 November   Class: Year 2

> By looking at this plan I know what the learning objectives are for my group – as well as the class.

Learning objectives:

Collect words and phrases to write poems – ponds.

Design simple poems or patterns of words – swamps.

Express their views about a story or poem – rivers and puddles.

Identify words or ideas to support or back up their view – rivers and puddles.

Whole class work	Individual/group tasks	Plenary session
Model how to collect words and lines from different poems. Read several poems with the children first. Talk about writing down some of the words and ideas that we like	**Rivers and puddles** – with Mrs Goldbottom **Swamps** – with Miss Moss **Ponds** – with Miranda Marshall Higher ability groups will have already selected an idea for a poem. They need to be encouraged to collect words and phrases related to that idea from a range of books. Lower ability groups to read books on their table and to write down some words and sentences that they like. TA will need to assist with spelling and handwriting skills.	Ask pupils to read out what poems they liked best. Ask pupils what it was that they liked about these poems. Ask pupils what words and sentences they have collected for their poem.

> I am working with the lower ability group, **Ponds.** I have two students with IEPs. I need to be familiar with their targets as I will need to give additional feedback to the teacher. regarding their progress in meeting their targets.

> The teacher discussed the books/resources needed.

> Knowing the learning objectives allows me to focus my feedback on whether the pupils met their learning objectives and how much support they needed.

The importance of planning and evaluation of learning activities

Planning is an important part of teaching. In a sense, teaching can be seen as a cycle and TAs will have a vital role to play in this cycle.

Teachers plan the lesson

- The teacher may show the TA weekly plans and ask for the TA's comments and suggestions.
- An important part of planning a lesson is stating what the learning objectives are. The teacher will inform the TA of the learning objectives.

Teachers and TAs deliver the lesson

- During the delivery of the lesson the TA and the teacher may ask for feedback from the pupils regarding their understanding.
- Sometimes it is necessary to think on your feet and adapt or modify the lesson if some pupils are struggling.

Teachers and TAs will evaluate the lesson

- Evaluation will include feedback on whether the pupils achieved the learning objectives or outcomes.
- Evaluation will also include comments on what went well with the lesson and what areas could be improved for next time.
- Evaluation will also include personal reflections regarding how you could improve on the way in which you supported the session.
- All these comments will be fed into future plans.

Teachers will plan the next day's lesson

- On the basis of previous evaluation the teacher will revise or adapt the lesson plan as necessary. In this sense we can see planning, delivering/teaching and evaluation as a never-ending cycle.

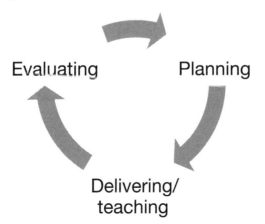

Figure 1.2
A never-ending cycle

Your experience and expertise in relation to supporting learning activities and how this relates to the planned activities

It is the responsibility of the teacher to plan, deliver and evaluate the learning activities. It is the role of the TA to assist the teacher in this task. In self-assessment activity 1.2 many examples of the support TAs offer are given; however, there are blank sections which you are invited to fill in.

Self-assessment activity 1.2

Preparation and planning

Support TA can provide	Examples of TAs using experience and expertise	How teachers can use TA experience	Give an example of how you have accomplished this
TAs can offer suggestions as to the type of support they can provide to the planned activities	'The class was to discuss World War II. I told the teacher that I had some interesting books and some old photographs my Nan took during the war that I could bring in.' 'I have attended adult education classes in cake decoration. I told the teacher I would be happy to help the class decorate their Christmas cakes.'	If teachers know the skills you have to offer, they can use your skills to enhance the quality of the lesson.	**Examples of suggestions**
TAs can point out any difficulties they see in the proposed plans	I mentioned to the teacher: 'I didn't think that pupil could cope with that work.' 'I thought that the pupil would find working in the corridor outside the classroom too disruptive as they would be distracted by all the comings and goings.' 'If I am to help the pupils with ICT skills I could benefit from some additional training myself.'	Teachers value and respond to your comments regarding pupils.	**Examples of difficulties to proposed plans**
TAs can make sure that they are prepared for their contribution to the lesson	'In a secondary school – I always make a point of trying to get to the class before the pupils so I can have a quick word with the teacher before the class starts.' 'I always make sure I have a supply of pens and pencils in case any of the pupils have forgotten their material.'		**What you can do to prepare for lessons**

Delivery of the session

Support TA can provide	Examples of TAs using experience and expertise	How teachers can use TA experience	Give an example of how you have accomplished this

Evaluation

Support TA can provide	Examples of TAs using experience and expertise	How teachers can use TA experience	Give an example of how you have accomplished this
After the lesson is over it is important that TAs offer feedback to the teacher	'I always make a point of telling the teacher who has achieved the learning objectives and who would require additional work on that area.'	Teachers need this information to plan future sessions.	
Provide the teacher with relevant information for records and reports	'Part of my role is to hear the pupils read and to record this information in their reading diaries. From my comments the teacher can get a sense of how the pupil is progressing.' 'I am responsible for recording the information from the pupils' end of term tests.'	Supporting learning is teamwork.	

Formative and summative assessment

Assessment is part of evaluation. Assessment is important as it establishes what the pupil has learned and what still needs to be learned. Assessment is an ongoing process. There are two types of assessment: **summative assessment** and **formative assessment**.

Summative assessment records what the pupil knows at a certain point in time. Examples of summative assessment are various types of tests. These tests could be:

- national tests, for example, **SATs**;
- end of term tests;
- commercially produced tests.

TAs may be involved in administering, marking and recording the results of the tests.

Formative assessment refers to continuous assessment that is carried out on a regular basis. Examples of formative assessment could be:

- comments made in reading diaries;
- marks and comments made in pupils' books.

TAs will be involved in formative assessment.

Table 1.1 Age-related expectations

Age (years)	Class	Key Stage	Expected attainment levels for the majority of pupils
4–5	Reception	Early Years Foundation Stage	
5–6	Year 1	Key Stage 1	
6–7	Year 2		SATs Level 2B
7–8	Year 3	Key Stage 2	
8–9	Year 4		
9–10	Year 5		
10–11	Year 6		SATs Level 4b
11–12	Year 7	Key Stage 3	
12–13	Year 8		
13–14	Year 9		Levels 5/6
14–15	Year 10	Key Stage 4	
15–16	Year 11		GCSE 5 A–C grades

Formative assessment also involves the pupils' participation in evaluating how well they think they are doing. In recent years emphasis has been placed on **Assessment for Learning**.

Assessment for Learning entails evaluating the lesson as it is progressing and involves the pupils in evaluation. This means asking the pupil as they go along – 'How is it going?' or 'Do we understand this?'

In order for the pupils to make comments on their learning they first have to know what it is that they have to learn. Often teachers will write aims or learning objectives on the board. Some schools will use systems such as WALT (What are the lesson targets) or WILF (What I'm looking for).

In asking pupils how it is going, some schools may use a traffic light system where pupils will hold up a:

- green card for 'I understand';
- orange card for 'Some things I understand and others I don't';
- red card for 'I don't understand – I'm confused'.

Other schools will use a thumbs up, thumbs down system.

The advantage of using these systems is that it gives you information on which pupils understand the lesson. If there are pupils who don't understand it is important for the TA to modify their approach.

In Assessment for Learning the pupils are also encouraged to review their work and identify what they need to learn next. A TA can help the pupil do this.

As a TA it is also useful to know the **attainment levels** that the pupils should be working towards. Your teacher will have detailed knowledge of this.

The basic principles underlying child development and learning; the factors that promote effective learning; and the barriers to effective learning

Active learning

'Active learning' is a generic term that links with a social constructivist theory of the development of cognition and learning such as developed by Vygotsky (see pages 33–4).

What is active learning?

Active learning means children being involved in their own learning. Children are not passive objects in school who have something 'done to them' in order for them to be educated. In order for effective learning to take place, children need to be actively and consciously involved in their learning – both in the content of learning and in the process of learning.

Rather than simply being present in class like absorbent sponges, children need to be involved. They need to be consciously aware of the learning process; of what they are being asked to participate in and they need to be able to have some control over what is being asked of them. Having said that, children are not mini-adults and they will require adult involvement to give direction and purpose to their learning.

Means of promoting active learning

Where adults talk to the class for extended periods of time, expecting them merely to listen and absorb the information presented to them, active learning will not take place. Where children are presented with endless series of worksheets to complete, active learning will not take place. Where the subjects taught bear no relation to the reality of the lives of the children in the lesson, active learning will not take place.

Both teachers and TAs can promote active learning by:

- extending the learning of the children through questioning and discussion;
- planning for individual children rather than the class as a homogenous whole;
- creating an atmosphere of acceptance whereby children feel confident to experiment, to 'have a go', even if they make mistakes;
- presenting children with learning activities with which they connect and which make sense to them;
- presenting children with genuine choices in their learning;
- taking time to reflect upon their own teaching in the light of what children are learning.

Factors to consider when supporting learning

The key factors that can affect the way pupils learn include age, gender, and physical, intellectual, linguistic, social, cultural and emotional development and family background.

Factor	Questions relating to learning
Age	When are pupils ready to learn?
Gender	How do males and females approach the learning situation in different ways?
Physical	How do physical changes, such as puberty, influence learning?
Intellectual	Does the ability to think change with age?
Linguistic	How does the ability to understand and communicate influence learning?
Social	How do others (pupils, teachers, TAs) influence the learning process?
Cultural	How does cultural background influence the learning process?
Emotional development	How does the ability to deal effectively with emotions influence the ability to learn?
Home life	How does family life impact on education?
School environment	How does the school environment impact on pupils?
Health	How does being healthy (for example: diet, sufficient sleep) impact on pupils' ability to learn?

Self-assessment activity 1.3

The following worksheet asks you to consider factors relating to learning and how these factors can both promote and hinder the learning process. NVQ candidates were encouraged in groups to fill in this worksheet and to share their ideas. Outlined below are some of their ideas. What would you include?

Factor	Examples of how this factor relates to my school	When is this factor a barrier to learning?	When does this factor promote learning?
Age	I work in a reception class and I noticed that some children take to reading like ducks to water, but others take a long time to get it.	I wonder how children who find it difficult to read react to those children who find it easy. If children constantly compare themselves to those who are more able that could result in feelings of frustration.	
Gender	I work in an infants' school and I noticed that the boys in particular find it very difficult to sit still during carpet time.		
Physical			
Intellectual			
Linguistic			
Social	In my secondary school there are a large number of Eastern European students. I have noticed that they tend to spend all their spare time together.		As a group they could support each other in adjusting to school in a new country.
Cultural			
Emotional development			
Home environment			
School environment			
Health	I work in a junior school and have noticed a number of the girls throwing away their packed lunches.		

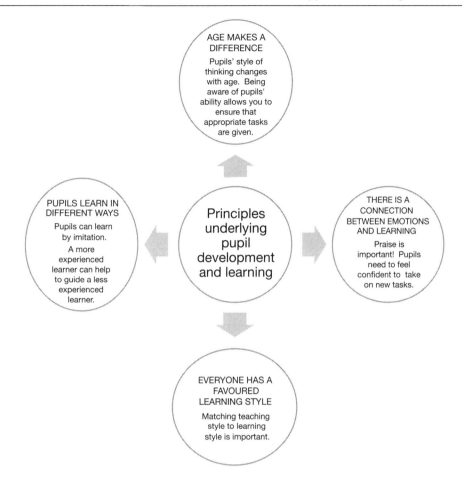

Figure 1.3 The basic principles underlying pupil development and strategies to enhance learning

Strategies to use for supporting pupils' learning as individuals and in groups

In reference to supporting learning in groups, we have already mentioned strategies to encourage participation and co-operation (see pages 15–16), we now turn to look at matching **teaching style** to **learning style**. Learning styles refers to the preferred manner in which an individual would choose to learn. There are many measures of learning styles. It is helpful to teach pupils in their preferred learning style. This is especially true with pupils who are struggling. Some schools are now giving pupils various questionnaires to measure their learning styles. If your school is doing this, then as a TA you can take advantage of this information. However, if you don't have this information you can watch how pupils learn and notice how they learn best.

With knowledge of a pupil's preferred learning style you can vary your approach. For example, use a visual approach for a visual learner.

As one TA comments: 'I was working with Sam helping him with a worksheet on maths co-ordinates; he was finding this very difficult to understand. I knew that Sam was a visual learner, so I quickly drew a treasure map with clues pointing to the location of the treasure. The clues were in the form of co-ordinates. Sam found this really interesting and quickly grasped the ideas of co-ordinates.'

Although it is useful to adapt your style to the learning style of a pupil, it is also true that all pupils will benefit from information being presented in a variety of styles. Though individuals will have their preferred learning style it is also important to be able to learn in a variety of ways.

Self-assessment activity 1.4: learning styles

The following worksheet outlines various learning styles and gives you the opportunity to fill in examples of how these theories relate to the pupils you work with.

Learning styles	Variations		
Perceptual learning style – which senses are being used	**Visual** Individuals prefer to be taught and learn more when teaching activities involve visual materials (videos, pictures, maps).	**Auditory** Preference to learn by listening. Preferred teaching activities would include listening to tapes and lectures.	**Kinaesthetic** These individuals prefer hands on, physical involvement. Preferred teaching activities would include making things or role-play.
Getting to know the pupils I work with	**Pupils who have a visual learning style are:**	**Pupils who have an auditory learning style are:**	**Pupils who have a kinaesthetic learning style are:**
Preferences in processing information	**Global** When a topic is introduced, global learners need to see the complete picture before they can begin to look at the details.		**Analytic** When a topic is introduced, analytic learners would prefer to proceed step by step. For them, being presented with the big picture could prove too overwhelming and confusing.
	Examples of pupils who have a global style are:		**Examples of pupils who are analytic are:**

	Impulsive This refers to the preferred pace of thinking. Impulsive learners like to jump in, start activities, make decisions and finish work quickly. However, in the rush mistakes are often made.		**Reflective** This refers to the preferred pace of thinking. Some pupils prefer to take their time over their work. They like to have time to think and consider the possibilities. However, it could be that the pupil spends so much time thinking that they don't get around to actually doing the work.	
	Examples of pupils who are impulsive are:		**Examples of pupils who are reflective are:**	
Environmental learning style	**Preferences in background noise**	**Silence** Some pupils prefer to work in absolute silence.	**Some noise** Some pupils prefer some background noise.	**Specific preferences in terms of noise** Pupils will differ in terms of what they would like to listen to when they learn, be it classical, jazz, rap, or hip-hop.
		Examples of pupils who prefer to work in silence are:	**Examples of pupils who prefer some noise are:**	**Examples of pupils with specific preferences in terms of noise are:**
	Preference in regard to temperature	**Cool**	**Warm**	**Hot**
		Examples of pupils who like a cool environment are:	**Examples of pupils who like a warm environment are:**	**Examples of pupils who like a hot environment are:**
	Preferred classroom design	**Traditional desk and chair placed in rows**	**Chairs and tables arranged in groups**	**Desks arranged in semi-circle**	**Sitting or lounging relaxed on carpet or floor**
		Examples of pupils:	**Examples of pupils:**	**Examples of pupils:**	**Examples of pupils:**

	Preferred level of lighting	Bright	Moderate	Subdued
		Examples of pupils:	**Examples of pupils:**	**Examples of pupils:**
Emotional learning style	**Preferences in responsibility**	Work independently without any supervision.	Some adult supervision.	Frequent adult supervision.
		Examples of pupils:	**Examples of pupils:**	**Examples of pupils:**
	Preferences in structure	Need to be told in exact and precise terms what the task is, how to do it and what is expected.	Students would prefer to be given the objective and then given the freedom to decide how they will accomplish the objective.	
		Examples of pupils:	**Examples of pupils:**	
Physiological learning style	**Food and drink intake**	Prefer to have no food or drink when learning.	Prefer to have some food or drink when learning.	
		Examples of pupils:	**Examples of pupils:**	
	Time of day	Learn best in the morning.	Learn best in the evening.	
		Examples of pupils:	**Examples of pupils:**	
	Need for mobility	Preference to sit still while learning.	Need, sometimes unconsciously, to move their body while learning. Often these individuals cannot keep still.	
		Examples of pupils:	**Examples of pupils:**	

Self-assessment activity 1.5

Inclusion involves changing the educational environment to match the individual needs of the pupil. As a TA you need to answer the following:

• How do the pupils I support learn?
• What range of teaching strategies do I use?
• How do the teaching strategies I use match how the pupils learn?

Figure 1.4 Learning styles super heroes

The basic principles underlying child development

Age makes a difference

Theorists, such a Jean Piaget (1970), state that children's thinking changes with time. Piaget states that children go through stages reflecting their thinking abilities or cognitive development. The precise age when a child will go onto the next stage will vary from child to child. However, all children will go through all stages in the same order:

Stage	Age
Sensori-motor	0–2
Pre-operational	2–7
Concrete operational	7–11
Formal operational	11+

When a child first starts school Piaget would describe them as pre-operational thinkers. This stage lasts from 2 years to 7 years. Children within this age group are learning at an incredible rate. However, Piaget states that their learning is limited by egocentrism and the failure to conserve.

Children between the ages of 2 and 7 are egocentric

Egocentrism refers to the difficulty in seeing the world from another's point of view. The classic test for egocentrism is known as the 'Three Mountains Test'. Here a child is presented with a model of three mountains: one with snow on the top, one with a cross on the top and one with a cabin on the top. The child is then shown a range of pictures of this model. The child has to choose the picture showing the view that they see. This the child can do.

Then the test gets more complicated. The child is shown a doll and the doll is placed at a point around the model of the three mountains. Then the child is asked to select the picture that the doll sees from where the doll is sitting. Often the child will select the picture that they can see.

From this test Piaget concluded that a young child tends to think that others see the world as they do. It is not until a child is 8 or 9 that they will realise that others will have their own viewpoint on the world and correctly select the picture that the doll can see.

Though this Three Mountains Test seems obscure, the fact that a child has difficulties appreciating another's viewpoint has implications for those working with children in this age group. The ability to see the world from another's viewpoint is related to the ability of empathy, where a child can imagine what another child would be feeling.

Teaching assistants can encourage children to think about how other children think and feel.

Children between the ages of 2 and 7 have difficulties conserving

Piaget also said that this pre-operational stage was dominated by the inability to conserve. Conservation, or to conserve, requires an individual to hold two apparently conflicting ideas in their mind at the same time. Again this idea seems complex.

Let's take an example of conservation of liquid.

Two children aged 4 and 8 are given one can of fizzy drink to share.

For the children involved it would be very important that each has the same amount.

As a TA you select two identical cups, two short, clear and wide cups, and very carefully measure the same amount of liquid into each cup.

At this point, after some consideration, the children will probably agree that there is the same amount of fizzy drink in each and that this is fair.

Figure 1.5
The 'Three Mountains Test'

Figure 1.6
Conservation
skills

However, if at that point you realise that one of the cups is chipped and pour the amount into a different shaped cup, let's say a clear tall thin cup, you may have problems convincing the younger child that there is the same amount in this cup.

A younger child of 4 might say that this is no longer fair as the tall thin cup has more liquid. It looks like it has more, therefore it has more.

An older child might reason that, as one cup is short and fat, the other cup is tall and thin. An older child will realise that although the cups holding the fizzy drink look different, actually they hold the same amount of liquid.

This skill of logic, involving holding two apparently conflicting views in your mind, is the ability to conserve. TAs can help pupils develop skills in logic by encouraging pupils to experiment and discover things for themselves.

Children of 7–11 are concrete thinkers

Children can do more complex operations such as multiplication and division and fractions but can only do these calculations on objects that actually exist, hence the word concrete. For example, three-quarters of 12 can be calculated but '*3/4 of x*' does not make sense.

Children of 11 plus move into the stage of formal operations

Piaget felt that children do not gain the ability to think abstractly until they reach the final stage of formal operations. This stage applies to children of the ages of 11 and over. It is for this reason that algebra is not taught to children until they are this age.

Factors that promote effective learning and the barriers to effective learning

Pupils learn in different ways

TAs can help pupils develop skills in logic by encouraging pupils to experiment and discover things for themselves. Pupils learn new information more easily if you can give them specific examples of real-life experiences that they can relate the new information to. Pupils benefit from using real apparatus.

If we remember, Piaget said that though children will go through all the stages in the same order, the age with which they can enter the next stage will vary from child to child.

Therefore, although the curriculum in secondary school assumes that older children can think more abstractly, some pupils who are struggling will not have this skill and will benefit from being given specific examples related to real-life objects. Though they are older, Piaget might say that they are still thinking at a less advanced level.

To learn children need to be actively involved

Piaget felt that a child's thinking ability was influenced by the age of the child and the interaction the child has with their environment.

Certain topics cannot be taught to a child until the child is biologically, or mentally ready to understand these concepts. Piaget talks about maturational readiness. If a child in Reception is having difficulties learning to read, perhaps it is because they are just not ready and that when they are ready they will learn.

However, to learn a child needs to be actively involved in the learning process. Piaget sees children as little scientists and who need to discover knowledge for themselves.

Piaget believed that when we learn information we store this information in the form of schemas. Schemas are units of mental thought.

Schemas are developed through the process of assimilation and accommodation.

Assimilation involves taking in new information and filing this information into an existing schema.

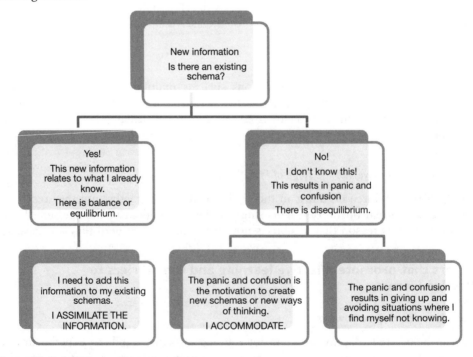

Figure 1.7 Assimilation and accommodation

Figure 1.8
The perils of
discovery learning

Accommodation is involved in the creation of new schemas or new ways of thinking.
   Accommodation is more complex. To create a schema or unit of new knowledge the individual first has to realise that:

- there is a gap in their understanding;
- others are seeing things differently;
- they are wrong and that they need to think in a different way.

Piaget called the state of being aware that there was a gap in understanding, cognitive dis-equilibrium. Piaget said that being in a state of cognitive dis-equilibrium was unpleasant but that it was a motivating force to learn new information. In a sense, what Piaget is saying is that to learn new information you first have to realise that there is something you don't understand. However, realising that you don't know can equally lead some students to give up and to avoid situations in which they are faced with the realisation that they don't know. As a TA you need to help students see that not knowing, not understanding, is OK and that it is an important step in the learning process. As pupils need to discover things for themselves, TAs can create situations or ask questions so that children can realise for themselves that there are things that they don't understand.

A more experienced learner can help to guide a less experienced learner

While Piaget stated that children learn new information through the process of discovery, Vygotsky (1986), another theorist, argued that children learn by being guided by a more experienced learner. This experienced learner could be the teacher, the TA or a more

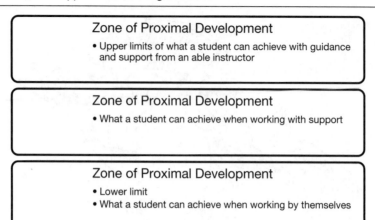

Figure 1.9 Zone of Proximal Development

able pupil. One of Vygotsky's key ideas was the Zone of Proximal Development. The Zone of Proximal Development states that what a pupil can do with assistance or help today they could do by themselves in time. Of course, to guide a pupil in learning is easier said than done. Successful guidance involves communicating knowledge to the pupil in a way that they can understand. Finding suitable questions is important.

Often it is TAs who work with 'pupils who find learning difficult'. A TA will usually need to explain a concept several times and perhaps in several different ways before the pupil shows some understanding. As pupils can learn from more experienced learners, TAs can encourage more able pupils to help pupils who are struggling. These pupils may be able to find the right words to explain the concept that the pupil finds so difficult to understand. As pupils can learn from each other it is helpful in group situations to encourage children to not only share the answers, but to share how they came to that answer. It is also important to communicate to the pupils that there are sometimes many ways to solve a problem.

Children learn by imitation

As we have mentioned previously, some individuals have a visual learning style; that is, they learn best by watching and imitating. To an extent all children learn by this process. If learning was just about watching what others do and imitating them, learning would be easy. But what makes imitation difficult is knowing what to pay attention to and being able to copy that behaviour when it comes to your turn. We have all had experiences when someone has said: 'Right this is easy, watch what I do and then you do it next.' However, whether they are demonstrating how to mend a photocopier, how to parallel park or how to make a soufflé, it is not quite that easy. Often the task is difficult to imitate because there are many steps involved and each of these steps involves practice.

As a TA, when you are asking a child to watch what you are doing and then imitate the task, it is important that you:

- Make sure the pupil is paying attention.
- Break the task into small steps. This allows the pupil to both remember the activity to be imitated and to recall what needs to be done when required.

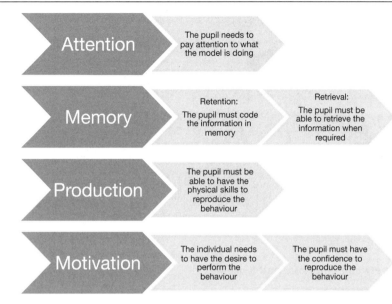

Figure 1.10 Observational learning requires ... (adapted from Santrock 2008)

- Praise effort and encourage the pupil to practise the steps on their own. Encouragement increases the pupils' confidence that they can do the activity.
- Explain to the pupil the reasons for and benefits of imitating the behaviour. This increases motivation.

The use of role models

One way of assisting a pupil to learn a task is to ask them to watch another individual (pupil or adult) who has mastered the task. There are two types of role model:

- Mastery models are individuals who can easily do the task. Here you are asking the pupil to watch another individual (pupil or adult) who is an expert. From watching this expert, the pupil can see how it is done and pick up tips.
- Coping models are individuals who have had difficulties with learning and have made their share of mistakes. However, these individuals do not give up; they learn from their mistakes and move forward.

Self-assessment questions

1   Benjamin has difficulties with maths and gets easily frustrated when he makes a mistake. As the TA, you want Benjamin to work with another pupil who could assist him. What type of model would you use, a mastery or coping model?

2   Maisy learns very quickly. The class has been given ten minutes to do the worksheet and Maisy has finished the worksheet in two minutes. You then ask Maisy to sit with Omar, a gifted pupil, who has been given extension activities. What type of model is Omar?

Figure 1.11 A novice can learn from an expert

Connections between emotions and learning

How children feel about themselves influences their ability to learn. When we talk about connections between emotions and learning we often refer to the importance of self-esteem. Those individuals with high self-esteem are prepared to take on new challenges. Individuals with high self-esteem are prepared to make mistakes and to learn from their mistakes. As we have said before, getting stuck, not knowing the answer, is the first step in building new ways of understanding. Unfortunately, some pupils are afraid of making mistakes and would rather not do the work, than try to do the work and fail. As a TA you will need to encourage pupils to take on new learning challenges and help them to deal with setbacks in a positive manner. As a TA you will need to praise the pupil. Praise should be given for the effort that they have put into the task rather than whether they got the question right or wrong.

School policy on the use of rewards and sanctions

Rewards

To encourage pupils to choose to act in a manner that is focused on learning and that is respectful and co-operative, the school will produce policies and procedures on rewards and sanctions.

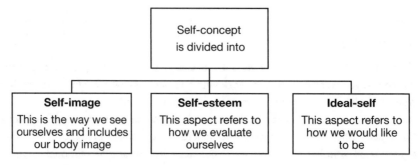

Figure 1.12 Components of the self-concept

Positive rewards include:

- verbal praise;
- rewards such as stickers and house points;
- positive notes or phone calls home;
- special privileges, for example, a pupil being able to work on a favourite activity, being first in line or first out of the class;
- special recognition from class or school.

Sanctions

Pupils need to know that there are limits and that there is a structure within the school that will create a safe and productive learning environment.

A behaviour policy will outline what constitutes disruptive behaviour and what the appropriate levels of intervention are in your school.

Possible levels of intervention

- Warning and reminder of appropriate behaviour.
- If inappropriate behaviour continues a consequence is delivered. This consequence could be in the form of a detention or missing break time.
- If inappropriate behaviour continues to be an issue a letter is sent home and if deemed necessary meetings are held with parents. Very serious incidents of inappropriate behaviour may result in an exclusion.

Remember:

- Sanctions are important in setting limits and boundaries.
- Sanctions should never be psychologically or physically harmful.
- Pupils need to perceive that sanctions are applied consistently and fairly.
- Sanctions should be delivered in a calm manner.
- Sanctions need to be focused on inappropriate behaviour and not the person.
- Pupils need to know why they received a sanction and what they should have been doing.
- Staff should know what sanctions are appropriate in what circumstances.
- Pupils need to know how they can make amends and move forward.
- Be Proactive! Pupils respond more positively to praise. It is important to catch the pupils when they are behaving well.

Many schools will involve pupils in formulating fair systems of both rewards and sanctions.

Self-assessment questions

1   What policies does your school have in relation to behaviour?
2   How does your school inform pupils of appropriate standards of behaviour?
3   How does your school involve pupils in formulating standards of behaviour?

Self-assessment activity 1.6

Table 1.2 Roles and responsibilities relating to behaviour

Routine	School and class rules	Role and responsibility of yourselves and others			
	Pupils are expected to:	I (the TA) will intervene when:	I (the TA) can use these strategies:	I (the TA) will inform the teacher if:	The teacher will:
In the playground	• Play safely • Play kindly with other pupils • Stay in designated areas	• A child is in out of bounds area • A child is not playing safely on equipment or leaving equipment lying around so that it is a danger for others • If a child is alone	• Remind them of the rules for play • Remind them of the consequences of not behaving • Praise good behaviour • If a child is alone encourage them to play with others	• A child refuses to behave after I have reminded them and told them of the consequences • Report any incidents of fighting, bullying or accidents	• The teacher has the authority to have pupils miss break and put their name in red book
Standing outside in the corridor waiting to come into class	• Stand in separate lines • Class helpers to go to front of line • Whatever line is the quietest gets to come in first	• The pupils are making too much noise or pushing in their line	• Remind them of the rules: be quiet, no pushing • Praise good behaviour	• A pupil refuses to get into line • If fighting occurs • A pupil refuses to behave when asked	

Beginning of the day	• Enter quietly • Hang coats up • Put book bags in right box • Put lunchbox on shelf in corridor • Put water bottle in tray • Sit quietly on carpet	• Remind pupils to hang their coats up • Remind pupils not to step on others' coats	• Praise for good behaviour	• Report to teacher if any pupil was upset
Where to sit				
When wishing to participate in class				
When requesting help				
Going into assembly				
Walking in corridors				
Using ICT equipment				

Of course, how you fill in this chart depends very much on your role.

Figure 1.13 Pupils' behaviour can sometimes present challenges

The importance of working within the boundaries of your role and competence and when you should refer to others

Part of behaving professionally is to know what you can do (working within your own sphere of competence) and when you need to refer situations or seek advice from others. Though mutual roles and responsibilities have been established there may be times when you feel you are struggling.

In terms of *supporting learning* there may be times when you feel you are not getting through to a pupil:

> 'No matter how I have tried to explain multiplication – he is just not getting it.'
> 'I know that part of my role is to support this pupil – but she has made it clear that she does not want me to help her.'

In terms of *supporting the curriculum* there might be areas that you as a TA feel the need for further input:

> 'I used to work on the interactive whiteboards but in the last year I have been working one-to-one with a pupil. However, now that I have been assigned to a new class I will be expected to use the interactive whiteboards again. Help!!!'

Being a professional requires a TA to recognise when further support is needed. Once you know that you need further support it is your responsibility to actively seek out the support. One area where it is crucial to know the boundaries of your role and when to refer to others is when you are *supporting standards relating to behaviour*. All school staff have a role to play in encouraging good behaviour and dealing effectively with disruptive behaviour. As a TA you will need to know what *you can do* to manage behaviour. Specifically, you will need to know the rewards, sanctions and strategies or techniques you can use. A TA will need to know when to consult the teacher and what strategies the teacher alone can use. In order to know what your role is in managing behaviour you will need to discuss this with the other staff. To help you do this, fill in Table 1.2. To help get you started let's look at how one TA has started to fill in her chart.

Self-assessment activity 1.7

The sorts of problems that might occur when supporting learning activities and how to deal with these	Possible explanations and strategies that can be used to support learning
Pupils may find the task too difficult.	Possibly the student is not ready (maturational readiness). I need to make sure that the task set is achievable. This will help to raise confidence and self-esteem.
Pupils say that they are bored and they don't want to do the task.	Perhaps the pupils are saying they are bored due to not being able to do the task. Again, I need to check to see if the task set is achievable. Perhaps I need to involve the pupils more in the activity. I need to remember that students learn when they are actively involved and that teaching style should match learning style.
Pupils who always ask me to do the work for them.	Possibly the student is lacking confidence and needs encouragement. I need to remember to encourage pupils to become independent learners. To begin I could help them, but slowly over time I would help them less and less and expect them to do more and more of the task by themselves.
Pupils who find it difficult to pay attention.	Perhaps there is a reason why they are finding it difficult to pay attention. I need to talk to the teacher about this. When working with the younger pupils I can remind them that they need to pay attention with their eyes, their ears and their hands. If they have targets regarding paying attention on their IEP, I will read the IEP so I know the strategies that I could use to help them.
Pupils who always want to have things their way.	
Pupils who feel they are not as good as other pupils.	
Pupils who make fun of other pupils that are struggling with their work. Pupils who refuse to do what I ask them.	
When working with groups one pupil may not want to join in.	
Even when the group is set by abilities there still may be a range of abilities within the group. How do I meet every pupil's needs?	
When working with groups one pupil always wants to dominate the group!	
When playing a game there is one pupil who always wants to go first.	
When playing a game there is always one pupil who finds it hard to lose.	

**rts of problems that might occur when supporting
activities and how to deal with these**

In this chapter we have talked at length about how to interact effectively with pupils. To test your knowledge have a go at filling in self-assessment activity 1.7. To help you get started a few examples and ideas for support have been given. Of course, for whatever problem that might occur when supporting learning activities, there are always numerous ways of dealing with the situation. A template for this is in the Appendix (see pages 238–9).

How to give feedback in a constructive manner and in a way that ensures that working relationships are maintained

Constructive feedback involves giving both positive comments and helpful suggestions but in a manner that is perceived as helpful.

Consideration is needed in doing this as helpful suggestions, if not carefully phrased, might be interpreted as put-downs or as criticisms.

As a TA you will need to give constructive feedback to both pupils and other teaching professionals you work with.

Consider how you would comment on the situations given below.

Self-assessment activity 1.8: what would your response be?

Situation	Possible reply
Mr Telford in the maths class is having difficulties in controlling the class. You notice that although he threatens to give the pupils detentions he never does. Mr Telford remarks to you that the class is still out of control. **What do you say?**	
Amy, a Year 2 pupil, has asked the supply teacher if she can sit next to her best friend. The supply teacher has agreed but you know that the regular teacher never allows this and that Amy and her best friend sitting together is a recipe for disaster. **What do you say?**	
Lincoln has worked very hard on his essay and is very happy with it even though he has made many mistakes. The pupil besides him leans over, looks at his work and remarks loudly that it is rubbish and that he can't read a word of it. **What do you say?**	
Shona has worked very hard on her poster on Global Warming. Shona has almost finished the poster but is becoming very frustrated as it is not quite what she wants it to be. You notice her becoming tearful and angry. She remarks that she wants to rip it up. **What do you say?**	

Checklist

✔ Know the learning objectives for the sessions you are supporting.
✔ Be aware of the individual targets for the pupils you are working with.
✔ Match teaching styles to pupils' learning styles where possible.
✔ Remind pupils that making mistakes is part of the learning process.
✔ Praise pupils for effort.

Further reading

Dean, J. (2006) *Meeting the Learning Needs of All Children*. London: Routledge.
Pound, L. (2005) *How Children Learn: From Montessori to Vygotsky – Educational approaches and theories made easy*. London: Step Forward Publishing.

Chapter 2

Unit 2: Support children's development

In this chapter we will look at four elements:

1 Contribute to supporting children's physical development and skills.
2 Contribute to supporting children's emotional and social development.
3 Contribute to supporting children's communication and intellectual development.
4 Contribute to planning to meet children's development needs.

The purpose of careful observation

Observing what is happening around us is something we do all the time in our day-to-day lives. However, when we are carrying out observations in the classroom we need to be careful and considered. There is an art to observing. In carrying out observations we need to ensure that the observations are:

*   fit for purpose, that is, focused on the aim of the observation;
*   detailed and accurate, that is, we try to record exactly what has happened;
*   free from assumptions and biases, that is, we record what we see, not what we think has happened.

Careful observation has many uses. Observation enables teaching professionals to understand the development of a pupil. Observation allows us to evaluate the pupil's responses to activities and experiences, which in turn will help inform planning of future activities. Often if there is an issue of concern for a certain pupil, careful considered observation can shed light on the reasons for the behaviour. Observations that are undertaken can be formal in that what is observed is written down or it can be informal, in that you verbally feedback your observations to relevant others.

The value of an observation lies in the quality of the observation; the degree to which information gathered is shared and discussed with relevant teaching professionals and how the information from the observation is used.

As someone who works with pupils, you will need to make careful observations and to share this information with other teaching professionals. More information on observations can be found in Unit 9.

The importance of checking your observations with others

In carrying out observations, a word of caution is needed. One observation can be compared to a snapshot, in that it records what is happening at one point in time. This information is useful but we cannot say that what is observed is typical of a pupil's behaviour or that it tells the whole story. To make sense of what we observe we need to talk to other teaching professionals, seeking their opinions and advice. Of course, there may be situations you observe that require an immediate reaction. See Unit 9 for further discussion on this matter.

Case study: being observant

Jason was enrolled on a NVQ course and was at college discussing with his colleagues the importance of observation. Jason described an incident that happened in the infant school at which he worked. A girl came into the school wearing shiny red Wellington boots. As the little girl took off her boots the other children noticed that there were red marks all over her legs. The children made comments such as: 'Is it blood?', 'Do you have a disease?' and 'Did someone hit you?' Jason admitted that he too was concerned and then the little girl said: 'Look – it comes off with water.'

What lessons can be learned from this story?

Figure 2.1
Be wary of jumping
to conclusions

Where to refer concerns you may have about children's/young people's development

If you have concerns about pupils' development it is important that you pass this information on. Therefore, it is important to know who to go to. In primary schools it may be the teacher or a more senior teaching assistant. In some cases it may be the **SENCO** or the **Designated Officer for Safeguarding Children**. What is more difficult is knowing the appropriate level of response.

Self-assessment activity 2.1: consider your responses to the following situations

Situation observed	Possible responses					
	Make a mental note	Write it down	Formal observation	Share with others	Immediately report it	Who would you report it to?
Child of 7 walked to school by themselves						
Pupil made a brilliant poster						
11-year-old girl throwing away most of her lunch						
Pupil with behavioural targets behaving really well in class						
15-year-old visibly withdrawn. This is very uncharacteristic behaviour for this pupil						
Examples of situations that I have experienced	• _____ • _____ • _____					

Importance of confidentiality, data protection and sharing information according to the procedures of your setting

Some observations will involve the recording of information. Some of this information may refer to pupil progress. Whatever the focus of the written information, your school will have a procedure in regard to how the information is to be shared, that is, who should have access to this information and how this information should be stored. Information regarding pupils is confidential and should never be left in a place where anyone can find it. Though you will need to discuss your observations with relevant teaching professionals, such discussions should take place at an appropriate time and place.

The school policy for storage and security of pupil records, including confidentiality requirements

Schools will have in their possession many records and documents, some of which are sensitive and many containing information of a confidential nature. Only those with genuine reason should have access to these records. You need to find out exactly how your school responds to this. Most schools will, however, employ similar principles:

- Whole school records and pupil files will be kept in the school office in lockable filing cabinets with the keys held only by the office staff and head teacher or member of the senior management team.
- Pupil files will not be let out of the school office, which ensures that persons viewing them can be monitored by office staff.
- All school office computers will have personal passwords that are known only to those who operate them.
- Memory discs containing information will be locked away when not in use.
- Class records will be kept safely and placed out of reach of children (in the case of primary schools).
- Individual pupil records kept by SENCOs and others with school-wide responsibilities will also be kept in a secure place – often in the school office or in lockable cabinets in those people's rooms.

Figure 2.2 Don't let paperwork overwhelm you

• Any unwanted paper records must be disposed of appropriately – shredded if possible – to ensure that they cannot be read later.

Whatever the case in your school, there should be clear procedures in place and you need to become aware of these.

However, it is not records who talk, it is people. All school staff must be aware of their duty of confidentiality. This means that no one, teachers or TAs, should discuss information regarding pupils with any unauthorised person. Trust takes time to build, but can be destroyed very quickly and schools need to operate in an atmosphere of trust between staff and between school and parents. More details about data protection can be found on pages 161–2 and 232.

The role of play in development

Play is one of those terms that we use all the time. But what is play? One definition of play could be an enjoyable spontaneous activity. Interestingly, psychologists and educationalists have argued about how to define play. Despite offering different definitions all psychologists agree that play is vital to all aspects of development. Further psychologists note that the way in which children play changes as they grow older. More will be said on play in Unit 15.

Areas and goals of development

Area of development	Physical	Communication and intellectual	Emotional and social
Goals of development	Gain control over their bodies	To develop reasoning and problem-solving skills	Ability to express feelings
	Develop spatial awareness	To develop concentration and listening skills	Develop self-esteem and sense of self
	Develop hand and eye co-ordination	To develop observational skills	Interact with adults
	Being able to manipulate objects	To develop a system of communication through gestures, expression and language	Interact with peer group and develop friendships
	Fine motor skills such as writing or using a pair of scissors	To develop imaginative and creative skills	Develop confidence
	Gross motor skills such as running, skipping or hopping	To develop the ability to remember information	Ability to cope with fears and anxieties
		To grasp concepts relating to science, maths, English, etc.	To develop an awareness of the needs of others
			Developing skills of co-operation such as sharing and turn-taking

Case study: the role of play in development

Everytown Infant School and the doctor's surgery

In the reception class it was decided that part of the activity corner would be made into a Doctor's Surgery. There was a desk for the receptionist with telephone and pencils and papers. There was a doctor's office with equipment such as a plastic stethoscope and needles, cloth bandages, prescription pad and pencils. There was also a collection of dressing up costumes, for doctors and nurses. In addition, there was a collection of books regarding visiting the doctor's office.

Self-assessment questions

1   What areas and goals of development are being encouraged in the above example?
2   How do you think the staff would be supporting the play activities?

Influences that affect children/young people's development

There are many factors that will impact on a pupil's development, such as their background, health or environment. Figure 2.3 is a simplified version of Bronfenbrenner's 'Ecological Theory' (Cole and Cole 2001), which focuses on how social context will influence a child's development. Who we are is a complex interaction of many factors.

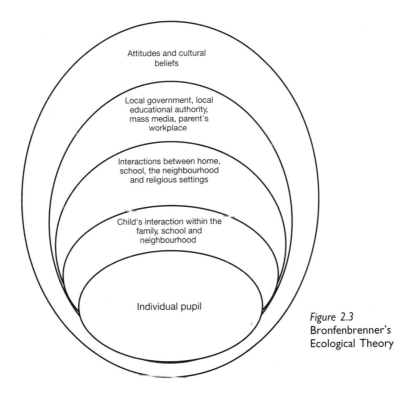

Figure 2.3
Bronfenbrenner's
Ecological Theory

Self-assessment questions

1   Think of a pupil you work with who is succeeding. What factors do you think influence their development and learning?
2   Think of a pupil you work with who is struggling. What factors do you think influence their development and learning?

Children's and young people's development is holistic and each area is interconnected

To really understand children's and young people's development there is a need to look at the whole child, that is to take a holistic approach that recognises that there are links between physical development, communication and intellectual development, and emotional and social development.

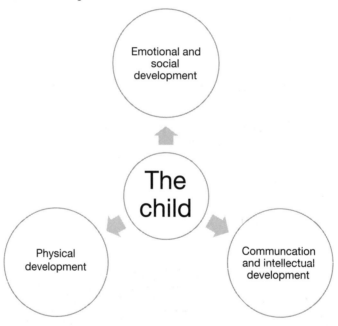

Figure 2.4 The interaction between different types of development

---

Physical development: at the end of the first year children develop the ability to point. This is a physical milestone.

Communication and intellectual development: parents will often respond to pointing by saying the word that corresponds to the object that the child is pointing at. This activity is key to the development of language.

Emotional and social development: these exchanges provide children opportunities to develop relationships with others.

Figure 2.5 Developing milestones at the zoo

Case study: how different aspects of development interact

Jason has just started junior school. Jason has been diagnosed with **developmental co-ordination disorder**. Though Jason's language and understanding is good for his age, he has difficulties with fine and gross motor skills. Jason finds handwriting difficult and is always bumping into things and falling over. Many other boys of his age have joined football teams – but Jason's attempts at playing football have always resulted in disaster. Jason does compare himself to others and wishes with all his heart that he could be good at football. Jason feels left out when the other boys play football at break time. It has been noticed at school that Jason is becoming more withdrawn and that he is no longer putting any effort into his work. Jason confided in his teaching assistant that he was lonely and that he felt his work was no good.

Self-assessment questions

1   How is Jason's ability in terms of physical development influencing his development in other areas?
2   What would you do to encourage Jason?

In planning activities for pupils, activities will often aim to develop goals from different areas of development.

Self-assessment activity 2.2

For the examples of activities given, state what goals are being developed.

Examples of activities	Physical development	Emotional and social development	Communication and intellectual development
Working in a group to carry out a science experiment			
Filling in a maths worksheet			
Participating in a team sport			
Examples from your own practice			

Children and young people develop at widely different rates, but in broadly the same sequence

Developmental psychologists will argue that there is a pattern of development, that is, a sequence or order in which development usually occurs. Remember that Piaget (see pages 29–33), in talking about cognitive development, or how children's thinking changed with time, stated that there were stages of development and that children progressed through these stages in the same order. However, Piaget also noted that there were differences between children in terms of when they progressed to the next stage. Every child is unique! In talking about development, psychologists talk about milestones, that is, development abilities that on average develop at a certain age. Often, in discussing milestones, relevant professionals give a range. For example, let's consider the age at which a child takes its first steps. A child who is an early developer might walk at 10 months. On average, most children will take their first steps at around 12 months, while some children won't be fully confident at walking until 18 months. All children are different! When a child is very late at reaching their milestones this can indicate an issue of concern. It is useful for anyone working with children and young people to be aware of milestones.

Basic outline of the expected pattern of children and young people's development: understanding how all children develop

Table 2.1 Patterns of development

Physical development	Communication and intellectual development (to include language development)	Social, emotional and behavioural development
By the end of the first year		
Walks holding on to furniture May walk two to three steps without support Uses pincer grip Points with index finger	Uses simple gestures Pays attention to speech Uses first words, such as mama, dada	Shy or anxious with strangers Starts to imitate others Preference for mother or regular care-giver
By the end of the second year		
Walks alone Begins to run Stands on tiptoe Scribbles Begins to show a preference for using one hand over the other	When an object is named, can point to the object, illustrating comprehension of word Uses two- to four-word sentences Follows simple instructions Begins make-believe play	Increased imitation of others Begins to show defiant behaviour Increased awareness of self Enjoys the company of other children
By the end of the third year		
Climbs well Runs easily Hold pencil in writing position Can turn book pages one at a time	Can sort objects by shape and colour Can complete simple puzzles with three or four pieces Uses four- to five-word sentences Can say own name, age and gender	Engages in turn-taking Expresses a wide range of emotions
By the end of the fourth year		
Can go up and down stairs without support Can kick a ball Draws circles and squares Begins to copy some capital letters Draws a person with two to four body parts	Speaks in sentences of five to six words Uses basic rules of grammar Correctly names some colours Begins to have a sense of time Understands the concepts of the *same* and *different*	Co-operates with other children Becomes involved in fantasy play
By the end of the fifth year		
Hops May be able to skip Copies triangle Prints some letters Dresses and undresses without assistance	Can count 10 or more objects Better understanding of time Speaks in sentences of more than five words Uses future tense Say name and address	Friends are important Can understand and agree to rules Able to distinguish fantasy from reality
Middle childhood (6–8 years)		
Can dress themselves Can tie shoelaces Can easily catch a ball with their hands Fine motor control involved in skills such as writing, sewing, playing a musical instrument develop	Rapid development of mental skills	Greater independence from parents Stronger sense of right and wrong Beginning awareness of future Greater awareness of others

continued

Table 2.1 (continued)

Physical development	Communication and intellectual development (to include language development)	Social, emotional and behavioural development
Middle childhood (9–11 years)		
For some children physical development associated with puberty will start	Becoming fluent in reading and writing skills	Stronger and more complex relationships with peers Growing independence from parent More peer pressure
Early adolescence (12–14 years)		
The changes of puberty will impact on all children	More ability for complex and abstract thought Relates to Piaget's formal operational stage	More influence from peer group Greater importance given to friendships Concern about physical appearance Moodiness
Middle adolescence (15–17 years)		
Most girls will be physically mature, while boys may still be maturing physically	Thinking about future educational and vocational choices Developing independent study skills	Increased interest in developing intimate relationships More time spent with peers than parents Developing a stronger sense of identity

(www.allthedaze.com, www.cdc.gov/ncbddd)

Quiz

Draw lines to match age with developmental milestones below.

Malcolm is 5	• **Friends are important**
	• **Uses joined-up writing**
Shona is 9	• **Engages in make-believe play**
	• **Can tell the time**
Leon is 12	• **Can distinguish between reality and fantasy**
	• **Can understand abstract problems such as algebra**
Rory is 15	• **Eating disorders can be a concern**

Supporting children's and young people's development at different ages

This course requires you to understand how all children should develop; however, for the age of children you support you need to provide your assessor with specific evidence of how you do this. In this section issues relevant to stages of development will be discussed. Some examples of how TAs support pupils' development will be given.

Issues common to all stages of development

The environment

Children and young adolescents need to feel safe and settled in order to develop to their potential. Whatever their age children need to feel confident to take on new challenges. Staff, though encouraging independence, should ensure a safe environment and help pupils to recognise dangers.

EXAMPLES: HOW TO DO THIS

Age 3–7: safe, secure and encouraging environment   When I am supervising pupils at break I encourage children to use the play equipment safely. We have a climbing frame at our school. Some children are very reluctant to use this as they fear they will fall while others are too confident. I encourage the timid children to have a go by offering lots of praise. I also ensure that the over-boisterous children do not hurt themselves or others. I always explain to them why some actions could be dangerous.

Age 7–12: safe and encouraging environment   Children of this age need to be encouraged to take responsibility for the safety of their environment. The children that I work with in Year 5 were asked to create a class charter regarding what makes for a safe classroom. I circulated around the classroom and encouraged discussion.

Age 12–16: provide an encouraging and safe environment that recognises approaching adulthood
Some pupils find the environment of a secondary school overwhelming. Pupils now have the responsibility of having to remember what classes they have to go to on what day and where these classes are. It is important that these pupils develop the confidence to do this for themselves. To help them in this I have held sessions after school with a few Year 7 pupils, where I have helped them draw personalised maps and have practised various routes around the school with them.

Make sure all the children you work with can take part equally, including those with disabilities and special educational needs

All children and young adolescents, regardless of ability, should feel valued and should have equal opportunities to participate in school activities. This is central to **inclusion**. See pages 12–16, 148–9 and 183–4.

EXAMPLE: HOW TO DO THIS

Age 3–7   Wilf is in a wheelchair and is the only child who needs a wheelchair in our school. When we are playing team games in PE, I help Wilf in his role as referee. In this way Wilf knows that he is playing an important role in the game.

Develop consistent relationships and work to support children's emotional well-being, confidence and resilience

Positive and supportive relationships are central to emotional and social development. Children need to feel that they are valued and special in order to develop a healthy level of self-esteem. Recent interest has centred on happiness and well-being. Layard (APPG 2007) argues that one of the aims of education is to help children to lead happy lives. Happiness and well-being involves managing your emotions and the ability to feel compassion for others. Individuals who have high levels of emotional well-being are more likely to be resilient, that is, to be able to cope with difficult situations that come their way. On the other hand it has been found that individuals who are less happy are constantly comparing themselves to other people. The SEAL (Social, Emotional Aspects of Learning) programme is now being run in both primary and secondary schools; as a teaching assistant you might be involved with this programme. Five aspects of learning that are covered within these sessions include self-awareness, managing feelings, motivation, empathy and social skills.

EXAMPLES: HOW TO DO THIS

Age 3–7   I work in the reception class. Within the SEAL programme we were looking at the topic of understanding feelings. We showed the pupils various pictures of children doing things and looking happy. We asked the pupils what they thought the person was feeling and why they thought that. Then we asked the children to make a happy face and to say what makes them happy. The children in the class really enjoyed this. To encourage some of the more timid children I made a happy face and talked about what makes me happy.

Age 7–12   I work in Year 5. Following the SEAL programme we had the children working in groups to create a book regarding friendship problems and how to solve them. This activity encouraged the pupils to feel empathy for others and to look at situations from many perspectives. I circulated around the groups and encouraged the children in what they had to say.

Age 12–16   When working in a small group within a Year 9 class, one of the students was very upset as they had been dumped by text message. I took the student out and just listened to him. Though I didn't say much I think this student really appreciated that I cared enough to listen. I mentioned this to the teacher and we decided to have a discussion with the class on text etiquette.

Give meaningful praise and encouragement

Is praise always a good thing? Praise can raise self-esteem, give the person on the receiving end that feel-good factor and encourage the person to repeat the behaviour for which they were praised. However, praise will not be effective if it is not perceived as genuine. For example, a pupil might turn around and say: 'You don't really mean that . . . You are just saying that . . . You say that to everyone'. Praise is most effective if it is focused on effort rather than ability. Though 'Well done' and 'Great work' are nice to hear, praise such as 'I know you found that worksheet very difficult – but you tried very hard and I am proud of you', will encourage the pupil to associate effort with achievement. Praise can be more meaningful if it is combined with constructive and helpful feedback that tells the pupil what they did well and what they need to do next.

EXAMPLES: HOW TO DO THIS

Age 3–7 When I first worked with the pupils in reception class, I told all the pupils that their work was brilliant! Now I make a point of also saying one thing about why I thought their work was brilliant.

Age 7–12 In the Year 4 class I find that many of the pupils are very quick to compare themselves with others. I make a point of trying to help the pupils realise their own unique strengths.

Age 12–16 Some pupils in secondary schools find receiving praise difficult as they think it is not cool or that they will be called a swot. With pupils of this age, I usually give them a 'thumbs up'. Many pupils appreciate this.

Case study: pupils comparing themselves to others

TA: Jimmy are you good at reading?

Jimmy: I'm in the swamp group and we are reading the yellow books. Amy is better than me, she is a river. In the river group they are reading the red books. But I'm better than Todd – he is a puddle. The puddle group is still on the green books.

Self-assessment question

How would you respond to Jimmy?

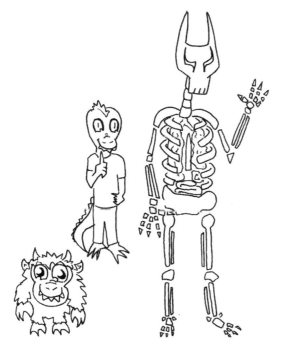

Figure 2.6
Making comparisons: I am not as scary as the tall bloke, but I am scarier than the little guy

Be a listening ear when needed: encourage positive communication, being available to support, listen and encourage

Pupils develop emotionally, socially and cognitively in an atmosphere where they feel valued and listened to. When pupils feel valued and listened to they are more likely to feel able to express their worries and anxieties. TAs are there to listen and to respond sensitively and appropriately in the event of disclosures (see pages 76–8 for disclosures and pages 102 and 106 for **active listening**). TAs and other teaching professionals can act as role models in regard to dealing positively with disagreements, conflicts and anxieties.

EXAMPLES: HOW TO DO THIS

Age 3–7   I work in a Year 2 class. The girls in my class are constantly falling out with their friends. When I am supervising at break time there is always someone who is upset because her best friend is playing with someone else. I am always there to listen to their concerns. I try to explain that part of being a friend means sharing that friend with others.

Age 7–12   I work in a Year 5 class. One of the boys that I support just loves football. However, he confided to me that he feels left out as all his friends are in football teams. He said that he tried out for the team but was turned down. He said that he was very upset and felt rejected. I can't make everything better for him – but I can listen and I do try to get him to appreciate all the things that he can do well.

Age 12–16   I work in a Year 11 class. Though some of the students I support know what they are doing after GCSEs, some of them have no ideas. I talk to the students about how I didn't know what to do when I left school and how worried I felt about what to do. I then advise them to explore as many options as possible. Though I can't make their decisions for them, I think that being there to talk things through is very important.

Be realistic, consistent and supportive in your responses to children's behaviour

In terms of being realistic in regard to your expectations of the pupil's behaviour, it is important not to expect too much nor to expect too little. As a TA you will need to know both what constitutes age-appropriate behaviour and what the individual pupil is capable of. In dealing with pupil behaviour it is important to be consistent, fair and measured. In order to achieve this you will need to know and follow the school's behaviour policy. It is not only essential that you deal with inappropriate behaviour but that you recognise and reward good behaviour. Sadly many pupils still comment that they are never noticed or praised when they are behaving well. When dealing with pupils who find behaving appropriately a challenge it is important to praise them in their attempts.

Allow children to assess and take risks without over- or under-protecting them

As a TA you will need to provide a safe nurturing environment where pupils feel confident to undertake age-appropriate risks. Taking risks can lead to an increase in self-esteem, confidence and independence. However, there is a fine line between over-protection and under-protection. Under-protection could lead to pupils being placed in potentially dangerous situations where they could experience harm, for example being allowed to play on an outdoor climbing frame in wet weather. On the other hand, over-protection could lead the pupil to doubting their own ability to cope with new situations and challenges, for example not letting a pupil have a go on a climbing frame just in case they fall. Risks arise when an individual is placed in a new situation where they feel unsure of how to respond. Risks might involve physical or emotional harm. An example of emotional harm could be a pupil feeling humiliated when giving the wrong answer to a question. To help a pupil deal with new situations a TA needs to discuss the potential risks and ways of responding to these risks. It is hoped that by having such discussions the pupil will eventually be able to assess and deal with the risks of any new situations for themselves. This is a very important life skill.

Use appropriate activities, materials and experiences to support learning and development

As a TA you will discuss with the teacher appropriate activities, materials and experiences to support learning and development. In a sense, when we are talking about matching appropriate activities, materials and learning experiences to the learning needs of individual pupils, we are talking about **personalised learning**. When deciding how to personalise the learning experience consideration needs to be taken regarding:

* how much support should be given to a pupil by the teacher or TA;
* the task required;
* the outcome expected;
* the resources available to support the learning;
* the level of negotiation the pupil has in deciding the task;
* whether the task involves individual or group work.

All this may seem complicated but these decisions about how to plan learning activities are ones that you discuss with the teacher on a daily basis.

Identify activities and equipment to support children's play, creativity and learning, including how these are used to best effect

Again it is the role of the TA to work with the teacher to support children's play, creativity and learning. Creativity is now seen as essential to learning. Traditionally it was thought that only a few rare and gifted individuals could be classified as being creative. Nowadays schools focus on a more democratic definition of creativity where every child is considered to have creative potential and to be capable of creative expression. The emphasis is now on the creative process. The creative process involves the use of imagination and the pursuit of originality, which is coming up with new ideas. It is through this creative process that pupils have the opportunity to develop communication skills, problem-solving skills and thinking skills. Mellou (1996) states that creativity can be developed through creative environments, creative programmes, creative teachers and creative ways of teaching. Edwards and Springate (1995) state that teaching professionals can encourage creativity by encouraging experimentation, modelling creative thinking and behaviour, asking open-ended questions, accepting that for some questions there is no one right answer and praising pupils who provide novel answers.

Provide opportunities for exploration and different experiences

Pupils of all ages learn and develop by being encouraged to explore their environment and to partake in different types of experiences. There is a tendency for some pupils to want to stay in their comfort zone, that is they choose to participate in activities that are known and familiar. This is fine to some extent but it does not stretch the pupil. To grow intellectually, socially and emotionally pupils can really benefit from new experiences. School can provide a wealth of new experiences, for example field trips to museums, theatre productions or activity centres. On a more day-to-day level pupils can be encouraged to explore different types of reading books, working with different pupils or playing different types of games at break time. The role of the TA is to give pupils the confidence to value and engage in a variety of experiences.

Use every opportunity to encourage children's communication, literacy and language development

TAs have many opportunities to encourage pupils' listening and speaking skills. These skills can be developed through interactions with individual pupils, through encouraging small group discussions and whole class debate. Some pupils who are shy or fearful that they will give the wrong answer will need encouragement. Talking and listening are important skills as they are essential in the development of thinking and reasoning skills. Children who have additional language needs or children who come from bilingual or multilingual backgrounds will need more support. See Unit 11 for what schools can offer.

Contribute to an environment that supports children's physical skills and confidence in movement

One aspect of a pupil's **self-image** concerns their physical abilities and skills. Certainly physical skills are practiced and developed formally within PE lessons. However, on an informal basis these skills are practiced at break time through participation in numerous games and activities. On another level fine motor skills are involved in tasks such as writing. Pupils will vary in their physical abilities and skills and pupils will be aware of how they compare to others. Part of the TAs role is to encourage pupils whatever their ability to have a go and to encourage the pupils to value effort. It is not the winning that counts. It is also important to recognise that physical activities might need to be adapted so that all pupils can participate.

Issues facing children of different ages

Supporting children's development from 3–7 years: support children's interest in numbers, counting, sorting and matching

Being numerate, that is, being able to understand and use numbers, is an important skill in today's world. Too often, adults will struggle with this. Many adults will say that their dislike or fear of numbers began when they were very young. In schools there will be certain parts of the day when the focus will be on developing mathematical skills. It is important that young children's experiences of learning about numbers, through counting, sorting and matching, is experienced as an enjoyable and fun activity. Further, it is important that young children see that numbers are important and relevant to many aspects of their life. As a TA you can help children to develop an interest in numbers. See Unit 6 for further information.

HOW WOULD YOU DO THIS?

Play with and alongside the child, sensitively supporting their play   Play is an important part of the early years curriculum. Here the emphasis is on playful learning and purposeful play where academic skills can be encouraged through play. Young children should feel that they have ownership of the play, that is, they are not being controlled by the adults around them. However, skilful teaching practitioners can support children in extending their play by giving them ideas and making play opportunities for learning by engaging the pupils in conversations that have an educational purpose. See Chapter 13 for further information.

Supporting children's development from 7–12 years: recognise and acknowledge children's particular needs as they enter puberty

The age in which individual children will enter puberty will vary. However, all children will experience changes in appearances during puberty and will face challenges as they begin to forge a new identity as an adolescent. Individuals who are early or late developers may experience particular difficulties as they feel out of step with their peer group. In today's society the media provides a very powerful image of ideal body shapes that many young people aspire to. Incidences of eating disorders, such as anorexia and bulimia are increasing as is the rise of obesity. Earliest indicators of eating problems can emerge during this stage. TAs can be sensitive to these changes and be there to listen and support pupils.

Support young people's development from 12–16 years: recognise and acknowledge young people's particular needs as they go through puberty and adolescence and become adults

Pupils of this age will be faced with changes in appearance and these changes will impact on their self-image and self-esteem. TAs can support pupils in feeling good about themselves. Individuals who are slow developers may experience particular difficulties at this stage. Eating disorders become a real issue for this age group. TAs should try to encourage pupils to focus not on the shape of their body but the shape their body is in, by encouraging healthy eating and healthy lifestyles. Additionally pupils of this age will be faced with challenges of developing relationships, facing pressure of their peer group and making choices regarding their future life. Adolescents need positive adult role models and concerned adults who value them and take a personal interest in their hopes and ideals.

HOW WOULD YOU DO THIS?

Provide information for young people, when requested, about things that concern them   In the transition to adulthood, teenagers will face many challenges regarding relationships, friendships and choices in regard to lifestyle. Alcohol and drug abuse, teenage pregnancy, juvenile crime, including knife crime, are real issues in society. Teenagers will ask questions and will need honest and factually correct answers about the issues that concern them. TAs need to respond appropriately and sensitively, being aware of how to deal with disclosures (see pages 76–8) and when to refer individuals to others professionals for support. TAs do not need to have all the answers but they do need to know who to go to for these answers.

Supporting children and young people of all ages through transitions in their lives

Transitions or changes are a fact of life. In some respect these changes can be seen as rites of passage. A child moves from pre-school to school, from primary school to secondary school, from secondary school to college and from the world of education to work. Different phases of education involve different educational environments, different manners of teaching and different views in regard to what is expected from the student. From the pupil's perspective these changes can be exciting and challenging but at the same time frightening as they might require making new friends, settling into new routines and meeting new expectations in regard to work. Schools nowadays spend much time on devising programmes to ease the transition. Such programmes include taster days, school visits and buddy schemes, whereby new students are paired with older students. There is evidence that the better prepared a pupil is for the transition, the quicker they will settle into the new routine and the sooner the pupil will be ready to learn. No matter what transition programmes are in place there will be some pupils who, for whatever reason, find the transition difficult. These pupils will need additional support that a TA can provide. Transitions or changes are not easy but dealing positively with the challenges these changes bring can give a pupil the confidence to deal with future changes. Perhaps the greatest gift a TA can give a pupil is to help them develop the confidence to deal with these challenges.

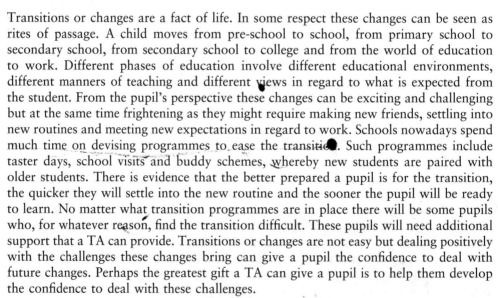

Self-assessment questions

1   In your school what transitions are required of the pupils?
2   How does your school support these transitions? What programmes do they offer?
3   How do you support pupils going through these transitions?
4   How do you give pupils confidence to cope with the transitions?

Checklist

✔ Remember every child is unique!
✔ Know the developmental milestones for the age group with which you work.
✔ Share concerns with other teaching professionals.

Further reading

Bee, H. and Boyd, D. (2006) *The Developing Child*. London: Pearson Education.
Keenan, T. (2001) *An Introduction to Child Development*. London: Sage.

Chapter 3

Unit 3: Help to keep children safe

This unit contains four elements:

- Preparing and maintaining a safe environment.
- Deal with accidents, emergencies and illness.
- Support the safeguarding of children from abuse.
- Encourage pupils' positive behaviour.

School policies and procedures

Every member of staff in a school has, as a primary duty of care, to give consideration to the health, safety, security and well-being of both pupils and adults. It is everyone's responsibility to ensure that the school environment is both safe and secure for all the community.

Every school must have a Health and Safety Policy, which should:

- outline the responsibilities of staff;
- state how a healthy and safe environment will be established and maintained;
- stipulate procedures for recording and reporting accidents, injuries and emergencies.

Staff need to follow procedures for external and internal security. Every member of staff has a responsibility to challenge anyone on the premises they do not recognise who is not showing appropriate identification.

The laws governing safety and safeguarding children

Health and safety

Various Acts of Parliament and government regulations relate to health and safety in schools. Some of the most significant are:

- The Health and Safety at Work Act, 1974.
- Health and Safety (First Aid) Regulations, 1981.
- The Manual Handling Operations Regulations, 1992.
- The Health and Safety of Pupils on Educational Visits Act, 1998.
- Health and Safety at Work Regulations, 1999.

Probably the most familiar government publication is *Every Child Matters (ECM)*. Two of the five ECM outcomes relate to health and safety – Be Healthy and Stay Safe.

Figure 3.1 Security is important

Safeguarding children

A large number of Acts of Parliament and government publications relate to safeguarding children. Among these are:

- The Children Act 1989;
- The Education Act 2002;
- The Children Act 2004;
- Safeguarding Vulnerable Groups Act 2006;
- *Circular 10/95 Protecting Children from Abuse: The role of the Education Service* (DfEE 1995);
- *Every Child Matters: Change for children* (DfES 2004a);
- *What to do if you're worried a child is being abused* (DfES 2006);
- *Working Together to Safeguard Children* (HMSO 1999, revised 2006).

While you do not need to be familiar with the details of all these, you do need to know how they impact on schools (see Chapter 18 for more details).

Safe working practices

A number of procedures are mandatory for all schools and local authorities:

- A Child Protection Policy must be in place.
- CRB (Criminal Record Bureau) checks for all staff, governors and regular volunteers must be made.
- Information must be shared within and between agencies.
- The school **governors** must ensure that a '**Designated Officer for Safeguarding Children**' (DOSC) is in place with responsibility for child protection and that that person has received appropriate and up-to-date training.

- The DOSC needs to make sure that all school staff receive training every three years to inform them of up-to-date issues and procedures.
- Local Safeguarding Children Boards (LSCB) must be established in every region with core members coming from local authorities, health bodies and police.
- Each **local authority** must have a senior officer responsible for co-ordinating policy and action on child protection.

Important concepts

Four categories of abuse are identified by law – neglect, sexual abuse, physical abuse and emotional abuse. Children can be considered to be at risk of abuse if their basic needs are not being met or if those needs are in some way being violated. Concepts such as 'significant harm', 'joint working' and 'abuse of trust' must be understood within all schools. The overarching principle is that the welfare of the child is paramount.

'*Significant harm*' – an official term used to indicate when compulsory intervention in family life will take place, which can be as a result of children witnessing domestic violence even though they may not have experienced this themselves.

'*Abuse of trust*' – it is illegal for an adult in a position of trust (which includes all school staff, governors and volunteers) to engage in sexual activity with any person less than 18 years of age with whom they have a 'relationship of trust'. This is the case whether or not there was consent from the young person.

'*Joint working*' – all agencies need to work together, including sharing information, in order to safeguard children and young people.

Physical contact with pupils

Young children and even older ones who are distressed may look for physical contact with adults for comfort. In such cases there are no concrete legal requirements; staff need to use their own discretion, taking into account the principles below.

Physical contact:

- must be normal and natural, not unnecessary or unjustified;
- should not persist for long;
- should not be with the same pupil over a period of time.

Adults:

- should be aware that physical contact could be misinterpreted;
- must never touch pupils in ways which might be considered indecent;
- should avoid being alone with a pupil in confined or secluded areas.

Regulations covering manual handling and the risks associated with lifting and carrying children

It is illegal to use any form of physical punishment, although pupils can be physically restrained in certain circumstances – dealt with in your school's Physical Intervention Policy.

Some pupils may require manual handling, for instance those whose physical disability necessitates them being turned by others or who need help with toileting. In such situations, schools will need to put an Intimate Care Policy into place and TAs involved in such support will need to receive specialised training from health professionals. No one should be asked to manually handle pupils without adequate and appropriate training.

There are a number of risks associated with manually handling or lifting pupils, perhaps the most obvious of which is the physical risk of injury to either the pupil or the person lifting. Improper lifting can seriously injure either pupil or adult, or both, which is why proper training is essential.

Safety factors and recognised standards of equipment and materials for children

Teacher responsibility – the 'prudent parent'

Teachers are responsible both for the safety of their learning environment and for the children in their care. This begins with the legal responsibility to take registers at the start of each morning and each afternoon. All staff should act like a 'prudent parent' in the event of an accident, injury or emergency, reporting any such incident in line with school procedures. They should also ensure that the working environment is safe for pupils; this includes making sure all areas are free of obstructions, exits are clear and that all equipment used is both safe and is being used in compliance with the manufacturer's instructions.

All employees have a responsibility to maintain a safe and secure environment, including the appropriate disposal of waste. Nobody can say it is somebody else's job. The school is required to ensure that all facilities, including washrooms and toilets, are regularly cleaned and inspected for health and safety.

Whole school environment

Part of safeguarding pupils is to ensure that those with **special educational needs** and/or **disabilities** are safe and secure in the school environment and that the physical environment is adapted as much as possible to meet their needs.

Visual impairments

Pupils with visual impairments can be helped by having appropriate lighting not only in the classes, but also in the corridors and in every other part of the school. Décor is also important – contrasting paint for doors and walls can help pupils with visual impairments orientate themselves around the school. It is essential that corridors and doorways are kept free from clutter so that pupils with visual impairments are not hindered in their movement around the school.

Hearing impairments

Acoustics are very important for pupils with hearing impairments, with the aim of maximising any residual hearing. Background noise needs to be reduced as much as possible, which can be done by the use of carpeted areas, acoustic baffle boards hung from ceilings and by seating pupils away from distracting noises.

Physical disabilities

Wheelchair access to the school building and to classrooms should be made possible. Within classrooms and corridors, enough room needs to be made so that wheelchairs can be manoeuvred. Pupils with physical disabilities may need to be seated near exits so they can enter and leave the classroom as easily as possible. It may also help to have their time of arrival and departures made flexible to avoid the melee experienced by other pupils at such times.

Many pupils benefit from postural supports. This can be as simple as a wedge-shaped cushion, but it could also be a special chair that may well be larger than normal classroom chairs.

Moving equipment

You yourself are required not to try and move objects beyond your strength and where you have children under your direct supervision, it is your responsibility to instruct them in how to safely move equipment, should that be needed. They should never be allowed to move awkward objects such as pianos or televisions. It is also your responsibility to ensure that children under your supervision are wearing appropriate safety equipment, such as goggles when using potentially dangerous science or DT equipment.

Safe layout and organisation of rooms, equipment, materials and outdoor spaces

Inside the school building you may work in classrooms, halls, general working areas, ICT suites, science laboratories, gymnasiums, cooking areas, workshops and many others. Each of these will present different issues of health and safety, which must be considered and responded to carefully.

Figure 3.2 Don't strain yourself

You may also work outside of school buildings with children – the school playground, during sports activities, on educational visits, joining residential trips and so on. These too pose issues of health and safety that must be responded to appropriately.

Safety and security also relates to pupils arriving at and departing from the school. Care needs to be taken that younger children are met by appropriate adults while older students must be protected from dangerous traffic or from undesirable activities outside the school gates.

The context of the school

Issues of safety and security are likely to be different for village schools than for those situated in busy and crowded inner cities. Where schools are located on main roads, safety will relate to road crossing patrols, whereas village schools may face issues of pupils needing to be escorted along narrow roads without pavements, possibly with poor street lighting in the winter.

Road safety

While travel to and from the school is the responsibility of parents and carers rather than school staff, the school has a duty to teach and train the pupils in road safety. The school may have a policy on using bicycles, skateboards or roller blades to come to school. You must be familiar with this and reinforce school procedures whenever the occasion arises.

Safety issues and concerns when taking children/young people out of the setting

Pupil–teacher ratio

When taking pupils out of the school on educational visits and the like, the level of pupil–teacher ratio required by law varies according to the age of the pupils and the type of activity engaged in. The younger the pupils, the higher ratio of adults to children will be required. The essential factor is that there are enough adults to ensure the safety and well-being of the pupils both at the place of the visit and on the journey there and back.

Risk assessments

When taking children on trips the lead teacher is required by law to complete a risk assessment, indicating the risks that have been thought about and consideration given to reducing those risks. Below is an example of a completed risk assessment with an associated accident report log. Both are imaginary events, but could actually happen!

Somewhere Junior School risk assessment and risk management form – educational visits

Location of the visit: City Museum

Purpose of visit: Local history study

Group on the visit: Class 3R

Leader: Mrs Russell (class teacher)

Other accompanying adults: Miss Begum (TA) and three mothers

Group size: 30

Adult–pupil ratio: 1:6

Identifying and assessing risks	What to do to reduce the risk
Location of visit Walk along a main road, crossing several smaller ones	Split into groups of six, each leader practiced in 'shepherding' pupils across roads
Risk rating high	**Reduced risk level** low
Complex corridors and rooms out of sight from each other	Group leaders regularly take head count
Risk rating high	**Reduced risk level** low
Risk to group as a whole 30 children mixed ability – get separated, misbehave	Low pupil–teacher ratio, pupils likely to misbehave placed with teacher or TA
Risk rating medium	**Reduced risk level** low
Risk to individual pupils Abigail – asthma – can develop symptoms after walking for only a short period of time	Discussion between TA, teacher and Abigail's mother – agreed TA to have Abigail in her group and take medication and mobile phone with her. Agreed procedures if asthma attack occurs (administer medication and contact school and mother and emergency services if serious)
Risk level medium	
	Reduced risk level low

Somewhere Junior School accident/incident log

Date of accident/incident: 2 June 2009

Time of accident/incident: 9.25 a.m.

Location of accident/incident: Princes Road on way to City Museum

Nature of accident/incident: Asthma attack – Abigail

Name and title of person dealing with the accident/incident: Nazreen Begum (teaching assistant) under the supervision of Mrs Russell (teacher)

Name and title of person completing this log: Nazreen Begum (TA)

Other person(s) involved including their roles/responsibilities: Mrs Katie Russell (class teacher)

Any follow up required:
None

Description of the accident/incident
Abigail was in my group on the way to the museum. We were nearly there when I noticed that she had begun to find it difficult to breath and was beginning to wheeze. She stopped walking and begun to inhale and exhale deeply and was obviously beginning to be distressed.

Response to the accident/incident
Abigail herself was used to what was happening, and I was prepared for it. I asked the whole group to stop and gave Abigail her inhaler. I made sure the other pupils gave her space as she used her inhaler. As soon as I realised Abigail was having an asthma attack I sent a pupil to go ahead to the front of the class to tell Mrs Russell. She stopped the class on the pavement as soon as she heard and came back to see how Abigail was. It took two minutes or so to take effect, during which time the whole class was waiting away from the kerb. After that she recovered and was able to reach the museum. At the museum I made sure she sat down and rested for ten minutes before engaging with the rest of the visit. There were no more incidents during the day.

Signature of person completing this form: Nazreen Begum (teaching assistant)

Date signed: 2 June 2009

Reasons for any delay in completing this form: I completed this form on return to the school after the visit to the museum.

Self-assessment activity 3.1

1   Name the information which should be found in a Health and Safety Policy.
2   What do you think acting as a 'prudent parent' means?
3   What responsibilities do you have for safety and security in your school?

Good hygiene practice: avoiding of cross infection, disposal of waste, food handling and handling bodily fluids

Your own protection

At all times you are to have concern for your own health and safety so, for instance, you need to wear protective clothing such as disposable gloves, when touching or potentially touching any bodily fluid. After any incident you should make sure that all involved wash their hands.

Health, safety and security education

One important aspect of ensuring the safety of children in school is the health, safety and security education they receive. The younger the children, the more need there will be to enforce consistent, explicit and firm rules for safe behaviour.

Health education is part of the **National Curriculum** and is normally covered within PSHE (Personal, Social and Health Education). The overall aim is to develop a sense of personal responsibility and pride in pupils and give them information to make informed choices about their lifestyles. This will be in keeping with the *Every Child Matters* outcome: be healthy.

Figure 3.3 TAs should wear protective clothing

The younger the children, the more need there will be to enforce consistent, explicit and firm rules for safe behaviour. Safety procedures and rules will need to be continually reinforced, particularly those relating to personal hygiene and to interacting with strangers ('stranger-danger').

As children get older they need instruction on how to play and explore safely, e.g. riding bicycles, swimming, road safety, going to and from school on their own. While all children need to learn to take responsibility for their own safety and well-being, this is going to be especially developed during their junior school careers. They must be allowed to participate more and more in decisions regarding their safety and their health.

Adolescents need to be given increasing responsibility and more flexible boundaries while maintaining limits. They need to be instructed and encouraged to discuss and respond to many dangers – abuse, use of weapons, criminal activity, gang culture, drugs, alcohol and irresponsible sexual activity. New levels of road safety are needed when they begin to ride motorcycles and drive cars.

Policies and procedures of your setting for responding to and recording accidents, injuries and emergency conditions; basic first aid and awareness of location and contents of first aid boxes

Emergency procedures

Each school must have emergency procedures in place as part of their preparation to respond to incidents such as a fire or bomb scare. Training in these procedures must be given to all staff and they must be practised, for example, it is a legal requirement that schools conduct a fire evacuation drill at least once a year. As a teaching assistant you may be asked to perform specific functions in respect to emergency procedures, for instance, checking the toilets or other non-teaching areas in the event of evacuation of the building.

First aid

Legislation requires that all schools have adequate first aid available – both in the form of appropriate equipment and in trained personnel. This applies whether on site or off-site on school activities. There are minimum requirements for the contents of first aid boxes and guidance is given regarding the numbers of trained first aiders who should be in place relative to the size of the school population.

Only those trained by agencies recognised by the Health and Safety Executive (HSE) should give first aid to pupils or staff, and these should not go beyond what their training allows. At all times care should be taken for personal safety and to the prevention of cross-infection. Disposable gloves must be worn when treating pupils, especially if there is the presence of blood or other body fluids. Only those members of staff with appropriate qualifications, training and recognition are to administer medication.

Legislation requires that schools must have an 'appointed person' to take charge of first aid arrangements. This person is *not* necessarily a first aider.

First aid boxes

First aid boxes should contain, at the very least, a guidance card, scissors, safety pins, disposable gloves, sterile coverings, individual sterile dressings, a cloth triangular bandage, medium dressings, large dressings and eye pads. Any use of materials from the first aid box must be reported to the appropriate person.

Storage and administration of medicines

Every school's Health and Safety Policy should address the type of medicines allowed in school, the measures taken to ensure their appropriate use and safe-keeping, the members of staff available to administer medicines and so on. National policy states that, while no member of staff has to administer medicines if they choose not to, schools must have someone on site trained to do so should the need arise.

If you are not a trained first aider, you should do no more than summon help and provide reassurance. You should avoid moving the person unless it is essential. The following suggestions about how to respond to specific emergencies are only outlines and *should not be regarded as full instructions.*

Do no more than you have been trained to do. Never take matters into your own hands. Always call for those with the training and the responsibility.

All accidents, injuries and emergencies must be recorded in accordance with school procedures. Records will include the time and date of the incident, details of how and where it happened and what response was given.

The importance of following instructions about children's diets to avoid allergic reactions, how you would recognise allergic reactions

Where individual pupils have medical conditions, including allergies, requiring specific responses, information needs to be shared with all adults coming into contact with those pupils. The relevant information will normally be in the form of a **medical protocol** which sets out the nature of the condition, the likely symptoms, the response required and people to contact. You need to be familiar with pupils in the classes where you work who have allergies and, consequently, specific dietary requirements such as not eating nuts or not being in the vicinity of eggs.

Figure 3.4 'Miss, I don't feel well'

Emergency	Responses
Severe bleeding	The flow of blood needs to be stemmed as soon as possible. This is best achieved by applying pressure to the wound for ten minutes if there is nothing within it. If there is a foreign body in the wound, this should not be removed but pressure should be placed around it without putting pressure on the object itself.
Cardiac arrest	If the patient is unconscious, place in the recovery position; if he or she is conscious have them half sit up, supporting them with cushions. Do not give them anything to eat or drink.
Shock/ anaphylactic shock	The victim should be lain down and any tight clothing loosened, particularly at the neck to help with breathing. If possible, raise the legs higher than the head and keep the victim warm. Do not give them anything to eat or drink.
Faints or loss of consciousness	If someone complains of feeling faint, sit them down and put their head between their knees. If they do faint, lay them on their back and raise their legs so the blood flow is increased to the brain. Tight clothing must be loosened to help with breathing.
Epileptic seizure	The patient must not be moved or restrained; any furniture or other people near them must be moved out of the way to prevent injury. Something soft should be placed under the patient's head if that is possible.
Choking and difficulty with breathing	If there is something actually choking the patient, encourage them to cough. If that does not work, bend them over with their head lower than the chest and slap them five times between the shoulder blades with the flat of your hand.
Asthma attack	Provide reassurance and administer medication (inhaler); possibly giving two doses. Encourage the casualty to breathe slowly. Call for an ambulance if the inhaler has not taken effect after five minutes.
Falls	All suspected fractures must be treated as actual fractures. The casualty must not be moved but a qualified first aider called for immediately. The casualty must be made as comfortable as possible without moving the limb injured.
Burns and scalds	The affected area needs to be cooled with cold water; any clothes attached to the wound must not be removed.
Poisoning	If possible, find out what the victim has swallowed and inform the medical team when they arrive. You should provide reassurance to the patient and watch for them becoming unconscious. Do not try and make them sick.
Electrocution	The source of electricity needs to be cut off, preferably by removing the plug from the socket. You should not touch the victim unless it is absolutely necessary. If you have to move them to remove them from the electrical source, stand on dry insulating material, such as paper or wood, and push the person away using an insulated item such as a stick or a chair. Once the person has been disconnected from the electricity source, place them in the recovery position.
Substance abuse	If you can, find out what they have taken and inform the medical team when they arrive. Do not try and make the patient sick. Provide verbal reassurance and comfort to the patient. Place them in the recovery position if they become unconscious.

Policies and procedures to deal with children/young people's illnesses

The following is a summary of the common illnesses you are likely to come across in school. Your responsibility is obviously not to diagnose illness, but you should be in a position to recognise common symptoms and have a working knowledge of what sort of response is required.

Illness and symptoms	Response
Colds and flu – runny nose, coughing, temperature, difficulty breathing	Rest at home; infectious; medicines available from a pharmacy; see GP if symptoms persist
Chickenpox – itchy red spots with white centres on parts of the body	Infectious; keep at home for five days after the rash begins; calamine lotion to ease itching; can be very serious in adults
German measles (rubella) – pink rash on head, torso, arms and legs, slight fever, sore throat	Infectious particularly before diagnosis is possible; keep indoors for five days from onset of rash; keep away from pregnant women
Impetigo – small red pimples on skin which weep	Infectious – stay at home until all weeping has stopped; treat with antibiotics from GP
Ringworm – infection of the skin, flaky circles under the skin	Contagious; see GP for antibiotics
Diarrhoea and sickness	Keep taking fluids; keep at home until 24 hours after sickness and diarrhoea has stopped; see GP if persists
Conjunctivitis – redness and sore eyelids and around the eyes, irritant	Infectious; swab with warm water; visit GP if persists; school may have a policy on length of time to stay at home
Measles – fever, runny eyes, sore throat and cough, red rash over the body	Rest; lots of fluid; visit GP if symptoms persist; some form of junior painkiller to reduce fever
Tonsillitis – very sore throat, tonsils enlarged, fever, earache	See GP and treat with antibiotics; frequent and/or severe cases may require surgery
Meningitis – severe headache, fever, stiff neck, rash on skin which does not go when pressed with a glass	See GP immediately or call ambulance urgently – can be fatal

Types and possible signs and indicators of child abuse

Signs of abuse and/or neglect include:

* physical marks (cuts, bruises, etc.);
* sudden or prolonged change in behaviour;
* personal hygiene issues;
* language, terminology and subject matter used by the child in conversation;
* disclosure by the child to an adult (or to other children and reported to an adult).

Responding to disclosure

There are important guiding principles which must be recognised and adhered to when responding to children who disclose abuse:

- The prime consideration at all times must be the child's welfare.
- Children who are at risk of abuse have the right to be protected.
- Children who may have been abused will be treated with sensitivity, dignity and respect.
- Any person who feels that a child may be at risk has a duty to refer that child promptly to the appropriate person or agencies. It is not their responsibility to make a value judgement about what the child has told them.

A child making an actual disclosure of abuse is likely to do so because they trust that particular member of staff. Alternatively, children, particularly younger ones, may simply be talking with a member of staff about what is happening to them without being aware that it actually is abuse. Either way, the adult will need to respond very carefully. At one and the same time they must not destroy the trust shown in them but they must take action.

There are a number of procedures to follow when responding to disclosure:

- Listen carefully to the child calmly and dispassionately.
- Let the child recall events without interruption or comment.
- Any questions you ask must be to clarify what is being said. Do not ask leading questions.
- Do not offer alternative explanations for what happened.
- Explain to the child that you are there to help them and this involves telling others in the school who need to know. Assure them their information will not become common knowledge.
- Record the discussion using the actual words spoken by the child. Note when and where it happened and who was present. Make sure your name is on the record and that you have signed and dated it.
- Written reports should be based on evidence and be objective. They should distinguish between fact, observation, allegation and opinion.
- Report to the designated person in school as soon as possible, but certainly within the day.
- Be available for any follow-up investigation.

If a child makes a disclosure of sexual abuse, or sexual abuse is suspected, social care agencies must be informed and they will decide upon medical examination. To arrange a medical examination of the child is beyond the responsibility of the school.

Investigating disclosures

Schools are not investigative bodies. Any investigation of possible abuse is the responsibility of social care and/or the police. Every member of staff, however, has a duty to report any concerns they may have regarding a particular child. Often it is only as information from several sources is pieced together by social care or the police that incidents of child abuse come to light. The piece of information you hold could be significant in building up a picture of a particular child's situation.

Confidentiality

Confidentiality is a crucial issue, but you must never allow yourself to be placed in a situation where a child tells you something on the condition that you keep it to yourself.

Where there is a risk of abuse you have a legal duty to follow your school's procedures and report it to the appropriate person in the designated manner. Examples of records to be completed are given below.

Cultural considerations

For children who are learning English as an additional language (EAL), the provision of a bilingual interpreter may be an important part of the process, bringing extra security to the child. Cultural norms, however, must never be a 'cover' for abusive situations or activities.

Case study: concerns over possible abuse

Sadie Molapo is a TA working in a junior school. She provides general support for pupils in Year 3. From the records provided by the infant school, Sadie and the class teacher (Katie Russell) were aware that concern had been expressed in the past about one of the pupils, Eric.

By the middle of the first term, Sadie and Katie had both noticed changes in Eric's behaviour. They had observed marks on his arms which could not easily be accounted for and had overheard some of his conversations with other children where he had been using vocabulary and language not expected from a 7 year old. On one occasion he had grown very angry with another pupil, which was unusual in itself, but then he shouted, 'I'm going to kill you. I'll strangle you until you're dead and it'll really hurt.'

Sadie completed a Safeguarding Children Report and a Skin Map each time the concerns were observed and gave these to the Designated Officer for Safeguarding Children (DOSC). The DOSC logged these in the appropriate file and asked Sadie and Katie to closely monitor the situation.

One week, Eric was absent for the first three days. This was the first time he had been absent from school. When he returned to school on the Thursday, Sadie and Katie knew right away something was wrong. He was not only withdrawn, he also seemed frightened. Sadie took Eric for a walk by himself in the playground and asked him if everything was all right. He immediately burst into tears and told her about the abuse he had been experiencing on and off over the past weeks and months. It turns out that his father, who he sees at weekends, is violent towards him and hurts him badly. His father has told him that he must not tell anyone; if he does he will kill him. His father, according to Eric, drinks a lot and is violent when he gets drunk. His mum did not want anyone to see what had been happening and so kept him off school until the bruising had died down.

Sadie listened to all this without comment or showing shock and knew that she must not ask any leading questions. When Eric finished talking Sadie reassured him of her concern for him and told him that she needed to write down what he had told her and that she needed to tell the head teacher. Eric silently nodded.

She completed another Safeguarding Children Report, as accurately as she could, using the actual words Eric had himself used. She handed this report to the DOSC, verbally telling him what happened as well and he immediately referred the matter to the duty officer at social care.

The importance of encouraging and rewarding positive behaviour

Encouraging positive behaviour is always preferable to trying to sort out poor behaviour after it has occurred. Each school will have a Behaviour Policy with which you must be familiar. This policy is likely to set out both rewards and sanctions. Pupils are to be encouraged when they behave appropriately, usually this will be in the form of verbal praise, rewards such as behaviour points leading to some kind of certificate, letters of commendation home and the like (see pages 36–7). Recognition is to be given to those pupils who always comply with school and class rules, and also to those who find this hard to do, but nevertheless make the effort.

Pupil's positive behaviour can be encouraged through various means:

- All adults working with them treating them with respect and dignity.
- Class rules discussed and agreed among the pupils themselves with teachers and TAs acting as facilitators.
- Pupils given the space to make their own choices.
- Ensure that the work given them is appropriate to their needs and abilities.
- Listening to pupils and taking them and their views seriously.
- Those who do move beyond the boundaries set are seen to be responded to quickly, justly and fairly.
- Clear reward and sanctions in place which are followed consistently throughout the school.

Checklist

✔ I am familiar with my school's Health and Safety Policy and understand its implications for my role and responsibility.

✔ I understand my school's procedures for ensuring the safety and security of the pupils.

✔ I know how to respond to accidents and emergencies, keeping within the boundaries of my role and responsibilities.

✔ I am familiar with school policies and procedures with regards to safeguarding children.

✔ I know what signs to be aware of in children regarding possible abuse.

✔ I am familiar with the procedures in place to encourage positive behaviour.

✔ I am aware of my responsibility to treat all pupils fairly and with respect and to expect the same from them to me.

Figure 3.5
Some activities
are safer than
others

Examples of forms regarding safeguarding children

ANYWHERE SCHOOL
SAFEGUARDING CHILDREN REPORT

NAME OF ADULT REFERRING:

NAME OF PUPIL:

DATE OF BIRTH OF PUPIL:

DATE: LOCATION:

NATURE OF CONCERN:

REASONS FOR CONCERN (give details of why you are referring to the DOSC, where possible use the actual words spoken by the pupil):

RECORDS COMPLETED (date and time):

SKIN MAP COMPLETED: Y/N

REPORTED TO DESIGNATED SENIOR PERSON (date and time):

REASON FOR ANY DELAY:

Signed: _____

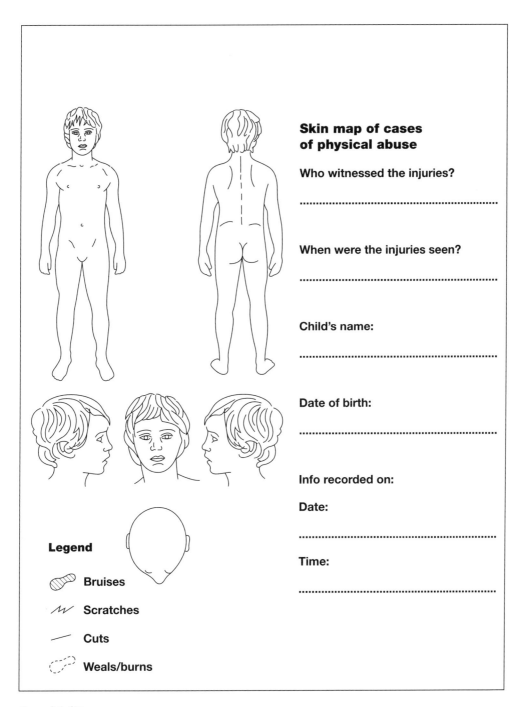

**Skin map of cases
of physical abuse**

Who witnessed the injuries?

....

When were the injuries seen?

....

Child's name:

....

Date of birth:

....

Info recorded on:

Date:

....

Time:

....

Legend

🖐 Bruises

/\/\/ Scratches

— Cuts

⌒ Weals/burns

Figure 3.6 Skin map

Further reading

Baginsky, M. (2008) *Safeguarding Children and Schools: Best practice in working with children series*. London: Jessica Kingsley.

Bentham, S. (2006) *A Teaching Assistant's Guide to Managing Behaviour in the Classroom*. Oxford: Routledge.

Birkett, V. (2006) *How to Manage and Teach Children with Challenging Behaviour*. London: LDA.

Lindon, J. (2008) *Safeguarding Children and Young People: Child protection 0–18 years*. London: Hodder Arnold.

Wilson, K. and James, A. (2007) *The Child Protection Handbook*. Oxford: Bailliere Tindall.

Websites

www.bbc.co.uk/health/first_aid/
www.childline.org.uk/
www.everychildmatters.gov.uk/
www.everychildmatters.gov.uk/socialcare/safeguarding/
www.hse.gov.uk/firstaid/
www.nspcc.org.uk/
www.safeguardingchildren.org.uk/
www.teachernet.gov.uk/wholeschool/familyandcommunity/childprotection/

Unit 4: Contribute to positive relationships

In this chapter we will look at four elements:

1 Interact with and respond to children.
2 Interact with and respond to adults.
3 Communicate with children.
4 Communicate with adults.

The importance of giving children and young people full attention when listening to them and how you demonstrate this through body language, facial expression, speech and gesture

Communication can take many forms

The first point to make is that we communicate both verbally and non-verbally. Verbal communication refers to what we say while non-verbal communication focuses on the manner in which we communicate. Non-verbal communication strategies include: facial expressions, body posture, gestures, eye contact and proximity. Non-language, verbal strategies refer to volume, tone and pitch of voice. Communication is complex in that individuals do not always say what they mean or mean what they say. Communication involves much more than just listening to what is being said but involves paying attention to non-verbal communication.

Figure 4.1
Communication is not always straightforward – 'I am fine sir, really I am!'

Self-assessment question

Can you describe a time when you used non-verbal communication to help you understand what a pupil was saying?

Why it is important to listen to children and young people

Listening communicates value

It is not only important that we listen to what pupils have to say but that we listen in such a way that pupils feel they have been listened to. When individuals feel that some-one has taken the time to listen to them and has really heard what they have had to say they feel supported and valued. **Active listening** skills involve: making time to listen, giving your full attention to listening, using appropriate body language and giving supportive feedback.

Listening allows pupils to share concerns

When pupils feel they have been listened to they are more likely to come back to that person for further support. Pupils who feel that they are listened to are likely to feel more comfortable in discussing problems they are encountering. These problems could involve difficulties with not understanding work, in relating to other pupils or staff, or could involve serious matters regarding bullying or abuse. For further information on disclosures see pages 76–8.

Listening gives information on pupils' thinking processes

When we listen to pupils explaining how they have solved a problem we get a glimpse of their thinking processes and strategies they have used. If pupils are having difficulties in understanding, then knowing how they are approaching a problem can give a TA useful information necessary to help move the pupil forward.

Consider the following:

TA: What is the answer to 12×12?
Pupil: 23
TA: How did you get that?
Pupil: 12 plus $12 = 23$, no 24
TA: Does the question ask you to add or multiply the numbers?

In terms of listening to children and young people, specific challenges can arise. For details regarding issues relating to clear communication in bilingual and multilingual settings see Unit 11.

Why it is important to give all children and young people the opportunity to be heard and how you do this in a group

Pupil voice

When teaching professionals talk about the importance of pupils being heard, they will often talk about pupil voice. Pupil voice involves listening to what pupils have to say about their experiences of learning and what they say would improve their learning experience. By involving the pupils in the process of learning, pupils feel more engaged and motivated. Nowadays, most schools will have school councils and pupil suggestion boxes while some schools have gone further and have decided to become a 'rights respecting' school. A 'rights respecting' school bases their school ethos on The UN Convention regarding the Rights of the Child. The UN Convention states that children should have the right to express their views about what should happen to them in situations where adults are making decisions about them and that the adults should take their views and opinions into account. Of course, with rights come responsibilities. In trying to develop an understanding of rights and responsibilities within a pupil group, pupils will need to develop an understanding of how what they do impacts on others. Developing an understanding of rights and responsibilities enables pupils to make a positive contribution in that they are developing skills in reasoning and decision making and developing their self-confidence. Making a positive contribution is important as it is one of the government's **Every Child Matters** goals. But how do you develop an understanding of rights and responsibilities within a pupil? How do you involve pupils in the learning process and take account of their views in regard to what would improve the learning process for them? Here it is important to talk to pupils about responsibilities, rights, what they have learned, how they think they could improve on their learning and what could you do to help them learn more.

Case study: language found in a rights respecting school

Jimmy is in the playground and has left all the play equipment (balls, skipping ropes) near the door. The TA could say either:

'Now – it is important to put away all the play equipment as some other pupil might trip over them and hurt themselves.'

or

'It is your right to be safe and it is the right of other pupils to be safe therefore it is your responsibility to put away the play equipment so others don't fall over and hurt themselves.'

Which version is reflective of a rights respecting school?

How do you inform pupils of their rights and responsibilities in your school?

Self-assessment activity 4.1: student voice, roles and responsibilities

	Does my school do this?	How is this done in my school and why is it important?
School Council		
Involving pupils in creating classroom rules		
Having pupil suggestion boxes		
Involving pupils in target setting		
Helping pupils to review their learning		

Ways of encouraging participation

As stated above, it is important that all pupils contribute and participate in the learning process. However, it is clear to those involved in teaching and supporting learning that some pupils need encouragement to participate. There are certain strategies that TAs can use. These include:

- Create an atmosphere where all comments are valued and mistakes are seen as an important part of the learning experience. As a TA you need to find value in all responses. Praising pupils for their attempts to answer questions will encourage them to answer further questions.
- Discuss with pupils the importance of listening to each other and respecting each other's comments.
- Encourage pupils to talk to each other. There are a number of ways to do this when working with a group. Sometimes after working individually you can ask pupils to share their ideas with a partner. After sharing their ideas with a partner they can then share their ideas with the group. This is a great way to draw pupils who are shy into the discussion.
- At times you can encourage pupils to write their answers on individual whiteboards so that they can show each other their answers. Nowadays, with technology, pupils can be actively involved with lessons (see Unit 8).

Much of the work that TAs carry out involves working with groups; however, working with groups present many challenges as Figure 4.2 illustrates.

Figure 4.2 Challenges of working with groups

Self-assessment activity 4.2: how do I work with groups?

Challenge	Why is this important?	How do I do this?
Ensuring that all pupils understand the task		
Balancing the needs of all pupils		
This will include pupils who are very able, very needy and demanding, and very needy but quiet		
Ensuring that all pupils have the opportunity to participate and contribute		
Using opportunities of pupil talk to develop thinking skills		
Checking that all pupils have met the **learning objectives**		

An outline of how children and young people's communication skills develop within the age range 0–16 years

Age	Skills
0–6 months	During this stage various emotional stages develop. Usually by 2 months a baby expresses enjoyment by smiling while the ability to laugh emerges usually by 3 months. By six months a child will be able to vocalise with intonation, or in common language will be able to babble. A child will recognise and respond when they hear their name. Children will be able to correctly identify friendly and angry voices, and will respond accordingly.
6–12 months	The use of babbling increases during this stage resulting in a child being able to use one or more words with meaning by 12 months. A child will be able to understand more than they can say and by a year should understand simple instructions especially if they are accompanied by gestures. In turn a child will use a combination of sounds, words and gestures to communicate. Increasingly during this time a child realises the social value of language, that is, language can be used not only to request desired objects but to share interests.
12–18 months	Usually by the age of 18 months a child will have a vocabulary of five to twenty words, most of these words being nouns, that is, words denoting a person, place or thing. Between 15 months and 18 months most children begin to enjoy language games such as 'show me your hand . . . show me your leg'.
18 months–2 years	By the age of 2 most children will be able to combine words into short sentences. These short sentences are often combinations of nouns and verbs. Words such as 'my' and 'mine' begin to emerge by the age of 2. By the age of 2 most children will have a vocabulary of between 50 to 200 words and be able to follow simple instructions.
2–3 years	This year sees children making significant progress in language comprehension and language expression with many children having a vocabulary between 200 to 300 words and some children having a vocabulary of between 900–1,000 words by the age of 3. It is during this stage that children begin to use pronouns (I, me and you) correctly and begin to use the plural form of words as well as the past tense. Most children will be able to use three word sentences and will be able to tell you their sex, name and age by the age of 3.
3–4 years	By the age of 4 most children will be able to name common objects and know one or more colours. Children of this age will use language to participate in make-believe play.
4–5 years	By the age of 4 or 5 most children will be attending school and obviously skills in language comprehension and expression will enable them to participate to a greater extent in the learning environments that schools provide. Most children of this age should be able to follow more complex instructions, to recount things that have happened to them, to listen attentively to stories and to tell their own stories. In a sense most children of this age become skilled at having conversations.
6–12 years	During the years at primary school, children become more adept at language. The questions children ask become more complex and they are able to adapt their style of communication depending on the audience. For example, the way in which they communicate with their friends will differ from the way in which they communicate with their teachers.
13–16 years	During this age most adolescents and young adults become skilled at using more abstract forms of language.

(www.medem.com)

Quiz

Can you match up the skill, to the age in which it develops and to an appropriate example?

Age	Communication skills	Examples of communication skills
6–12 months	Skilled at conversations	Child in front of biscuit tin, jumping up and down, pointing and saying: 'Oooh, ooooh, bic, bic!'
4–5 years	Uses a combination of sounds, words and gestures to communicate	Child to friend: 'Gimme the ball.' Child to teacher: 'Miss, can I please play with the ball?'
6–12 years	Uses abstract form of language	Adult: 'Do you know where your daddy works?' Child: 'Well – actually no – but it is somewhere in the city. Where does your daddy work?'
13–16 years	Can adapt style of communication to audience	The posters the students worked on had the following slogans: 'Overturn the barricades!' 'Pledge to end cycles of despair.' 'Down with tyranny!'

Why it is important to give children and young people sufficient time to express themselves in their own words

Giving pupils sufficient time to express themselves is very important, as Figure 4.3 illustrates.

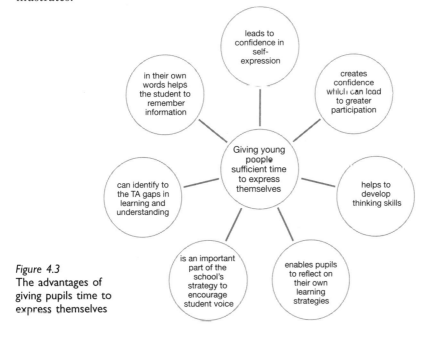

Figure 4.3
The advantages of giving pupils time to express themselves

As a TA it is also essential to know how to give students the necessary time to express themselves. For example, a TA can:

- ask open questions;
- not answer the question for pupils;
- rephrase the question if the pupils is having difficulty in knowing what to say;
- praise the pupils for their attempts.

Why it is important to help children and young people make choices and how you can assist them to do this

Giving pupils choices is said to have a number of advantages. Choice is seen as empowering and can lead to a sense of self-determination. Further, daily decision-making opportunities assist both personal and academic growth. However, choices and decision-making opportunities need to be considered. Too many choices can lead to confusion and less participation. Some individual pupils may feel uncomfortable with choices and prefer to be told what to do. The first point to consider is what choices are available to the pupils you work with? Self-assessment activity 4.3 presents types of choices available. What you will notice is that the examples given of choices involve small everyday interactions.

Modelling choices can be helpful

Some pupils have limited experiences of making choices. Other pupils may lack the confidence to make a choice and prefer to be told what to do. With such pupils TAs can model or show what is involved in a choice making process (Sanacore 1999). For example, consider the choice of selecting a book to read.

Case study: modelling choices

Sandy – a TA in a primary school explains:

I work with a small group of pupils who have been described as reluctant readers. When I took the group to the library to help them select a reading book – I decided to show them how I selected a book to read for pleasure. I told them that first I think about what books I enjoy reading. I said: 'I like to read about horses.' I then picked up a book about ships and quickly looked at it saying well this is not about horses – I need to find another book.

The children found this amusing. I repeated picking up the wrong book and realising that it was the wrong book for me several times to show the pupils that it takes time to choose books. Then I found a book on horses. As I picked it up I pointed out that the book had no pictures and lots of words. I said that though this book was on horses, I wanted a book with words I could read and pictures. Eventually I found my book.

Then I asked the pupils what books they liked to read. I gave them ten minutes to look for a book. I also asked them to bring back to the table not only the book that they had chosen but the books that they looked at but decided not to choose. I asked each pupil to describe how and why they had chosen their particular book.

Self-assessment question

How do you model choices?

Self-assessment activity 4.3: types of choices available

Choices available	For example	Examples of choices I can give pupils in my school
Where to work	The pupil may choose to work on their maths sheet at their table or they can do their work at a quiet area at the back of the class.	
What materials to use	When working on a maths sheet pupils can choose the materials or resources to support them. Some pupils might want to use number lines or they might choose to use multi-link.	
When to start to work	You have chosen your book – are you ready to start to read?	
Who to work with	In some activities – group projects – pupils can select the members of their team.	
What activity to do first	What do you want to do first – your maths work sheet or practise your spellings?	
When to finish an activity	Have you finished your painting?	
What activities you wish to do next	What do you want to do next – your spellings or work on the computer?	
The right to refuse to do an activity	Do you want to continue to play football?	
The right to choose an alternative activity	If you don't want to read this book, what do you want to do?	

(Jolivette et al. 2002)

Pupils need the opportunity to learn from making the 'wrong' choice or decision.

To truly appreciate what choice involves, pupils need experience of making choices. Likewise, to appreciate the consequences of making decisions, pupils need to experience the consequences of their decisions. A widely used behaviour strategy is to state choices and consequences to pupils. For example, a TA may say to a pupil: 'If you continue to disrupt the others in your group – you will receive a detention – the choice is yours.' If the pupil makes the wrong choice, and continues to disrupt other pupils, then they will face the consequences. Hopefully the pupil will learn through the process of making choices and facing consequences.

Often, to make an informed choice pupils need to have an opportunity to try out a variety of activities or options. Consider a pupil who always chooses to select books on dinosaurs and states that he doesn't want to read anything else. To truly make a choice, the pupil needs to have the experience of reading or being read other books on a variety of topics.

The key features of effective communication and why it is important to model this when interacting with adults, children and young people

As a TA it is important to remember that pupils will watch and imitate what you do; therefore TAs are in a powerful position in that they can act as role models for effective communication. See Chapter 1 (page 35) for further discussion on the modelling process. Figure 4.4 illustrates some of the key features in effective communication. Can you think of any others?

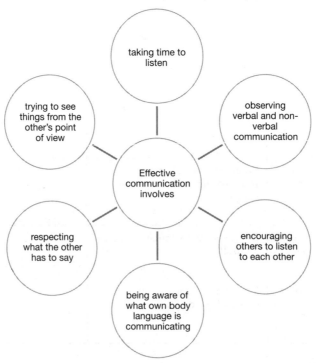

Figure 4.4 Key features for effective communication

The main differences between communicating with adults and communicating with children and young people

One of the main differences between communicating with adults and communicating with children and young people is the language that we use. The language that we use should be appropriate to the individuals we are talking to. Common mistakes include:

- Using phrases and words that are not appropriate for a particular age group.
- Assuming that if a pupil nods in agreement and states that they understand that they actually do. Sometimes pupils are afraid to say that they don't understand. As a TA it is always important to check for understanding. One strategy is to have the pupil repeat back to you what they have heard you say. Sometimes TAs can use a simple system of thumbs up (Yes – I understand this), thumbs down (No – I don't understand) and thumbs sideways (I understand parts, but can we go over this again).
- Not recognising the particular language needs of a pupil, for example some pupils have difficulties understanding metaphors and idioms. So expressions such as 'it is raining cats and dogs' and 'do you have ants in your pants?' will be interpreted literally.

Case study: effective communication

A TA talking to a reception class states:

Holding a spider, also known as an arachnid, can create different physiological responses in individuals dependent on their unique temperament and psychological profiles.

What should the TA say?

A head teacher in a staff meeting for all staff states:

A representative from the LA will be coming to the next PaRM meeting to discuss changes to SEN and ESBD provision and the new CAF within the ECM agenda.

What should the head teacher do to ensure understanding?

How to demonstrate that you value other adults' views and opinions and why it is important to the development of positive relationships

Demonstrating that you value what other adults say is an important part of working effectively as a team. Further, as a TA you can help pupils understand the skills involved in relationships by demonstrating how you value your colleagues' views and opinions. Remember you are modelling to the pupils what positive relationships looks like.

For example, a TA can:

- make time to listen to other adults;
- make a point of being friendly and courteous to all adults;

- always say please and thank you;
- be seen to share equipment and resources;
- be aware and concerned for others' feelings;
- be prepared to say sorry and to accept others' apologies;
- support the authority of other teaching professionals.

Communication difficulties that may exist and how these can be overcome

Problems or difficulties in communication are frequent and can happen between:

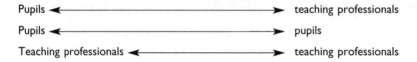

Pupils ◄────────────────────► teaching professionals

Pupils ◄────────────────────► pupils

Teaching professionals ◄────────────────────► teaching professionals

Common communication difficulties can stem from any of the following triggers.

Poor communication

This sometimes results from individuals not quite hearing what has been said or mis-interpreting what has been said. On a day-to-day level we often talk about getting the wrong end of the stick or our wires crossed. If we don't understand then it is important to say so.

Not saying what we mean and not meaning what we say

Good communication is important in a school. Though we need to be honest, we also need to be tactful and constructive in our comments. Pupils and are colleagues are very quick to realise if someone is not being genuine in their remarks.

The effect of mood

Sometimes our mood and our assumptions we hold about someone influences how we interpret what they say. For example, if we are feeling down and someone compliments our work we might think: 'I know they said my work was great – but I know they didn't mean it.' On the other hand sometimes we only hear what we want to hear.

On another level there can be specific speech difficulties, as Table 4.1 illustrates.

As TAs often work with pupils who have specific speech difficulties this information is useful. For further information regarding language difficulties see Unit 14.

How to cope with disagreements with adults

Valuing and respecting your colleagues will lessen the likelihood that major disagreement will occur. However, disagreements do occur between staff even in the best run schools. It is important to resolve disagreements at an early stage. Ignoring a problem is seldom an effective strategy. It is sometimes first helpful to talk directly with the person concerned. Again such conversations need to be constructive and respectful and held in a suitable place and at a suitable time. Confidentiality is important. Colleagues will

Table 4.1 Speech difficulties

Difficulties with fluency (flow of language)	Stuttering	Repetitions or the prolonging of sounds and syllables that interrupt the flow of speech
Difficulties with articulation (difficulties in the production of individual speech sounds)	Substitution	When a sound an individual can't make is substituted for a sound which they can make
	Omission	When a sound an individual finds difficult to pronounce is left out
	Distortion	A sound that is difficult to pronounce is not left out or substituted for another but altered in some way so that it does not sound quite right
	Addition	This occurs when an extra sound is added
Difficulties with voice	Pitch	Voice can be too high or too low
	Loudness	Voice can be too loud or too soft

often have very different views and sometimes it is important to agree to disagree. If disagreements continue and if you feel these disagreements are impacting on your work with pupils you will need to seek advice from a senior staff member.

Case study: dealing with conflicts

Sandy was new to working at Everytown Secondary School. Most of the staff were very kind and supportive. However, Hilary, the TA, she worked with twice a week, seemed to Sandy to always be criticising her. Hilary had worked at the school for five years and had told Sandy that she knew all there was to know and that she didn't need a qualification to know what to do.

1   What should Sandy do?
2   Who should Sandy talk to?

Why it is important to reassure adults of the confidentiality of shared information and the limits of this

Organisational policy regarding information exchange

At many times in this textbook we have talked about confidentiality. In terms of sharing information, information can be categorised in terms of which information is shared and with whom the information is shared. Some information is strictly confidential, other information is shared on a need to know basis and some information needs to be communicated to all staff members. For further detailed information on relevant legal requirements and procedures covering confidentiality and the disclosure of information see pages 76–8. For further details on information regarding record keeping and the need for confidentiality see pages 47–8 and 161–2.

Self-assessment activity 4.4: to what extent is the following information shared?

	Shared on a need to know basis (Yes/No)	Who needs to know and why?	Does everyone need to know?
IEP targets			
Behaviour targets			
Parent contact details			
Pupils' attainment on reading schemes			
Details of behaviour incidents			
Allergies			
Details of disclosures			
Details regarding parents' change of circumstance, e.g. parental divorce			

The importance of communicating positively with children, young people and families

For a child to achieve their potential schools make enormous efforts to work positively and constructively with families. TAs can assist in this process. When parents, schools and children are all working together the sky is the limit in terms of what can be achieved. Often it is the small everyday interactions that are so important to communicating to parents that they are valued. If parents feel valued they are more likely to share their concerns with the school and are more likely to take on the advice and suggestions that the school has to offer.

Case study: welcoming parents

Barbara works in a reception class and is always there with the teacher to welcome the students and the parents at the beginning of the day. Barbara states that she always has a warm smile and words of greeting for each parent as they drop off their children. Barbara also states that she makes a point of getting to know all of them and specifically knowing how they wish to be addressed. Some parents like to be addressed formally by their title, such as Mrs Smith, while some parents preferred to be addressed by their first name. Barbara says that she knows that this is a small detail, but the fact that she has taken the time to ask how they wish to be addressed makes the parents feel welcomed and valued. According to Barbara if parents feel valued and welcomed they are more likely to stop and chat and to pass on small but relevant bits of information that are important for the teaching team to know.

Self-assessment activity 4.5: it is the small everyday interactions that are important

Example of everyday interactions	Do I do this?	How do I do this?
Communicate in school/parent communication records (reading diary, etc.)		
Talk to individual parents		
Answer phone in office		
Work with parent volunteers in the classroom and on school activities		

How children and young people's ability to communicate can affect their behaviour

In Figure 4.3 we talked about the advantages of encouraging pupil self-expression. As pupil self-expression can encourage self-confidence and thinking skills, so difficulties in communication can have an adverse impact on behaviour.

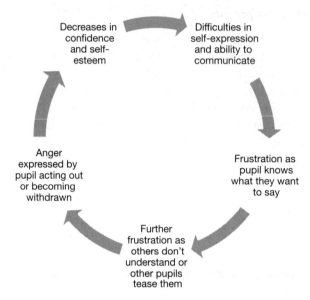

Figure 4.5 Possible consequences of communication difficulties

---

Self-assessment question

What can a TA do to intervene in this negative cycle?

Checklist

✔ Make time to listen to your colleagues and the children and young people you support.

✔ Create an atmosphere where comments are valued.

✔ Give the children and young people you support time to express themselves.

Further reading

Cheminais, R. (2008) *Every Child Matters: A practical guide for teaching assistants*. London: David Fulton Publishers.

Layard, R. and Dunn, J. (2009) *A Good Childhood: Searching for values in a competitive age*. London: Penguin.

Chapter 5

Unit 5: Provide effective support for your colleagues

In this chapter we will cover two elements:

1 Maintain working relationships with colleagues.
2 Develop your effectiveness in a support role.

School expectations and requirements about your role and responsibilities as set out in your job description

Every member of staff will have a job description. This job description will outline your responsibilities within the school. However, responsibilities within schools change as a result of government policies and initiatives. Of note within the past ten years there have been documents such as 'Every Child Matters', the extended schools initiative and the Remodelling Agenda. By 2010 it is proposed that all schools will be open from 8am until at least 6pm covering a range of services to include breakfast clubs, after-school clubs and drop in centres for parents. Some TAs will have a role to play in these new initiatives. As part of the Remodelling Agenda a list of additional tasks was developed. These tasks were jobs that teachers were no longer required to undertake. These tasks include such responsibilities as: classroom display, invigilating examinations and managing pupil data. What these changes mean is that the role of a TA is becoming increasingly varied, as a TA may be asked to take on a diverse range of roles and responsibilities within the school. For example, a TA may also work as a midday meal supervisor or in an after-school club. In addition, many schools now rely on volunteers coming in on a regular basis. If you are working within a school on a volunteer basis there should be a designated member of staff to whom you are responsible. Further, some schools will have a job description for volunteers. Whatever your role or responsibility within a school it is important to be familiar with your job description and that your job description is reviewed on a regular basis.

Self-assessment activity 5.1: Workforce Remodelling – which task do you do?

Task	Never	Sometimes	Always
Collecting money			
Chasing absences			
Copy typing			
Bulk photocopying			
Producing standard letters			
Producing class lists			
Record-keeping and filing			
Classroom display			
Analysing attendance figures			
Processing exam results			
Collating pupil reports			
Administering work experience			
Administering examinations			
Invigilating examinations			
Administering teacher cover			
ICT trouble shooting and minor repairs			
Commissioning new ICT equipment			
Ordering supplies and equipment			
Stocktaking			
Cataloguing, preparing, issuing and maintaining equipment and materials			
Doing the 'minutes' of meetings			
Co-ordinating and submitting bids			
Seeking and giving personnel advice			
Managing pupil data			
Inputting pupil data			

Self-assessment questions

1   What does my school offer in regard to extended services?
2   Do you have any additional roles within the school?

A summary of a typical job description for a primary teaching assistant could look like this. Many job descriptions will include more details than the one mentioned below.

Anywhere Primary School

Job title:	Teaching assistant.
Job purpose:	To ensure, in collaboration with other teaching professionals, that the aims and objectives of the school are achieved through the delivery of the National Curriculum and the provision of other activities which promote optimum child development.
Responsible to:	Initially to class teacher and ultimately to head teacher/deputy head teacher/SENCO.
Accountable for:	Providing classroom, small group and individual support as required.

Key responsibilities

1   To assist with the organisation of the classroom and preparation of activities.
2   To observe pupil behaviour and to share in the responsibility for the well-being and discipline of all pupils.
3   To assist in the teaching and learning process as required.
4   To work in co-operation with other teaching professionals to ensure that equal opportunities and equal access to the curriculum exists for all pupils across all age groups.

A summary of a typical job description for a secondary teaching assistant could look like the following example:

Wherever Secondary School

Job title:	Teaching assistant.
Job purpose:	To support teachers and students in the classroom. To support students in examinations. To help with clerical work in the department.
Accountable to:	SENCO.

Key responsibilities

1 To support pupils in the classroom.
2 To read texts and scribe responses for designated pupils as appropriate.
3 To help pupils plan and organise their work.
4 To explain work to pupils as necessary.
5 To give social and emotional support to all pupils and in doing so help to build positive self-esteem.
6 To work with individuals, groups or classes as required.
7 To assist teachers with the **differentiation** of work.
8 To keep necessary records as required.
9 To support designated pupils in exam settings as required.
10 To help with clerical work in the preparation, photocopying and organising of materials as required.
11 To communicate effectively with pupils and all members of staff.

The roles and responsibilities of colleagues with whom you work and how these relate to your own role and responsibilities

Teaching assistants do not work in isolation. An effective school relies on teamwork. The table on pages 103–5 shows a list of 'Who's who' in a school.

Basic principles underlying effective communication, interpersonal and collaborative skills

Communication and interpersonal skills involve **active listening**.

Active listening involves being able to acknowledge your own feelings and being aware of how they might influence your reactions to others

> Teaching assistant: Sometimes I can have a very stressful morning. I am on my own with three children and it takes a lot of work to get them ready for school, their lunchboxes prepared and the youngest dropped off at my mother's before I can get to school. If I have had a particularly difficult morning I can get quite snappy and abrupt especially with the new TA who has just started helping out in the class. I know that I need not to take things out on others or lose my patience with other members of staff.

Active listening means really listening to what the other person has to say

> Teaching assistant: I find accepting feedback difficult. I know that sometimes my teacher is just trying to give me suggestions about how to do things better next time. But it is like when I hear them say 'you should have done that', I just shut down and get angry and upset. In fact sometimes I am so upset I really don't hear what they have to say. I know I have to learn to take comments and feedback on my work as suggestions rather than criticisms and over time I am getting much

Position	Duties	Examples of how a TA interacts with these professionals	In my school this position is held by
Governors	The governors with the head teacher make the final decisions about how the school is run. The governors will deal with issues relating to finance, curriculum and special needs. The governors will include members of the community, parents, teachers and representatives from the local authority.	The governors are there to give assistance and advice as required. As a TA you might meet one of the governors when they visit the school. Some TAs themselves are governors and gain a useful insight on the school from this role.	
Head teacher	The head teacher is responsible for managing all aspects of the school. The head teacher needs to ensure that the curriculum is effectively taught and that the well-being of the pupils is ensured.	Head teachers are busy people, but they make time to listen to all those involved with the school.	
Deputy head teacher	The deputy head teacher is second in command. The deputy is there to assist the head in managing the school and will take the responsibility for the school when the head is absent.		
SENCO/ inclusion manager	The Special Educational Needs Co-ordinator is responsible for all pupils registered as having special educational needs. The duties of the SENCO will involve monitoring pupils, writing, updating and reviewing IEPs.	SENCOs are very busy people. They are also have a wealth of information regarding how to deal with pupils who face particular challenges. They will offer advice to teachers and teaching assistants on what strategies could be used with pupils who are having difficulties.	
Designated officer for safeguarding children	A senior member of staff who has responsibility for overseeing all aspects of child protection.		
Secretarial and administration staff	These members of staff are responsible for greeting visitors, answering phone calls, typing, sending out required correspondence and maintaining necessary records.		
Bursar	The bursar is in charge of the finances of the school.	The bursar will know how much money the school has to spend on training and continuous professional development.	

continued

Position	Duties	Examples of how a TA interacts with these professionals	In my school this position is held by
Curriculum co-ordinators/ subject managers	These are teachers who are given special areas of responsibility. In this case the teachers will be responsible for a certain subject or curriculum area. In primary school this could be Key Stage 2 Maths or it could be Head of Maths at a secondary level.		
Heads of year/ key stage	These are teachers who are given the responsibility of meeting the pastoral needs of pupils within a year group or key stage.	At a secondary level if a pupil you are working with starts behaving in an uncharacteristic manner, the head of year is a good person to talk to. The head of year may be able to talk to the pupil's family to see if there are any issues going on that are affecting the pupil.	
Classroom teachers	Each teacher will have responsibility for planning, preparing, delivering and evaluating the learning for the classes that they support.	As a TA most of your work will be with the class teacher to which you are assigned.	
Senior teaching assistants or **HLTAs**	In some schools where there is a large number of TAs there may be one senior TA who has responsibility for organising the work of all the TAs within the school. Some TAs will have gained the status of HLTAs and will be given extra responsibilities.	Senior TAs or HLTAs can offer valuable advice and training to TAs who are just starting out.	
Teaching assistants	Teaching assistants can be assigned to work with a specific class or assigned to work with a specific pupil with special educational needs. In secondary schools TAs might be assigned to work with a specific year group supporting those pupils within the year group who are on the SEN Register. Some TAs at secondary school are assigned to work within departments.	The advice, encouragement and support you get from your fellow TAs is invaluable.	
Volunteer TAs	Volunteer TAs are dedicated individuals, who are interested in education and are giving up their free time to help teachers to effectively manage their classroom.	Often volunteer TAs go onto full or part-time employment within a school.	

continued

Position	Duties	Examples of how a TA interacts with these professionals	In my school this position is held by
School nurse	This member of staff is responsible for dealing with minor accidents, making decisions regarding when to call for further medical assistance and for administering necessary medication.	As a TA you will need to know who these individuals are.	
First aiders	These are members of staff who have taken courses in 'first aid' and know what to do in the event of medical emergencies.		
Cleaning staff	These members of staff start to work before other staff arrive for the day or when the teaching staff prepare to go home. They ensure that the working environment of the school is in a clean state.		
Site security	These members of staff are often found in large schools. These staff members are there to ensure the premises are safe from unwanted intruders. These staff will often have the duty of ensuring that the buildings are secure at the end of a teaching day.		
Caretaker	This member of staff is responsible for the maintenance of the school building.		
Midday meal supervisors	These individuals are responsible for setting up the dining hall for many hungry pupils. They are responsible for ensuring appropriate behaviour is maintained during the lunch hours and they are responsible for clearing up afterwards.	Some TAs may also work as midday meal supervisors.	

better at this. My difficulty with accepting feedback has helped me to empathise with the pupils I work with. I am really careful and considered about the feedback I give the pupils I work with.

Active listening means communicating to the other person that you value and respect them

Teaching assistant: It is important when working together to find something good to say about a person's work and not to take them for granted. After a very difficult day in the class I mentioned to the teacher that though the class was still difficult that there was an improvement and that it was very much down to her hard work with the group. The teacher was very touched and thankful for my comments.

Good communication skills involve knowing how to say difficult things in a positive manner

Teaching assistant: I always try to do this with pupils who are struggling – but it is more difficult with other staff members. Sometimes the teacher says to me after the class, 'that went well – didn't it?' However, sometimes the session did not go well at all! But what can I say to the teacher? In a sense I know that she is looking to me for reassurance and I am not sure if it is my place to criticise or make judgements.

Teaching assistant: I find the same difficulties, however the teacher I work with welcomes my suggestions and I always start by telling him what I thought went well with the session. I think it is important to be honest, but it is also important to be constructive – it is not what you say but how you say it!

Good communication skills involve dealing with issues before they become problems

Teaching assistant: I always find it helpful in the long run to be open about any problems. Last year at my school it was always the same TA who was chosen to go to any training days. Rather than just talk about this behind her back we decided to raise the issue of training at our next TA meeting. Well it was good that we talked about it. As it turns out the TA who was going on all those training days was due to start working with a pupil with complex special needs. The head teacher since that meeting has put all of the TAs down on a rota for training.

Good communication skills involve realising and valuing the contribution you can make towards the successful running of the school

Teaching assistant: When I first started working at the school I felt very overwhelmed and was very anxious about talking to teachers. Now I feel more confident about putting my ideas forward, not only to the teacher, but sometimes I will make suggestions in our staff and TA meetings.

Good teamwork involves knowing how to relate to each other on a professional basis

Teaching assistant: I see some of the staff members on a social basis and though we are very much first name basis in the pub – at school I will always address members of staff by their titles and treat them with respect and courtesy. I know that the children will be watching how we, the staff, treat each other and that the way we treat each other should be an example of how they, the pupils, should try to get on with each other.

Teaching assistant: An important part of your job involves maintaining confidentiality. There are some things in the school that are made known on a 'need to know' basis. This means that there are some things that you will be told in confidence and some details which while you can discuss them at school do not get discussed once you leave the school.

The lines and methods of communication that apply within the school setting

In addition to meetings, there are procedures whereby staff members can communicate with each other.

Watch the notice board

Often the notice board at school has a wealth of relevant information. Notes could include rotas for supervision at breaks, information on available courses and lists of pupils who have been currently excluded.

Memos, notes, filling in records and the like

Often if you wish to communicate with another member of staff, you can write them a note. This note might need to be written on a specially designed paper or possibly might need to be written in a specific book. For example, notifying the IT specialist that there is a problem with a particular computer requires filling in a specific report form. In some very large schools each member of staff will have their own pigeon hole where you can leave them information and likewise collect relevant information. In addition, school staff will often have their own email accounts.

Informal discussions

Often it is at break, during lunch hour, before class begins for the day or at the end of the day that you will have a chance to talk to the teacher about lesson plans, what went well, how a pupil coped with their maths worksheet and possible ideas for future sessions. In many schools a specific time in the day will be put aside for you to meet with your teacher.

The meetings and consultation structures within the school

In schools there are always meetings:

- *Planning meetings*: teachers, head teachers, subject co-ordinators will be involved with planning how the school will deliver the curriculum.
- *Meetings regarding individual pupils*: teachers, head teachers, SENCOs, members of outside agencies (for example **speech and language therapists**), parents and teaching assistants may be involved in meetings relating to **IEPs**.

- *Staff meetings*: all school staff may attend these meeting where specific issues relating to the whole school are discussed. Items on the agenda may include the upcoming Ofsted inspection, plans for future INSET days and where to go for the staff Christmas lunch.
- *Specific meetings*: there may be separate meetings for relevant members of staff (be they the senior management, governors, teaching assistants, teachers) to discuss issues specific to them. These meetings are held as the need arises. Some schools will have special forums for teaching assistants to meet and discuss issues relating to their work.

School expectations and procedures for fostering good working relationships, promoting team work and partnerships with colleagues

Working together

It has been said that no man is an island. While this is true for any individual it is especially true for those working in a school. For a school to run smoothly teamwork is essential. Key factors involved in effective teamwork are illustrated in Figure 5.1.

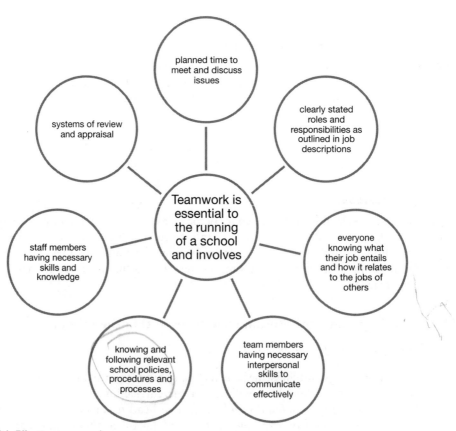

Figure 5.1 Effective teamwork

What makes for an effective team?

✔ *An ethos of collaboration*: an obvious point being that group members are willing and committed to working together.

✔ Clear objectives and focus: it is helpful if the group identifies and sets targets.

✔ *Agreed roles and responsibilities*: depending on the nature of the group there can be various roles such as team leader and secretary.

✔ *Necessary skills and knowledge*: what is deemed necessary skills will vary according to the function of the group. If the group's focus is to review pupils' IEPs, a personal knowledge of relevant pupils and the SEN Code of Practice would be necessary.

✔ *Set procedures for working together*: often meetings will have an agenda to follow.

✔ *Ways of reviewing and evaluating group progress*: often the outcomes of meeting are a set of action points. A review of whether the action points have been met can indicate the effectiveness of the group.

✔ *Conducive working environment*: an obvious but important point being that a group needs an appropriate place to meet that is free from interruptions and the necessary time to cover the required topics.

The differences between work relationships and personal relationships and how work relationships can be maintained effectively

Many people will say that they have made close personal friendships with those they work with. Further, many will spend time socialising with their colleagues outside of work hours. While personal friendships exist, staff know that within working hours they need to act in a professional manner.

Being a professional and acting as a professional requires:

- following a code of conduct
- being accountable for your actions
- being competent at your job
- being worthy of trust
- acting in a manner worthy of respect.

On a day-to-day level this means acting as a role model, addressing your work colleagues in a respectful manner, dressing appropriately and knowing what information needs to kept confidential.

Case study: example of good practice involving respecting confidentiality

Norma, a TA at a large primary school states that her sister works as a teacher at the same school: 'Obviously we do not work in the same class – but we always come into work together. As sisters we are very close. However, I know that there is information my sister knows about pupils and the school that is confidential. I wouldn't dream of compromising my relationship with my sister by asking her for information that she is not at liberty to discuss.'

Self-assessment activity 5.2: create your own code of conduct

(What follows is just a guideline to get you thinking about what it means to be a professional and to act in a professional manner)

Professional code of conduct for my school

As a school we believe that our classroom and school are places where our professional standards apply.

Dress code

Men: No to:
        Yes to:

Women: No to:
        Yes to:

How to relate to pupils

Yes to:

No to:

How to relate to other teaching professionals

Yes to:

No to:

How to behave during or after school events
The reality is that we are watched by parents and pupils and that as teaching professionals we are role models and representatives of the teaching profession.

Yes to:

No to:

Why team discussions are important and why you should contribute constructively to them

An important part of collaborative working relationships involves the ability to share your ideas, observations and comments in a constructive manner with other teaching professionals. Meetings between team members can be formal, as in a staff meeting, or informal as in a brief discussion at the end of the day over a cup of coffee. The strength of a team is its ability to draw out the talent and expertise of each member. Participating in team discussions effectively is a skill which needs to be developed.

Self-assessment activity 5.3: how do you rate yourself as a team member?

Task	I do this well. An example of this is:	I could do better. I need to do:	Help! There is definite room for improvement. My action plan for improving my practice involves:
I contribute to meetings			
I express my views in a way that my colleagues understand			
I am confident in expressing my views			
I wait until others finish speaking before responding			
I listen to what others say			
I make notes of key points in meetings			
I express my feelings in a professional manner			
I use appropriate body language (smiles, encouraging nods, relaxed body posture)			
I accept constructive feedback from others			
I encourage others to contribute			
I offer constructive feedback to others			
I carry out my team responsibilities			
When I can't carry out my team responsibilities I inform the relevant individuals			
I am positive and enthusiastic			

The importance of respecting the skills and expertise of other practitioners

First – the need to recognise the skills and expertise of other practitioners. As stated earlier, an effective school recognises and utilises the skills and expertise of its staff. As a TA you might have expertise in IT skills or be gifted in sewing. The first point in regard to sharing your expertise is to let others know you have something to offer. An effective team member does not 'hide their light under a bushel'. Once others know that you have skills and expertise to share then you need to find a way of sharing this information. One way of contributing is to offer to do tasks for other members of staff. For example, an expert in IT could make themselves available to sort out any IT difficulties. However, when we were talking about working with pupils we mentioned that if we always solved their problems for them, then they would not learn how to solve the problems for themselves. So following this logic, the IT expert can best share their expertise by teaching other members of staff how to become more proficient at using the relevant technology.

Figure 5.2 What can you offer?

Case study: an example of good practice – finding out what others can offer!

We have just had a new head appointed. At our first staff meeting – all staff: teachers, teaching assistants, cleaners, midday meal supervisors, volunteer TAs, secretaries and governors attended. As an ice-breaker we all had to write down our name and what we were good at. It is strange – I have worked in this school for five years and I thought I knew everyone – but there were surprises. I didn't know that one of the TAs was a former swimming coach, that our cleaner was the secretary of the local horticultural society and that one of our midday meal supervisors was involved in the local operatic society. Well the new head was thrilled with all the talent in the room and made a point of suggesting to every one of us other areas of the school in which we might wish to be involved.

Case study: respecting what others have to offer and encouraging others to contribute

Jean, a senior TA, at a large primary school was sent on an INSET day entitled 'Smarter Marking'. As Jean explained to the head teacher, the session described techniques that the teacher and the TA could use such as discussing the assessment criteria in language the pupils could understand before the task, telling pupils that mistakes to be corrected will be marked by a coloured dot and that for each assignment pupils should be given no more than three specific points to work on. Smarter Marking techniques stated that it was important to celebrate the successes made by the pupils and to note clearly how they could improve. Jean was so enthusiastic about the session, the head teacher asked her to give a 15 minute presentation with examples at the next TA meeting. However, Jean was aware that some of the newer TAs had been sent on INSET session regarding marking in their previous school. In particular Jean was aware that one of the newer TAs, though having great ideas was very reluctant to speak out in meetings.

Questions

1   How can Jean involve all the TAs in her session on 'smart marking'?
2   Why is it important that Jean do this?
3   How can Jean draw out the expertise of those TAs who are reluctant to share their opinions?

What has been stressed within this chapter is the importance of working as a team. All members of the team will have expertise and skills that they can offer. As well as sharing what you know it is also helpful to share the nature of how you approach your role. In a sense you are sharing with others how you act professionally.

Why it is important to continually improve your own work

The reality of being involved in teaching is awareness that supporting teaching and learning is not a goal but a process. No matter how long you decide to work in schools there will always be *new things to learn* and *new ways of doing* to be mastered. Everyone involved in teaching needs to reflect on all aspects of their role in order to improve their practice. What is helpful is to consider what aspects of your work could be improved. This is illustrated in Figure 5.3.

After identifying areas that are relevant to you, the next step is to ask yourself questions about your practice so that you can identify what areas to focus on, or targets to work on.

Remember the old adage about targets needing to be SMART:

✔ Specific: the targets should provide a clear and precise description of what you would like to achieve.
✔ Measurable: you need to state how you will know when you have achieved the target.
✔ Achievable: targets need to be realistic and achievable taking into account all other work and family commitments you might have.
✔ Relevant: the targets need to make a difference to you in terms of your personal development and/or your professional workplace practice.
✔ Time-limited: you need to give yourself a specific and realistic time to achieve your target. Meeting a target will give you the motivation to set new targets.

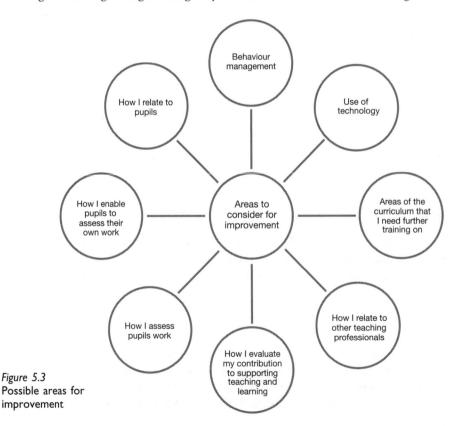

Figure 5.3
Possible areas for improvement

Self-assessment activity 5.4: questions to help you evaluate your practice

To help you get started a few suggestions are offered:

Topic: Behaviour management
Questions
Do I follow relevant policies?
Do I make a point of catching students when they are good?

Topic: How I assess pupils' work
Question
Do I give pupils constructive feedback?

Topic: Use of technology
Question
Do I need further training in any areas?

Topic: Areas of the curriculum that I need further training in
Questions
Am I aware of relevant changes relating from the renewed primary framework?
Am I aware of the SEAL initiative in my school?

Topic: How do I relate to pupils?
Question
Am I a good role model?

Topic: How do I enable pupils to assess their own work?
Questions
Do I ask questions that get students to recognise their mistakes/misconceptions?
Do I ask questions that help students to identify areas of progression?

Topic: How do I relate to other teaching professionals?
Questions
Do I make time to listen to my colleagues?
Do I value and respect their opinions?

Topic: How do I evaluate my contribution to supporting teaching and learning?
Questions
How do I feel the session went?
How do I think the pupils felt about the session?
What were the strengths of the session?
What did I find difficult regarding the session?
What would I do differently next time?

How to reflect on and evaluate your own work

Reflection is defined as the process of thinking about and critically analysing your actions with the goal of changing and improving occupational practice.

In order to increase professional knowledge and skills we need guidance and support. To understand and make sense of our experiences we need constructive feedback.

A TA's charter on reflection

To make sense of and learn from classroom experiences I can:

- Discuss and talk through issues with colleagues. I can ask for and seek advice.
- Gather feedback from others. Feedback could be comments from observations made on my practice. Feedback could be in the form of pupils' comments.
- Relate current classroom experiences to my personal history of experiences that I have had in the classroom.
- Relate classroom experiences to general life experiences as a parent and as a responsible adult.
- Relate classroom experiences to what I have learned on courses, training and INSET days.
- Read books, articles and conduct Internet searches.

In Chapter 2 we discussed how children learn. The same principles apply to us. We can learn:

- through discovery learning, that is, through trial and error;
- through being guided by a more experienced individual;
- by remembering that we need to be aware of what we don't know in order to learn.

Often the development of knowledge and skills has been seen as a cycle. Dennison and Kirk (1990) talk of a cycle of 'Do, Review, Learn and Apply'. Figure 5.4 illustrates this cycle.

Figure 5.4 The Do, Review, Learn and Apply cycle

Figure 5.5 TAs need to be able to multi-task

Professional development is a cycle, in that we never stop learning – thus the term continuous professional development.

The importance of taking feedback from colleagues into account when evaluating your own practice

Though we can be reflective about what we do, it is important to ask others for feedback. Sometimes others can help us see things from new perspectives. Feedback from colleagues can be gained in a variety of ways.

Case study: seeking feedback and asking for advice

Carole had just started working in the school. There was one pupil who Carole was due to support in the class; the only difficulty was that this pupil did not want to be supported. Whenever Carole went up to her – she was told to go away. The teacher had given her suggestions but they did not seem to work. Carole then approached a senior TA and asked her for advice. The TA said that she would make time to watch how Carole interacted with the pupil and give her feedback.

Self-assessment questions

1   Briefly describe a situation where you have asked for advice or feedback.
2   How did this feedback alter your practice?
3   Briefly describe a situation where you have given advice or feedback.
4   When giving advice and feedback is it important to think about how you deliver it?
5   How should advice and feedback be given?

Case study: seeking feedback from others to improve on practice

Jasmine, a senior TA, was given responsibility for introducing new TAs to the school. Though she had been doing this for several years she felt she needed feedback from the TAs on what they had received. To do this she handed out a questionnaire. Jasmine hoped that feedback from the questionnaire would help her to evaluate and improve her practice. The questionnaire asked the following:

1   What information did you receive within your first week?

2   Is there any information that you did not receive that would have been useful?

3   What information do you think should be highlighted within your first day in the school?

4   If a day's induction training was organised, what do you think should be included?

Self-assessment question

1   How does your school introduce new TAs?

Case study: coaching – an example of good practice

Coaching is a way to learn from each other. Peer coaching involves staff working together to plan and develop their own ways of improving an aspect of their teaching. Sandy commented that her school is involved in this initiative. Sandy said that she was paired with another TA and described how it worked:

> We initially met to discuss what specific area of our supporting teaching and learning we wanted to focus on. Interestingly we both wanted to look at how we used questions, in particular how we used questions to get students to think about their thinking processes and what strategies they used to solve problems.

> Then we each observed each other in a number of sessions. Afterwards we made time to discuss the session. As a coach you are acting as a critical supportive friend. You need to be a good listener. Coaching is not about giving suggestions but about helping your partner to reflect on how they use questions. Our teacher says that the advantage of peer coaching is that it is a form of discovery learning in that staff are more likely to remember something they have discovered for themselves.

The formal and informal staff appraisal/performance review opportunities available to you and how you can contribute to and benefit from these

In the changing world of education, teaching assistants need to constantly think about how they do their job and in what ways could they do their jobs better. One way of doing this is by having an official review with your teacher or SENCO on a regular basis. In some schools these reviews are called professional discussions and in other schools they are called appraisals.

An appraisal looks at the following elements:

- How you are progressing in your duties. What duties are you doing at the moment? Does your job description match what you are currently doing?
- The areas you feel confident in.
- The areas you find difficult.
- The areas you need further training in.

The outcome of an appraisal is that you set yourself targets that you would like to work towards for the upcoming year.

A clear example of the paperwork and thinking involved in this process is presented on pages 224–6.

The sorts of development opportunities available to you and how to access these

Things never stand still in the field of education as the following comments from TAs suggest:

'My school is now trying to become a dyslexia friendly school.'

'With the introduction of PPA time – I am now required to work with whole classes.'

'I have a new role within the school – working in the behavioural unit.'

TAs need to be aware of the diverse range of development opportunities on offer if they are to keep up with changes in the field of education, teaching and learning. Of course, keeping up with what's new and extending skills is an ongoing process, thus the term continuous professional development (CPD).

Opportunities available to TAs include:

- INSET or school-based training;
- having a Mentor with the school;
- attending networks or support groups for teaching assistants;
- enrolling on specific courses for teaching assistants;
- reading relevant publications;
- accessing relevant online material.

Figure 5.6 TA training: mission impossible

Checklist

✔ Make time to talk to your teacher.
✔ Participate in a self-appraisal and a formal review/appraisal if possible.
✔ Know relevant school policies.
✔ Use active listening skills.
✔ Take advantage of developmental opportunities that come your way.

Websites

www.dcsf.gov.uk
www.standards.dfes.gov.uk
www.tda.gov
www.tes.co.uk

Chapter 6

Gathering evidence

NVQs require the candidate to show that they are competent in relevant aspects of work. The role of the assessor is to help the candidate compile the evidence and to make links between what the candidate does and what the candidate knows. As stated before, evidence can come in a variety of formats to include:

- observations carried out by an assessor;
- expert witness/witness testimony;
- questioning/professional discussions;
- work products;
- case studies and reflective accounts of your work.

The emphasis for this qualification is on a holistic approach to evidence collection where there are clear links between knowledge and performance and the evidence which is collected is of high quality, detailed and relevant. Further, a holistic approach involves considerable cross-referencing. For example, one observation does not just focus on collecting evidence from one unit but from as many units as relevant.

In this chapter we will be looking at how one assessor works with one candidate to compile detailed, relevant and high quality evidence. As stated in the introduction, the revised National Occupational Standards for Supporting Teaching and Learning in Schools (TDA 2007) places greater emphasis on gathering evidence from observation and expert witness statements. The role of your assessor is to observe you engaged in real work activities and make judgements regarding what performance criteria and knowledge and understanding you have demonstrated. The process by which assessors work is guided by relevant documentation published by the exam boards, Centre guidelines and, of course, the NVQ Code of Practice (QCA 2006). The examples of documentation and evidence produced in this chapter, while paying heed to relevant guidelines, recognise that the documents can vary between centres. So – the documents you may be required to complete as an NVQ candidate will be similar, but not identical to the examples given. Further examples of evidence of performance can be found in Chapters 8, 10, 11 and 16. Of course the assessor and candidates are imaginary, though the work that they engage in reflects the process that many NVQ candidates are involved in.

Let's get started!

Terrie Cole informs her NVQ candidates that the first task they need to work on is to establish a course assessment plan that will be compiled for each candidate. The advantage of a course assessment plan is that it gives an outline of which specific units the candidate will be working on and how they will gather the evidence. Terrie Cole reminded the candidates that there were five mandatory units and an additional two optional units that they would need to select. What follows is the course assessment plan for Miranda Marshall who works in a primary school.

Assessment plan

Date 6 October 2009	Course NVQ 2 Supporting teaching and learning in schools	Venue EveryTown FE College
Name of candidate Miranda Marshall	**Assessor** Terrie Cole	

Any special assessment requirements (tick which applies) If yes, describe the requirements	Yes	No X
		How special requirements will be met

Unit(s) to be assessed (minimum of one full unit)
Mandatory: Units 1, 2, 3, 4, 5. Optional: Unit 6 (Literacy and numeracy) and Unit 9 (Observe and report on pupil performance)

Method of assessment (please tick those which apply)			
Observation	✓	Witness testimony	✓
Examine products	✓	Personal statements	✓
Candidate questioning	✓	Professional discussion	✓

Four observations to be undertaken throughout academic year
Portfolio to be assessed once per half-term
Feedback and action plan to be discussed with candidate following observations/assessments during which candidate will be asked questions

Details of those people involved in the assessment process other than the assessor and candidate	Yes X	No
	Mrs Higglesmith (classroom teacher and mentor) plus other teachers who Miranda works with on an occasional basis.	

Records to be completed by the assessor and candidate			
Assessor		**Candidate**	
Observation reports	✓	Witness status sheet	✓
Candidate feedback sheet	✓	Written evidence	✓
Professional discussion	✓	Record of achievement	
Evidence reference sheet	✓	Other	

Review arrangement for this plan			
Brief feedback following observations, more detailed feedback in class tutorials	✓	Comments We will meet next week to plan first observation session	

NVQ candidate signature:	Miranda Marshall	Date: 6 Oct. 2009
NVQ assessor signature:	Terrie Cole	Date: 6 Oct. 2009

Assessment plan adapted from Liron (2003)

The tutorial

At the end of college session three, Miranda stayed back after class to have a short tutorial with Terrie Cole:

Terrie: Well, Miranda, how are you finding the course? I know from my perspective that I really value your contributions in the class discussions.

Miranda: I really enjoy coming to class and I am finding out so much that I can relate to my classroom practice. I was a bit nervous to begin with but now I can really say that I am enjoying it.

Terrie: Now what we need to do is to arrange a time for me to visit you. Of course you will need to discuss this with your teacher.

Miranda: Do we have to do this so soon? I am alright in the class but if I know that someone is watching me – well I just don't know if I can handle that.

Terrie: I always say don't worry. But I know that every year when I arrange to visit candidates at their workplaces that they do worry – that is only natural. What will happen is that I will come into your class and you can tell me where I should sit, so that I can observe what you are doing. After a few moments you will forget that I am there.

Miranda: OK.

Terrie: What we are going to do next is to fill in an Observation Plan.

Miranda: More paperwork?

Terrie: This plan is both necessary and useful in that it lets you know what to expect. In some ways I see this plan as an aide-memoire.

Miranda: An aide-memoire?

Terrie: Let me say this is another way . . . the plan acts as a prompt or reminder for what I am looking for and what you need to do. Oh yes – remind your teacher that if possible I would like to talk to her for five to ten minutes regarding your work.

Miranda: OK, but do you have to?

Terrie: Don't worry it will be fine. After I observe you and talk briefly to the teacher it will take us probably to morning break. If possible could we sit in the staff room and that will give me a chance to feedback to you and ask you a few questions.

Miranda: OK.

The day of the observation – expect the unexpected

Miranda had discussed her assessor's visit with her teacher. In fact, to be honest Miranda had spent considerable time talking with Mrs Higglesmith about the visit. Miranda had notified the office that Terrie would be arriving at 9 a.m. When Terrie arrived she was shown to the classroom where Miranda was waiting for her. Miranda had her lesson plan to give to Terri but was quite flustered as Mrs Higglesmith had phoned in sick yesterday and was still off sick today and there was a supply teacher and what else could go wrong! Terrie encouraged Miranda by saying that this happened all the time and not to worry: 'If I had a pound for each time this happened I would be very rich!'.

Everytown FE College observation plan

Name of candidate: Miranda Marshall

Name of assessor: Terrie Cole

Location of assessment: Everytown Primary

Date of assessment: 20 Oct. 2009   Time of Assessment: 9:15 a.m.

Unit/element(s) to be assessed:
Focus on Unit 1: Provide support for learning activities, Unit 6 Literacy

Assessment methods to be used:
Direct observation of Miranda working with pupils
Short questions after session
Talk to teacher regarding Miranda's work (this will provide additional evidence)
Lesson plan (work product) to be given to assessor upon arrival

Action needed before assessment (including any special requirements):
Confirm with (class teacher) that this is a convenient time to observe the lesson and arrange with class teacher to provide a witness statement to support additional performance indicators

Candidate signature: Miranda Marshall
Print name: Miranda Marshall

Assessor signature: Terrie Cole
Print name: Terrie Cole

Session plan: written by Miranda Marshall after discussion with Mrs Higglesmith (teacher)

Activity: comprehension

Date: 20 Oct. 2009

Number in group: 5

Age: Reception

Description of the group

I will be working with the lower ability group.
Tyson and Matthew have difficulty paying attention.
Charlotte and Angie are very shy and need encouragement to participate in group discussions.

Aim of activity

Encourage pupils to contribute to group discussions.
To be able to answer questions regarding the story.
Draw a picture about the story and describe the picture.

Materials

The book we were to read was a story about a group of teddy bears that went on a picnic in the rain.

Methods to be used

Read story to children.
Ask children questions about the story. For example, what clothes do you wear when it is raining? What clothes were the teddy bears wearing?
Role-play – getting ready to go out for a rainy day picnic.
Ask children to draw picture of a rainy day picnic and discuss their picture with the group.

Key points to be developed

Have children think about the book and discuss the weather and what types of clothes they would wear for a rainy day.

Expected outcomes

Hope that all the pupils are able to answer questions relating to the story.

Evidence: observation form (written by assessor)

Observation NVQ Level 2 Supporting teaching and learning in schools

Candidate	Miranda Marshall
Assessor	Terrie Cole
Date	20 Oct. 2009
Time	9:15 a.m.
Place	Everytown Primary

Notes on observation	Performance Indicators covered
While the teacher was talking to children on the carpet, Miranda took the opportunity to collect her props and set up in the resource centre (1.2, P2; 1.1, P4). Having completed this task, Miranda returned to the classroom and collected the children she was working with and walked with them to the resource centre in a calm, quiet and orderly manner. This was important as everyone had to walk by a Year 6 class who were writing a test. Miranda had mentioned this to the group and praised them afterwards for being so sensible (3.4, P2). Before commencing the story Miranda reminded the pupils of how they were to behave during the session.	Unit 1.2 (P2) Obtain and use agreed learning resources Unit 1.1 (P4) Make sure you are adequately prepared for your contribution to the learning activity Unit 3.4 (P2) Praise and encourage children/young people Unit 6.1 (P2c) Support pupils in activities to develop their speaking/talking and listening skills
Miranda pitched the story correctly to the level of the children. Miranda was very good at engaging the children in the activity and encouraged them to both ask and answer questions. Miranda encouraged the more shy members of the group to participate and divided her attention between all members of the group. Miranda made sure that all pupils had an opportunity to contribute (6.1, P4). Miranda used constant praise, 'Well Done!' to help the pupils stay on task. A few of the children were unsure of what they had to do and asked Miranda for assistance. Miranda quickly put them at their ease and calmly explained to them in a language they understood, what they had to do (6.1, P4; 1.2, P3, 4, 5). At the end of the session she had each pupil stand up and describe their picture of a rainy day. After each pupil presented their picture she and the entire group gave the pupil a round of applause. A lovely use of role-play. I was very impressed with the work Miranda had put into the session.	Unit 6.1 (P4) Give encouragement and feedback using language and vocabulary that pupils are likely to understand Unit 1.2 Provide support as needed to enable pupils to follow instructions (P3) Make yourself available and easy for pupils to approach for support (P4) Use praise, commentary and assistance to encourage pupils to stay on task (P5)
Discussion with supply teacher (Mrs Carol Whitaker) regarding Miranda Planning for the session As I was not present to note Miranda's discussion regarding planning the session, I took a few minutes to talk to Mrs Whitaker (the supply teacher). Mrs Whitaker reported that she discussed the aims and lesson objectives for that day with Miranda and the individual learning targets for each pupil (1.1, P3). Miranda was asked to work with the Blue group for a brief 15-minute session. Several of the children in this group have difficulties with maintaining attention and are	Unit 1.1 (P3) Agree your role in implementing the learning activity

somewhat reluctant to participate. Mrs Whitaker reported that she showed Miranda the story she was to read and that Miranda suggested that she could bring in some props, various teddy bears, rain boots and umbrellas (1.1, P1). Miranda also suggested that to encourage the pupils to be involved in the activity they act out the book as they go along (1.1, P1) and noted that if they were to do this that they might disrupt other pupils working in the class and that fifteen minutes might not be long enough (1.1, P2). Mrs Whitaker reported that she agreed that Miranda's group would go to the resource centre and that they would be given an extra five minutes. Mrs Whitaker said that Miranda was a star!

Questions to Miranda
Question 1: Why is it important to know the learning objectives? (Unit 1, K5)
Answer: The learning objectives tell you what the pupils need to achieve at the end of the session. This is what you feedback to the teacher – how the pupils got on.

Question 2: Why is planning and evaluating important? (Unit 1, K6)
Answer: If you didn't plan you wouldn't know what you were doing. By setting learning targets you can measure progress. Evaluation means seeing how well the students did, or seeing whether you need to repeat part of the session for some pupils or saying how you would adapt the session in the future. All my feedback helps the teacher evaluate sessions and plan for future sessions.

Signed: *Terrie Cole*   Date: *20 Oct. 2009*

Unit 1.1 (P1) Offer constructive and timely suggestions as to the support you can provide to a planned learning activity

Unit 1.1 (P2) Identify and explain any difficulties you may have in providing the support needed

The tutorial

Terrie: Sit down Miranda – first I want to say how I was very impressed by the way you worked with your group.

Miranda: I was so nervous! I couldn't sleep the night before.

Terrie: I couldn't tell.

Miranda: You know – I couldn't look at you.

Terrie: I did notice that – but sometimes TAs find that not looking at the assessor is a helpful strategy to cope with having someone observe you. As you have more observations, this process will become easier.

Miranda: I hope so.

Terrie: This is very strong evidence for this unit. As you can see I have written at the side what performance indicators you have met. I know you were worried about finding evidence for *giving constructive suggestions*.

Miranda: I was convinced that I didn't do this.

Name of candidate: Miranda Marshall

Name of witness: Mrs Whitaker

Role of witness: Teacher (supply teacher)

Evidence (relating to discussions I held with Miranda on 20 Oct. 2009):

Offer constructive feedback on the learning activity in discussion with the teacher

Miranda reported on the pupils' responses to the literacy session in regards to who had successfully achieved the learning objectives and who had not. In fact all the pupils had achieved the learning outcomes. Miranda reported to me that all had done very well and that they all deserved a sticker for their hard work.

I value Miranda's comments, but what would have helped me to plan further activities would be to know *how much help and support each pupil had received*. With my encouragement, Miranda stated that Tyson had been able to answer questions but only after many prompts. Miranda has agreed that she will include more details in future feedback.

Identify and explain any difficulties you had in providing the support needed

Miranda reported that it was difficult carrying out the session in the resource centre as other pupils were coming and going returning and choosing new books. Miranda commented that it was hard work keeping the pupils focused. I will need to think of whether we can find a more suitable location.

Share your feedback with the teacher at an appropriate time and place, and in a way that maintains effective working relationships

Miranda reported on the students' progress to me, after the break. The pupils were there to hear her report and I could give them further praise regarding their efforts. However, it would be advisable if Miranda could catch me briefly at break to report in more detail regarding their progress.

Provide relevant information to contribute to the teacher's records and reports

For this session the feedback was oral in nature. However, there are times when written feedback is necessary and again the more detailed the feedback the more helpful the feedback is in regards to evaluation and planning for future sessions. Well done Miranda.

Signature: Mrs Whitaker (supply teacher)

Date: 3 Nov. 2009

Tip: when asking someone to provide a witness statement – it is really helpful to have them use the performance indicators as headings.

Terrie: Well, my report based on my discussion with Mrs Whitaker clearly illustrates that you did this: by suggesting a role-play activity and the types of props you could bring in, and by noting that fifteen minutes was not long enough for the activity.

Miranda: I guess this is what you mean when you said that sometimes you just don't think about what you do – or realise how much you do.

Terrie: I think you were reading too much into *constructive and timely suggestions* – in fact you probably make suggestions like this all the time. Remember teachers need and value your comments!

There are still a number of performance indicators to complete for this unit on offering constructive feedback regarding the activity and providing relevant information to contribute to the teacher's records. Here you could include a written account of the feedback you gave the teacher, including any forms or recording sheets you have filled in. You could ask Mrs Whitaker to write a witness statement regarding what you do. Well done Miranda! You are a star!

The next week Miranda brought in a witness statement from Mrs Whitaker. Miranda states that Mrs Whitaker sat down with her and discussed her feedback and showed her what she had written. Terrie noted that helpfully Mrs Whitaker had structured her feedback around the performance indicators for Unit 1.3. Terrie also noted that this expert witness statement would meet the criteria for Unit 6.1 (P6), 'Provide the teacher with relevant feedback'.

Back at the college: learning from others

Miranda at her next NVQ 2 college session was sharing this feedback with her fellow NVQ candidates. Terrie, agreeing with her teacher, commented on how important it was to give detailed feedback that included the degree of support given.

The secondary NVQ candidates commented that though Miranda worked in reception these constructive comments regarding feedback were also true for them. It was so easy to say that everyone had achieved the task but what was more important to mention was how much help was needed.

Chapter 7

Unit 6: Support literacy and numeracy activities

The school policies for mathematics and English

The job of a TA is to act as a bridge between where pupils are and the literacy or numeracy with which they need to engage. To do this effectively you need to be familiar with your school's policies for literacy and numeracy. These should set out the overall vision for literacy and numeracy, the objectives and reasons for teaching literacy and numeracy, and outline the ways literacy and numeracy will be taught throughout the school. Primary schools' literacy and numeracy policies will link with the **Renewed Primary Framework**. In secondary schools the policies will tie in with the **Framework for Teaching English** and the **Framework for Teaching Mathematics**.

Primary Framework for Literacy

As part of the Renewed Primary Framework, the Framework for Literacy was introduced to primary schools during 2007. It builds on and replaces the **National Literacy Strategy (NLS),** which has been in place since 1998. The renewed Framework takes into account the research into the early development of reading as outlined in the **Rose Report** (DfES 2006) and is described as an 'interactive planning tool', largely being accessed online (http://nationalstrategies.standards.dcsf.gov.uk/primary). Within literacy the Primary Framework emphasises what is termed the 'simple view of reading'.

The 'simple view of reading'

This understanding of reading development identifies two factors as being crucial for children to become fluent readers – word recognition and language comprehension:

- Word recognition is a matter of coming to know, understand and be able to use the full range of **phonic** skills, beginning with basic phoneme-grapheme correspondence (i.e. being able to read and write the letters of the alphabet).
- Language comprehension involves children understanding what they both hear and read.

Word recognition and language comprehension are related and both are essential if children are to learn to read; however, the balance should increasingly shift as children grow older and learn more. While during Key Stage 1 the emphasis will be on word recognition, during Key Stage 2 this should shift to language comprehension. As stated in the Rose Report, 'learning to read' should give way to 'reading to learn'.

Mini-quiz

Match the terms to the correct letters (note: there is usually more than one correct answer to each term). It may not be as easy as you think!

Phoneme	bl
	st
	e
Vowel	ou
	ough
	d
Consonant	le
	l
	pr
Initial consonant blend	ph
	ee
	mp
Final consonant blend	tr
	ai
	x
Vowel digraph	ie
	nk
	ck

The literacy hour

A major part of the NLS was the daily literacy hour. Although this is not as rigidly followed by schools as it was when it was first introduced, the four-part structure of the literacy hour continues to shape much lesson planning:

- *Shared text work*, when the teacher works with the whole class looking at texts and through this teaches reading and/or writing skills.
- *Shared word/sentence work*, when the teacher works with the whole class on phonics, spelling, grammar and/or punctuation.
- *Guided/independent work*, when the class is divided into groups and the teacher and teaching assistant each work with a group of children on reading or writing while the rest of the class work independently.
- *The plenary session*, when the whole class gathers together to discuss and reflect upon the lessons learned.

Framework for Teaching English

This is the national strategy covering the teaching of English in Key Stage 3. Like the Primary Literacy Strategy, it divides the subject into word level, sentence level and text level work and recommends what should be taught in each year group. TAs working in the secondary sector need to be familiar with this Framework if they are supporting students in English.

Primary Framework for Mathematics

Alongside the Renewed Primary Framework for Literacy, the Renewed Primary Framework for Mathematics makes up the Renewed Primary Framework which shapes the way all primary schools in England deliver the literacy and numeracy curriculum. There are significant differences between the Framework for Mathematics and the **National Numeracy Strategy (NNS)**:

*   It is electronic – allowing a much greater range and flexibility of resources to be accessed by teachers and TAs (http://nationalstrategies.standards.dcsf.gov.uk/primary).
*   The strands of learning are simplified to seven with learning objectives given for each strand to show how pupils should progress. These strands are:

    –   using and applying mathematics
    –   counting and understanding number
    –   knowing and using number facts
    –   calculating
    –   understanding shape
    –   measuring
    –   handling data.

*   There is clearer guidance regarding the use of calculators and how and when calculator skills should be taught.
*   There is an emphasis on standard methods of writing calculations for the four operations of number (adding, subtracting, multiplying and dividing).
*   As for the Framework for Literacy, sufficient time is allocated to topics to enable in-depth focus in teaching and learning.

The literacy and numeracy skills expected of the pupils with whom you work

Children develop their literacy and numeracy skills at different rates. Class teachers will have targets towards which each pupil in their class will be working. For the majority of pupils these targets will be in line with the **National Curriculum Level Descriptors** appropriate for their age range. Some pupils will be working ahead of the expected levels for their age group while others are going to be working at lower levels.

You can find out about the literacy skills expected of the pupils with whom you work by looking at class records, including **Individual Education Plans (IEPs)**, reading the National Curriculum Level Descriptors and through discussion with the class teacher or the school's **SENCO**.

How pupils develop reading, writing, speaking/talking and listening skills and the factors that promote and hinder effective learning

Just as there is physical development in children, so there is learning development – called *cognitive* development.

Speaking and listening

We learn how to speak through imitating those around us. This has significant implications for school life. Some children begin school already using a wide range of words and being able to express themselves very well. Others have a much more limited vocabulary. Encouraging pupils to express themselves verbally, and to listen to others in constructive ways, is an important aspect of developing their sense of identity and their self-esteem.

Reading and writing

To become fluent readers, four qualities are needed. Children need to know what the book is about (content); be skilled at decoding (phonics); understand the structure of the language used (grammar) and be able to read words on sight (word recognition). All these factors are interrelated, but different ones have more impact on reading development at different ages.

Younger children are more reliant on simple word recognition and begin to read high frequency words such as 'mummy' or 'daddy'. They also need to learn decoding skills – to recognise the names and sounds of individual letters and begin to put these together in phonically regular words, such as being able to read the sounds /c/- /a/ -/t/ and put these together to make the word 'cat'.

As they get older, content understanding (comprehension) and grammatical understanding become increasingly significant in the development both of reading and of writing. Fluency in reading will only come with understanding of meaning and an ability to make sense of the grammar of a text. The four skills needed for fluent reading are:

- understanding content
- phonic skills
- grammar recognition
- word recognition.

Memory plays a large part in the development of all aspects of literacy, and this, too, develops with age. A typical 4 year old will be able to remember two to three items of information said or shown to them; this increases to six items by the age of 12 and, at 15 and beyond they should be able to recall seven or so items. Older children develop more strategies for aiding memory than younger ones – this is a process which can continue throughout school life and into adulthood.

Neither reading nor writing is gained merely through imitation. Pupils make progress through interaction with others, particularly significant adults who teach them the skills and the knowledge they need to make that progress. Children need to be taught to read and write using apparatus that they can see and touch before they can progress onto more abstract ways of learning. This is called **'multi-sensory'** teaching and is a crucial part of most reading programmes.

Figure 7.1
TAs can encourage
reading

Children can be helped to make sense of texts by the use of pictures, suitable print size, the spacing of lines, the amount of words on a page, the complexity of sentences and the type of font used. Below is an example of two text layouts essentially conveying the same information, but one provided for younger readers or for older struggling readers.

Two texts

Snow in the winter

In winter the weather can become quite cold and when the wind blows from the north or the east we often have snow. In the south of England this does not happen very often, but it does further north and is often frequent and heavy in Scotland. When it does snow a lot, transport and utilities can be disrupted meaning that many people find it hard to move about the country or to heat their houses. When it snows, schools are often closed and children have the day off, which is enjoyed by many as they play snowball fights and go tobogganing.

Snow in the winter

When it is cold it can snow.
The wind blows, the snow comes
and the ground is white.
Roads can be blocked.
Houses can get cold.
Some schools are closed
and children have fun!

Writing, similarly, develops in stages as the following table shows:

Stage one	Beginning with scribbles on paper, children learn how to manipulate pencils and crayons.
Stage two	They move on to emergent writing when they begin to realise that they can convey ideas through putting pencil to paper.
Stage three	Gradually they learn the shape of letters, the sounds they make and the way to sequence letters into words and groups of words so that others can read what they write without having to have it interpreted for them.
Stage four	Children learn the rules of grammar, sentence construction, punctuation and how to construct different types of writing. They also learn how to spell, which is easier said than done given the complexity of written English.

The interactive use of speaking/talking, listening, reading and writing to promote literacy development in pupils

The Renewed Primary Framework stresses the interrelationship of listening, speaking, reading and writing. No one aspect of literacy is more important than any other and this should be reflected in the teaching provided for children of whatever age. Your role as a teaching assistant is part of the process of developing these interactive skills.

You can encourage timid or reticent pupils to share their ideas. You can help impetuous or impatient pupils to wait and listen before they leap into action. You can help pupils generalise their knowledge by saying something like, 'You remember what we talked about yesterday? Well, this passage is about the same thing.' You have opportunities to help pupils recognise the connection between what they hear and say, what they read and what they write.

Listening, speaking, reading and writing interact throughout the whole of literacy development. One reinforces and progresses the others – the more words a child can say and understand, the more they are likely to read and to understand what they read; the more they read, the more vocabulary they will gain; the more vocabulary they have, the more words they are likely to want to be able to spell and use in their writing. If the teaching of what the government terms 'high-quality' phonics is followed, children should learn the interrelated skills of decoding (reading) and encoding (spelling) over the same time period.

That speaking and listening are intimately connected with reading and writing development is evidenced in those who encounter problems in making progress in their literacy skills:

- Children who experience difficulties with speech or language are very likely to encounter problems learning to read, write or spell.
- If a child finds it difficult to pronounce certain sounds, they may not be able to correctly spell those sounds without intervention and specific teaching (see Chapter 11).
- A child with a large spoken vocabulary is likely to have a wider reading vocabulary, at least during the early years of schooling, than one with a more restricted vocabulary.

As part of the skill of reading involves the understanding of context, children with a rich spoken language background are going to be more advantaged than those who do not have this. Children with poorer spoken language backgrounds may well find it harder to understand written texts. As a TA, you could ask yourself and ask others: 'What can I do to enhance this?'

How pupils develop mathematical skills and the factors that promote and hinder effective learning

In developing numeracy skills, pupils move through stages of needing 'real' apparatus, such as small toys, beads, plastic or wooden blocks; then equipment such as number lines and number fans, before being able to think more abstractly. Pupils will move through these stages at different rates.

Numeracy can present significant difficulties to children:

- The range of vocabulary and the number of alternative methods available to solve any one problem may cause confusion.
- Some pupils will find it hard to remember all the pieces of information and steps required to solve a problem or complete a calculation.
- The speed or pace of the lesson may be too fast for some children and they get left behind.
- Pupils may have to move onto a new topic before they have fully understood the current one.
- There may not be sufficient use of concrete, 'hands-on' materials to enable children to fully understand the concepts being taught.
- Some pupils are able to do the numeracy, but struggle because they cannot read the questions or write down their answers.
- Numeracy can provoke panic, causing the brain to 'shut down' or the pupil to react aggressively.

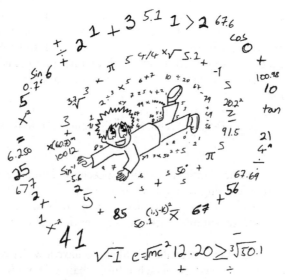

Figure 7.2 Some pupils can find numeracy an overwhelming experience

Confidence is important in learning any subject, but perhaps especially so for numeracy. Many children and adults too are simply scared of numeracy and freeze at the thought of doing it. To boost their confidence, pupils must be given tasks that they can complete effectively rather than activities which are always too difficult for them.

The nature of any special educational needs or additional support needs of pupils with whom you work

Some pupils will be identified as having **special educational needs**. Pupils with a specific learning difficulty, such as **dyslexia**, may be functioning within the average or above average range for science and numeracy, but struggle with reading and spelling. Other pupils may have plenty of ideas to write about and can structure a story verbally using a range of vocabulary but find it extremely difficult to physically write the words as they have **dyspraxia** (an aspect of the broader 'Developmental Co-ordination Disorder'). Pupils who experience a specific learning difficulty in numeracy may have 'dyscalculia'; in this case their literacy skills may be fine, but they find it very difficult to understand mathematical concepts.

Pupils with dyslexia are likely to be experiencing difficulties with **phonological processing** – they may, for instance, be unable to recognise vowels in the middle of words (medial vowels) or syllables in words they hear. They may also experience difficulties with short-term or 'working' memory. They are almost certainly going to find decoding hard. However, many of these children may have strengths in other aspects of reading, such as comprehension. It may be, therefore, that for a pupil with dyslexia their comprehension age is higher than their reading accuracy age and they compensate for their difficulties in phonic skills with their understanding of the content of texts and the context of words. They may have strong visual processing skills and are able to build up a large word-bank learned purely through sight recognition.

Those pupils who have an all-round global developmental delay may be functioning at two years or more below the level of most of their peer group in all areas of the curriculum, while other pupils are academically above average but are held back by challenging behaviour or disturbed emotions. Still others will experience **physical or sensory impairments** which impact on their learning to a greater or lesser extent. Each teacher will have records regarding such pupils, normally via IEPs. You need to be familiar with these records to support pupils appropriately.

The strategies and resources used at your school for developing pupils' reading, writing, speaking/talking, listening and mathematical skills and knowledge

There is a range of strategies you can use to support pupils in literacy and numeracy activities. Not all of them will be used all the time and not all of them will be used in any one lesson. They can be likened to tools in a tool-box upon which you can draw as and when needed.

Strategies available to TAs include:

- helping pupils to understand spoken and written instructions;
- prompting shy or reticent pupils to take part in conversations or small group/class discussions;

- encouraging pupils to use classroom resources such as dictionaries, word banks, or maths equipment;
- adapting materials used in the class;
- explaining words and phrases used by the teacher;
- giving specific reading or writing support as part of normal classroom practice, such as being an **amanuensis** or a reader.

Prior to the actual lesson you will need to ensure that you have all the learning resources you need; that all equipment required is both available and in working order; that you have access to the right quantity of written and curriculum materials. If some of the pupils you support require specialist equipment, you need to know it is available and in good working order.

Some general principles apply to supporting pupils in numeracy who experience a range of barriers to their learning.

You can:

- help pupils understand what is being said by repeating it in simplified language;
- help the pupil frame or formulate their own answers by asking questions such as, 'How could you explain that?' or 'Why do you think you got that answer?';
- remind them of what they have learned previously;
- use visual stimuli and concrete apparatus such as games, number lines, multi-link
- encourage a pupil who is easily distracted to focus on the lesson;
- ensure that all pupils understand what is being asked of them and can read any materials that have been handed out;
- go over the teaching points already made in the lesson, taking time to give more explanation if needed;
- provide adapted resources, including work in large print;
- work with pupils using ICT;
- prepare pupils to participate in whole class discussions by going over their answers with them, asking them for their ideas and suggestions, and encouraging them to speak up.

You are likely to use structured, cumulative (i.e. one fact or skill building upon another) and multi-sensory methods when seeking to develop numerical understanding.

Not too much at once

It is better to focus on a limited amount which can be understood, than to try and teach everything and end up confusing the pupil. For instance, you may be supporting a pupil who finds it hard to process information quickly. During a mental maths session, therefore, where the class are required to answer ten or twenty questions within a certain timeframe, you could encourage them to try and answer every other question. This will give them the opportunity to get at least half right, rather than seek to attempt all of them and, most probably, get most or all of them wrong.

'Can you explain how you did this?'

Asking pupils to talk about how they approached certain problems or arrived at particular conclusions is an important element of TA support. It may be that, by listening to what they say, you can see why pupils are making errors and can teach to that gap or misunderstanding. If, say, a pupil tells you that they worked out that 16 plus 23 made 48, they may be confusing the digits in the tens and units columns and you can teach specifically to this. This is more likely to be the case if they are adding in lines rather than columns (16 + 23 = ___). They may look at the first digit in the calculation (1) and add that to the last digit (3), then they may add the middle two digits (6 and 2) thus deciding the answer to the question is 48 (1 + 3 and 6 + 2).

Ensure the basics are in place

As pupils get older and begin to experience difficulties in maths, it is tempting to try and tackle the immediate presenting problem. This, in itself, may well be insufficient. You need to check that the pupil has a grasp of fundamentals first.

Use concrete apparatus

Using concrete materials can effectively introduce or consolidate concepts. Number lines and number squares, while being useful, rely solely on visual skills. More tactile equipment such as plastic or wooden cubes and rods are readily available in primary schools and in special needs departments of secondary schools.

Constant review

'Use it or lose it' certainly applies to maths. You can support pupils by ensuring concepts and facts they have been taught are regularly and frequently reviewed.

Your role is to create an environment of trust whereby pupils feel able to ask you questions about the tasks knowing that they will be treated seriously and not ridiculed. In responding to their questions you obviously need to explain and clarify tasks and answer their questions in such a way that they understand. Simply repeating what has already been taught in the lesson is unlikely to meet their needs. This necessitates that you yourself understand the tasks and are able to reshape the teaching content into a more understandable format.

Organising your support

Support that is effective in promoting children's progress does not simply happen because there is an extra adult in the classroom. Indeed, having a teaching assistant in the classroom can actually impede pupil progress if they do the work for children and thus promote 'learned helplessness' where pupils become dependent upon the TA rather than taking responsibility for their own learning.

The key is the class or subject teacher and the TA agreeing and planning just how that extra adult support will be used. A number of alternative organisational strategies have been used, all of which have shown themselves to be successful in helping pupils make progress (Cremin et al. 2005).

One organisational strategy is *zoning* – where the teacher and the TA each take responsibility for an area of the classroom, e.g. the TA supports two groups of pupils while the teacher focuses on the remaining three. Another strategy can be described as *room management* when the teacher and TA take on definite roles within the class, such as the TA working with specific pupils, thus allowing the teacher to give her attention to the rest of the class. A third organisational strategy is known as *reflective teamwork,* which involves teacher and TA spending time discussing their respective strengths in supporting pupils and agreeing how to play to those strengths, and then meeting after particular lessons to review how their respective support went and plan for future lessons. While all of these can be useful, the third strategy is obviously very time consuming and, in many settings, is likely to be impractical.

Self-assessment questions

1   What difficulties might pupils experience in literacy or numeracy?
2   How do children become fluent readers?
3   What difficulties might pupils experience in numeracy?
4   How might you best be able to support such pupils?

How to use praise and assistance to maintain the pupils' interest in and enthusiasm of understanding and using the full range of literacy and numeracy skills

Pupils experiencing difficulties in either maths or literacy (or both) are quite likely going to want at some stage to give up. Nobody wants to do day-in/day-out what they struggle with. As adults we can usually avoid such situations, but this is not so for children experiencing difficulties with learning. They have no choice – they must be in school and they must be in maths and literacy lessons. Frustration and a sense of despair can easily creep in. Part of your role as a TA is to counter this tendency.

Pretending that everything is OK is not going to do anything except make the problem worse. Children are not easily deceived – they know when they can do something and when they cannot. They compare themselves with each other and realise very quickly who is on the 'lowest' table. If you try and brush over their problems and concerns, telling them that 'It will be alright' they will simply not believe you and you will lose credibility in their eyes.

But all is not lost! Children, particularly younger ones, but older ones as well, *do* respond to genuine interest, understanding and praise from adults they respect. It may be that you need to alter the way you communicate praise and acceptance as they get older – teenagers do not often appreciated being sent to the head teacher to receive an 'I worked hard' sticker – but they nevertheless appreciate your comments.

Praise is one way to boost confidence – but praise must be genuine and it must be specific. Saying 'Well done' is essentially meaningless; 'Good work' is even worse. Children know when their work is good, at least when compared to others, and, whatever you say, if a pupil thinks their work is rubbish, it will be rubbish to them.

Many pupils say that what they find hard is no-one taking any notice of how hard they have worked, how much effort they have put in. Part of your role as a TA could be to make sure that you *do* acknowledge this, that you take time to find out about the effort and time pupils put in and praise them for that. Praise does not always need to relate to either quality or quantity of work produced.

Praise can be given in a number of ways. Most obviously is through verbal comment, which you can do at any time during or after a lesson. But praise can also be in the form of written comments. You need to check with the teachers you work with about whether or not you can make written comments on pupils' work, but if you can do this, you can give very specific praise, such as 'I am impressed with your use of vocabulary in this story'.

Praise can also be given through awarding achievement or reward points, whatever system is employed within your school. You need to become familiar with the system of rewards operating in the school and find out to what extent you can give out these rewards. For older children, sometimes even for the most 'cheesed-off' pupils, a note home to mum saying how hard they have worked can work wonders and is much appreciated by pupils.

Whatever you do in terms of praise, as has been said before, be genuine. Look for what the pupil really has done well or has worked hard at and respond to that. Do not try and patronise children by telling them they have done well when they, and everybody around them, knows this is simply not the case.

The sorts of problems that might occur when supporting literacy and numeracy activities with individuals and groups

Learning resources

Prior to a lesson you will need to ensure that you have all the learning resources you need; that all equipment required is both available and in working order; that you have access to the right quantity of written and curriculum materials. It is too late in the middle of the lesson to find out that half of the calculators you need have dead batteries. If some of the pupils you support require specialist equipment, you need to know it is available and in good working order.

Limited knowledge

The older the pupils you are supporting, the more knowledge of literacy and maths you yourself must know. One problem could be that they ask you questions to which you do not know the answer. You need to be honest with them, and tell them that you will find out to help them in a future lesson – but be sure that you do! This is one reason why it is important to be aware of the teacher's planning and objectives for the upcoming lessons. If you are aware of an area where you yourself have limited knowledge, you can brush up your own skills and understanding before the actual lessons are taught.

The importance of working within the boundaries of your role and competence and when you should refer to others

Some of the suggestions for support given above assume you as a TA have a large measure of independence within the class and can take a certain amount of initiative with pupils. This sort of thing must be agreed beforehand with the class or subject teacher. Your school may have established clear guidelines regarding what TAs can and cannot do within lessons. It is vital you keep to these and do not try to take matters into your hands that are beyond your responsibility. All sorts of tensions can arise if this happens.

There are two areas of possible tension regarding your role. One is that you feel you have a lot more to offer than is being asked of you – the issue of being 'underused'. The other is that you are asked to do more than you feel you have the competence to do – the issue of being overstretched. Both these scenarios are reasonably common and both need to be discussed with the teacher and/or the SENCO or the person in your school responsible for the deployment of TAs. You cannot let either of these situations continue for long without tensions arising within the class.

Checklist

✔ I am aware of the resources available in my school for supporting literacy and numeracy.

✔ I understand the basics of how children develop literacy and numeracy skills.

✔ I know where to find out about any special educational needs the children I work with may have.

✔ I understand the implications of these needs on their literacy and numeracy development.

✔ I am familiar with ways of supporting children in literacy and numeracy.

✔ I am able to discuss and plan with the teachers I work with in order to effectively support pupils.

Further reading

Clayton, P. and Barnes, R. (2003) *How to Develop Numeracy in Children with Dyslexia*. London: LDA.

Corbett, P. (2001) *How to Teach Fiction Writing at Key Stage 2 (Writers' Workshop Series)*. London: David Fulton.

Fox, G. and Halliwell, M. (2000) *Supporting Literacy and Numeracy: A guide for learning support assistants*. London: David Fulton.

Haylock, D.W. (2005) *Mathematics Explained for Primary Teachers*. London: Sage.

Lewis, M. and Wray, D. (eds) (2006) *Literacy in the Secondary School*. London: David Fulton.

Palmer, S. and Corbett, P. (2003) *Literacy: What works?* London: Nelson Thornes.

Websites

http://curriculum.qca.org.uk/
http://nationalstrategies.standards.dcsf.gov.uk/primary
www.standards.dcsf.gov.uk/phonics/rosereview/
www.teachernet.gov.uk/teachingandlearning/subjects/maths/numeracy/

Chapter 8

Units 7 and 8: Use information and communication technology to support pupils' learning

This chapter combines two units – Unit 7 *Support the use of ICT for teaching and learning* and Unit 8 *Use ICT to support pupils' learning*. The first focuses on the provision and maintenance of ICT, while the second, on the use made of ICT by pupils; but there is considerable overlap between the two units.

The potential learning benefits of using ICT in different ways to support learning

ICT involves both the discovery of information and the communication of knowledge gained. The skills developed within the ICT curriculum can have enormous benefits on pupils' thinking and learning in every area of the curriculum.

Skills acquired during ICT include:

- finding and processing information;
- analysing and interpreting information;
- presenting information for a variety of reasons;
- enquiry and decision-making;
- making judgements about the appropriateness and value of information;
- problem solving;
- creative thinking;
- synthesising (combining) information from a variety of sources;
- reviewing, modifying and evaluating work on an ongoing basis.

Websites can be a highly motivating tool to help develop higher-order thinking. The benefits of interactive whiteboards in classes include motivating pupils who are inspired by the graphics and range of material available on them.

Alongside developing thinking and learning skills, ICT can help promote a wide range of skills needed by pupils, including:

- collaborative working;
- communicating via a wide range of media and with a variety of people often in various parts of the world;
- sensitivity to the rights and feelings of others, for example, in respect of privacy.

Using a search engine can help promote pupils' skills of inquiry and analysis of information. There are many search engines to choose from, the most well-known being Google. But there are also specifically 'child-friendly' search engines such as 'Yahooligans' or 'Ask for Kids' which are worth exploring.

ICT is particularly adept at developing pupils' skills in narrative storytelling. This can apply cross curricular and not simply in literacy. Storytelling using animation, cartoons, sound effects, dialogue, importing backgrounds from the Internet and scanning in pupil drawings or artwork can be applied equally effectively in subjects such as history and RE.

Software packages can enable teachers and teaching assistants, as well as pupils, to produce excellent graphics which enhance teaching and learning via templates, inserting visuals, animation, multimedia writing frames and many more. There are many websites available at no cost for pupils and school staff; among the most obvious being Google Images and the BBC for schools websites (www.bbc.co.uk/schools).

Other types of ICT can be used to promote 'pupil voice' and pupil participation in class activities. Consider the following case study and note down the aspects of learning (both academic and social) that are potentially being experienced via the use of ICT in this lesson.

Case study: pupils casting votes in a science lesson

The setting is a Year 5 science lesson, part of the unit on solids, liquids and gases. The teacher is demonstrating the fact that placing salt on an ice cube makes it melt faster than if left to melt by itself. Each member of the class has a hand-held electronic voting machine linked via the class's laptop computer to the class interactive whiteboard.

Standing at the front of the class, the teacher places an ice cube in a glass container and asks the class what they think will happen when he adds a teaspoonful of salt. They have already seen how long it took a similar sized ice cube to melt in the container without any additional material. Most of the class say that the ice will melt more quickly, some that the addition of salt will not make any difference, and a few that the ice will actually take longer to melt.

The teacher then asks each pupil to vote for the time they think the ice will take to melt when the salt is placed on to it. They press the appropriate buttons on their electronic voters (e.g. pressing '5' if they think five minutes, '3' if they think three minutes and so on) and then they press 'Enter'. On the whiteboard a graph is immediately shown indicating the distribution of predicted times.

The teacher places the salt on the ice cube and the class time the melting process. Once the ice is melted, the class teacher uses the software on the class laptop to identify those pupils who estimated most accurately.

The sorts of ICT resources available within the school and where they are kept

---

Self-assessment activity 8.1

Complete the following table with a list of all the ICT resources and equipment you have in your school – don't forget things like calculators and cameras.

- Where are they stored?
- What are they used for – whole class work, group work or individual work?
- Which of these are you familiar with using?
- Which ones would you like training on?

ICT resources in school	Where they are kept	What they are used for	I am familiar with this	I would like training on this

---

The relevant school curriculum and age-related expectations of the pupils with whom you are working

ICT is a central part of the **National Curriculum** for both primary and secondary schools. The knowledge, skills and understanding for ICT are set out under four headings:

- 'Finding things out';
- 'Developing ideas and making things happen';

- 'Exchanging and sharing information';
- 'Reviewing, modifying and evaluating work as it progresses'.

The **National Curriculum Level Descriptors** give an indication of the standards expected at different ages:

Foundation Stage

Children in Reception/Early Years will begin to use computers and programmable toys such as Roamers. They will begin to use appropriate vocabulary.

Key Stage 1

Children will use a range of ICT equipment both in literacy and numeracy. They will begin to learn the basics of word processing and use a variety of ways to present information.

Key Stage 2

Pupils will become more capable in the use of ICT and develop skills in working with a greater range of software, including word processing, audio-visual presentations and the Internet. The aim is that using ICT becomes both natural and normal and it can be applied in a variety of subjects.

Key Stages 3 and 4

Students are expected to develop knowledge of technical aspects of how ICT works. They need to become proficient in the use of multimedia presentations and to collaborate in presenting information in a wide range of formats. They are expected to develop a good understanding as to when using ICT is appropriate and when it is better to use something else.

It is a statutory requirement that ICT supports every curriculum subject apart from physical education. In this way ICT becomes not just a subject taught in its own right but a means of learning other subjects as well.

Ways of selecting good quality ICT resources

A valid question has been asked of ICT – '*Is education driving technology or is technology driving education?*' How software and hardware is selected goes a long way towards answering that question.

All schools will have similar criteria when it comes to selecting software that will be used by pupils. This will include:

- being age-appropriate;
- being of sufficient substance and accuracy to promote learning;
- being 'user-friendly';
- being legal – i.e. not pirated;
- not being violent or immoral;
- not being stereotypical or racist.

Part of your role is to monitor how effective software is. It may be that, for some of the pupils you support, the loading process is too complex or the level of English used in it is too advanced for them to access independently. If you find this to be the case, you need to inform the class teacher. Discussion with the ICT manager or with the **SENCO** may give you some ideas about more appropriate software.

Pupils must be able to access and control software themselves and it must be something which actively promotes their learning rather than simply engages them in activities of stimulus-response. For instance, pupils may be accessing a program which is supposed to be teaching them their multiplication tables by presenting them with questions on the screen and providing them with three answers to choose from. Rather than thinking through the problem, pupils may simply be pressing any key until the right answer flashes up. There is no learning taking place here except improving the speed of keying in numbers.

There must be a sufficient range of material available to pupils in order for them to meet the requirements of the curriculum. There is a minimum of hardware and software material needed, included in which is:

- access to networked computers;
- access to email and the Internet;
- multimedia machines;
- printers – both colour and black and white;
- access to scanners, digital cameras, video cameras;
- software that enables pupils to word process, use databases and spreadsheets, develop graphic and painting skills;
- music software.

Pupils need to have time to become familiar with the ICT they are being asked to use. This is not simply playing around on it, but it may well involve exploring what the equipment or the software can do.

Relevant legislation, regulations and guidance in relation to the use of ICT

Schools are covered by legislation such as the Data Protection Act (1998), the Children Acts (1989, 2004) and the Freedom of Information Act (2005). Copyright legislation and software licensing law will need to be followed so that all programs are used legally. All members of staff are required to be aware of the implications of legislation when using ICT. Basically it is designed to ensure that information is used appropriately. One aspect of copyright law is that, normally, staff are not allowed to bring software from home and load it on to school equipment.

The school's policy for ICT

Each school will have a policy for ICT, included in which will be 'Internet rules' along the following lines:

- I will never give out my home address, personal email address or telephone number or arrange to meet anyone over the Internet.

- I will only use the Internet and search engines when I have permission to do so.
- I will only email people that I know or who my teacher has approved and when I have been given permission.
- Any messages I send shall be polite, respectful and sensible.
- I understand that the use of chat rooms is not allowed under any circumstances.
- I understand that the school can check my computer files and the Internet sites I visit.

The ICT policy should also make reference to health and safety aspects of using ICT, such as:

- Children shall not be responsible for moving equipment around the school.
- Food and drink may not be consumed near ICT equipment.
- ICT equipment must be stored securely and cleaned regularly.
- Staff should ensure that children are seated at the computers comfortably and must be aware of the dangers of continuous use (e.g. eye/wrist strain).

How to use ICT to advance pupils' learning, including those with special educational needs or additional support needs, bilingual pupils and gifted and talented pupils

Promoting inclusion

One of the benefits of ICT is that it can often be more readily adapted to meet the needs of pupils than standard reading and writing materials. The school's ICT policy

Figure 8.1 TAs should be alert to the dangers of using computers for too long

should expressly state equality of opportunity in accessing ICT along these lines: '*All children have access to the use of ICT regardless of gender, race, cultural background or physical or sensory disability.*'

The National Curriculum states that for **inclusion** to happen in a lesson, staff need to:

- set suitable learning challenges;
- respond to pupils' diverse learning needs;
- overcome potential barriers to learning and assessment for individuals and groups of pupils.

ICT offers an excellent opportunity to respond to these statements and promote inclusion as:

- **differentiation** is often more easily achieved with ICT than with traditional learning techniques;
- hardware and software can be adapted to meet the needs of individual pupils through the use of an enlarged font, speaking text, a larger mouse or keyboard and screen magnifiers;
- ICT can be used to provide resources for specific pupils such as printing text in Braille;
- many pupils who find writing difficult will be more confident using a word processor;
- pupils are often highly motivated by ICT.

Age, gender, needs and abilities

ICT can provide support for pupils with **SEN** and be used to challenge **gifted and talented** pupils. Many software packages contain a range of levels of activities, such as learning spelling rules or multiplication tables. For instance, when using these within one spelling lesson, some pupils may be learning to spell 'cvc' words while others are working on the '-ious' pattern.

Tools and techniques

In order to adapt ICT to the needs of pupils an essential prerequisite is that staff themselves are familiar with and confident in using the particular hardware and software they are being asked to adapt. You need to be able to explain how pupils should do things and why they should do them.

Techniques and tools in adapting ICT include:

- choosing one technique at a time to work on with pupils, for instance, highlighting text and then learning how to change the font size or colour;
- combining several techniques to produce a completed piece of work;
- making sure icons are understood and used by pupils;
- ensuring pupils know the basic techniques of ICT such as opening files and saving work.

Promoting independence

When supporting pupils in ICT it is easy to do the work for them, particularly in the early stages. Your role is to tell them how to develop the skills they need and, where appropriate, to model this for them. At all times you should encourage them to 'have a go' themselves and to develop their independent skills. You should remind them to continually save their work so it is not lost if something goes wrong.

Many pupils are more willing to experiment using ICT than when writing as they can edit errors out with ease. However, it is important to encourage them to keep records of their progress through saving work, even in the draft stages.

The importance of health, safety, security and access

All electrical and electronic equipment carries a certain amount of risk. It is the duty of the ICT manager or technician to ensure that all equipment is regularly checked and adequately maintained; however, all staff and pupils have a responsibility to be on the lookout for faulty wiring, unsafe cabling and so on. Any risk needs to be communicated to the appropriate persons as soon as possible.

Schools are likely to be protected by a 'firewall' from harmful Internet sites, but adult supervision is usually going to be required as well. Schools are likely to be relatively 'safe areas' for pupils using the Internet, but they need to be taught how to use it safely so that they are protected off-site as well.

Identifying sources of information and advice

Within school, information and advice may be gained from ICT Technicians or Managers employed in the school. One key to the successful development of ICT within a school is positive leadership given by those who know what they are talking about. Such people are invaluable to members of staff and pupils alike.

Outside of the school, your **local authority** may have advisers or experts who can give advice. There are also numerous websites to visit, such as that of Becta (British Educational Communications and Technology Agency) – www.ictadvice.org.uk

Figure 8.2 ICT can be a puzzling affair

The sorts of problems that might occur when supporting pupils using ICT and how to deal with these

Three practical problems present themselves to staff and pupils alike:

- It does not work – the hardware or software does not function properly.
- It is not available – the ICT suite is booked when you want it, there are not enough computers for everyone in the class to use at the same time and so on.
- I don't understand it – staff and pupils may not be technologically proficient enough to access what they want.

In order to alleviate or, better still, pre-empt, these sorts of problems you need to become familiar with your school's procedure for booking ICT rooms and equipment and the process for reporting difficulties.

Misuse of ICT

A minority of pupils misuse ICT, either using it against fellow pupils or against members of staff. While much of this happens outside of school, it will have an impact within the school. For the pupils and staff members at the receiving end of threatening, bullying or humiliating text messages, emails or messaging services, this can be an extremely damaging experience.

Known as 'cyber-bullying', there are calls for closer monitoring by Internet providers to ensure this type of activity does not take place. School anti-bullying policies should relate to bullying via mobile phones or the Internet and should also have rules as to the possession and use of mobile phones in school.

'Cheating' on learning

Concern has also been expressed, by adults and pupils alike, that ICT can also be misused in the learning process. Rather than aiding enquiry and research, pupils can simply 'cut-and-paste' from the Internet and cobble together a piece of writing that they then pass off as their own. Searching via Google may save time, but it can also be a form of cheating.

The types of support pupils may need to use ICT effectively and how to provide this support

Depending on their age, you can support pupils in their use of ICT by helping them develop a number of skills:

- Learning to turn on the computer, log on, use a mouse and keyboard.
- Selecting and using software packages – choosing those which will best help them learn in that particular lesson.
- Using CD ROMs, the school intranet and the Internet to access programs, using these programs as independently as possible.
- Using all of the above knowledge to gain information for other subjects.
- Using the Internet and communicating via email.

Keeping up in order to ensure you provide the best support and opportunities for pupils' learning through ICT

As a TA you probably do not need to know about all the latest design techniques in ICT across the world, but you do need to know what is being introduced in your school. Sufficient time needs to be given to all staff to train and experiment with new ICT before being asked to support pupils with it. If you are not sure about anything – ask.

Checklist

✔ I am aware of the benefits ICT can bring to learning.

✔ I know what ICT resources are available in school and where they are kept.

✔ I am familiar with school procedures for safely storing ICT equipment.

✔ I am familiar with school procedures for safeguarding pupils when using ICT.

✔ I understand how ICT can promote learning.

✔ I can select and adapt ICT resources to meet the needs of the pupils with whom I work.

Further reading

Braham, G. (2006) *How to Survive and Succeed with an Interactive Whiteboard*. London: LDA.
Elston, C. (2007) *Using ICT in the Primary School*. London: Paul Chapman Educational Publishing.
Loveless, A. (2002) *ICT in the Primary School (Learning & Teaching with ICT)*. London: Open University Press.
O'Hara, M. (2004) *ICT in the Early Years (Classmates)*. London: Continuum.

Websites

www.bbc.co.uk/schools
www.becta.org.uk/
http://curriculum.qca.org.uk/key-stages-1-and-2/subjects/ict/inother.aspx?return=/search/index.aspx%3FfldSiteSearch%3DICT
http://en.wikipedia.org/wiki/Information_technology
www.ictadvice.org.uk
http://schools.becta.org.uk/

◈ Gathering evidence

This example relates to element 8.1, *Prepare for using ICT to support pupils' learning* and is in the form of expert witness testimony. Nazreen's NVQ assessor had agreed with her that she could not observe this aspect of her performance and so had identified two professionals in the school who had agreed to act as expert witnesses – the class teacher and the ICT Technician.

Setting the scene

Mr Palmerston's Year 6 class have begun to study the Tudors in history and Nazreen has been asked to support them in the ICT suite where they are to use the Internet to help research information about Henry VIII.

Expert witness testimony

Name of expert witness: N. Palmerston (Y6 teacher)

Name of candidate: Nazreen Begum

School: Anywhere Primary School

Date: 2 May

I declare that the following conversation took place between myself and Nazreen which, in my opinion, meets the following performance criteria:

Staff signature   Name (printed and role)

N. Palmerston   Nicholas Palmerston, class teacher

8.1P1 Identify and agree with the teacher the opportunities for using ICT to support pupils' learning within the overall teaching programme

Nazreen and I discussed how ICT might be used to help the class develop their knowledge of Henry VIII, agreeing that they should use the Internet for research. We agreed that Nazreen, as preparation for the lesson, would find a few websites to which the pupils could be directed as an introduction to their research.

8.1P2 Discuss and agree with the teacher the criteria for ICT resources to ensure the appropriateness for all pupils with whom you work

We agreed she should use the following criteria when choosing websites:
• Be readily accessible by all pupils
• Be geared to junior school children
• Contain good visuals which could be downloaded or copied without breaking copyright
• Provide opportunity for more able pupils to go to links leading them to more detailed information
We also discussed policies and procedures for online safety and Nazreen made a point of reminding students about this.

8.1P3 Explore and evaluate available ICT resources and consider how these can be integrated into the planned teaching and learning programme

Before lunch Nazreen explored various websites, chose sites which she thought would be the most helpful, and during lunch showed them to me. They seemed to me to fit the criteria admirably.

8.1P4 Discuss and agree with the teacher how pupils' progress will be assessed and recorded

In our discussion we agreed that during this lesson the focus of her observations and assessment would be the pupils' ICT skills and progress – how pupils access and use the Internet to log on to appropriate websites; how well they use the websites to find out information; and how effectively they begin to write up what they have found out. She will record her observations in each pupil's ICT file.

Expert witness testimony

Name of expert witness: H. Walpole (ICT technician)

Name of candidate: Nazreen Begum

School: Anywhere Primary School

Date: 2 May

I declare that the following conversation took place between myself and Nazreen which, in my opinion, meets the following performance criteria.

Staff signature   Name (printed and role)

Howard Walpole   Howard Walpole, ICT technician

8.1P4 Plan to use ICT to support learning in ways that are stimulating and enjoyable for pupils, *according to their age, needs and abilities*

I observed Nazreen in the ICT suite finding websites for children who have difficulties with reading. One was a website for younger children that used larger format print and less technical vocabulary. The links were via pictures that the pupils were likely to recognise – some of them were only just round the corner from the school!

8.1P5 Identify sources of ICT materials which meet the needs of the pupils and the teaching and *learning programme*

Nazreen practised using ICT packages which support pupils' written communications – both those with difficulties (Textease) and those who were more able (PowerPoint). She was preparing herself to be able to support and extend pupils in the lesson to come.

8.1P6 Ensure a range of ICT materials are available which meet the needs of all pupils including those *with learning difficulties, bilingual pupils and gifted and talented pupils*

Nazreen discussed with me the relevant benefits of these packages which offer a range of ways that pupils can present their findings. Textease enables all pupils to present their findings very effectively with relative ease, but the more able pupils can use PowerPoint to produce more complex presentations.

8.1P7 *Adapt ICT materials as necessary to meet the needs of the learning objectives and pupils' age, interests and abilities within copyright and licence agreements*

Nazreen asked me about the needs of some pupils regarding reading text on the websites and I showed her how to use Windows Narrator. She spent time adapting two computers to access this accessibility support programme. I confirmed with her that this program is part of Microsoft's package and using it does not break any copyright or licence agreements.

Assessor's comments (email correspondence)

These witness testimonies show that you have carefully thought through many aspects of ICT. It would be useful to include some examples of pupils' work showing how your preparation supported their learning – please try and include examples from pupils who are gifted as well as those who have some measure of learning difficulty. Your work and these expert witness statements also contribute to evidence for 5.1, P11 (*provide, consistent and effective support for colleagues*) and 3.3, P1 (*at all time follow the policies and procedures of your setting with regard to safeguarding and protecting children and young people*) and other performance criteria for Unit 8. Next time at college we will sit down and have a discussion regarding the knowledge required for this unit. Have a specific look at the following: K2, K3, K5 and K10.

Signed: Terrie Cole
Terrie Cole, NVQ Assessor   7 May

Chapter 9

Unit 9: Observe and report on pupil performance

This unit contains two elements:

- Observe pupil performance.
- Report on pupil performance.

This chapter is one of the 'mini-chapters' focusing on key aspects of the unit.

Unit 9.1 Observe pupil performance

> You see, but you do not observe. You listen, but you do not hear.
>
> (Sherlock Holmes)

How and why to record features of the context and off-task behaviours when making observations of pupils' performance on specific tasks and activities

Although teachers are said to have 'eyes in the back of their heads' – this actually isn't true, and observing how particular individuals or groups of pupil are behaving or learning in a large class can be extremely difficult for a teacher. An effective role for TAs can therefore be observing within lessons.

Observing is more complex than it first appears and certainly involves more than simply 'looking' or even 'seeing'. To quote Sherlock Holmes, 'You see, but you do not observe.' If you are asked to observe, you are being asked to do more than see.

In order to observe effectively you need to be clear about at least three things:

1 Who or what you are observing.
2 How your observation is to be made and over what time period.
3 How your observations are to be recorded and communicated.

You may be asked to observe how particular pupils are performing, but you may equally be asked to observe how specific aspects of a lesson are being understood or responded to by pupils.

There are various ways to make and record observations; for example, you could be asked to make observations of behaviours using a checklist or you could be asked to complete an observation schedule whereby your record a pupil's or group's activities at certain periods of time. Examples of these sorts of observations are given on page 156.

Example 1: an on-task/off-task tally chart

Name of pupil: _____
Date of observation: _____
TA carrying out the observation: _____

Time	On-task	Off-task	Comments
11.00–11.05	III	II	Off-task – gazing around the room, not disturbing others On-task – making notes in his exercise book, reading the textbook
11.05–11.10			
11.10–11.15			
11.15–11.20			
Total			

In this observation you would simply put a tally every time you observed the pupil being on-task or off-task in periods of five minutes. You would need to agree at what time interval you put the tally – every 30 seconds could be a feasible interval. Over a 20-minute period you would end up with a detailed awareness of how much a particular pupil was on- or off-task. However, there are difficulties with this – if, for instance, the pupil is looking out of the classroom window, are they 'off-task', or are they thinking about what to write?

Example 2: an observation schedule

<table>
<tr><td colspan="3">Name of pupil: Fred
Date of observation:
Time of observation: 1.00–1.15p.m.
TA carrying out the observation:</td></tr>
<tr><td>*Behaviours observed*</td><td>*Frequency observed*</td><td>*Comments*</td></tr>
<tr><td>Looking at teacher</td><td>IIII</td><td>Represents about half the occasions when Fred should have been focusing on teacher</td></tr>
<tr><td>Looking at other pupils</td><td>IIII</td><td></td></tr>
<tr><td>Listening to teacher</td><td>II</td><td>Should have been listening a lot more than this Judged to be listening to the teacher when he was looking at the teacher and being quiet</td></tr>
<tr><td>Listening to other pupils</td><td></td><td></td></tr>
<tr><td>Speaking to teacher</td><td>I</td><td></td></tr>
<tr><td>Speaking to other pupils</td><td>IIII</td><td>No speaking related to the lesson</td></tr>
<tr><td>Working independently</td><td>II</td><td></td></tr>
<tr><td>Working collaboratively</td><td></td><td></td></tr>
<tr><td>Reading</td><td>II</td><td></td></tr>
<tr><td>Writing</td><td></td><td>Refused to write</td></tr>
<tr><td>Other (specify)</td><td></td><td></td></tr>
<tr><td>Other (specify)</td><td></td><td></td></tr>
</table>

In this example you would put a tally in the appropriate row every time you observed that particular behaviour. You would need to agree with the teacher over what time period this observation would take place. The comments column is important as you may want to make notes about what you observed. This sheet is partially completed to give an idea about what could be included.

Example 3: an events diary

Name of pupil(s): MK

Date of observation:

Time of observation: 11.20–11.40 a.m.

TA carrying out the observation: Miranda Appleton

Lesson observed

Numeracy Y6 lower set, mental maths starter followed by teacher instruction on shape

TA semi-participant observer – seated just outside a group of four pupils, available to answer questions but not otherwise directly involved in the learning.

Behaviours observed

11.20 a.m. Children writing on individual whiteboards, rest of class sitting on carpet listening to class teacher who had put four computation questions onto a flipchart. The four pupils were required to write answers to the questions on their whiteboards.

MK not writing anything, rest of group writing answers independently. MK says, 'There's one reason I hate doing maths, it's irritating.' He remains off task for two minutes, during which time the other three children have completed the task.

MK rocking on chair for most of this time.

11.30 a.m. Class teacher addressing whole class introducing the main part of the lesson – shape work. MK knows the answers to teacher's questions about shapes, but calls out rather than puts his hand up. JB puts hand up, but when asked, gives incorrect answer.

MK and RJ talking to each other while teacher talking to the class, teacher asks them to be quiet and pay attention. They do this for about a minute then start giggling together.

11.32 a.m. Teacher moves RJ to another part of the class, MK continues to mutter under his breath. This seems to be deliberately designed to wind the others in the group up and to annoy the teacher.

11.35 a.m. Shapes being put on interactive whiteboard by teacher. This seems to gain MK's attention. He is more focused than before, looking at the board and stops muttering. Teacher gives final instructions and pupils return to their seats for independent work.

11.40 a.m. MK has been singing to himself and muttering for the past four minutes. He has done very little work.

Factors to be taken into consideration

MK has been diagnosed with autism and find maths particularly challenging.

Comments

This is a typical lesson for MK, however he would normally have had my help. The teacher and I agreed for me to stand a little back from him to closely observe his behaviour without such close TA intervention keeping him on task.

This type of observation leaves a lot more to interpretation of the observer. Here you would note down what you consider the pupil (or pupils) to be doing over a pre-determined period of time. It might be that you are asked to observe one or more pupils in several lessons over a number of days; in which case you would keep a record of each lesson and compile those records together. You will need to note down any factors that may be influencing pupils' responses, such as there being a supply teacher for the lesson, or the lesson was interrupted by a fire drill.

Figure 9.1
Be aware of what is
happening around you

Potential sources of distractions and disruptions during observations of pupils and how to minimise these

The most likely source of distraction or disruption to you as a TA trying to observe one or more pupils in a lesson will be other pupils. They are used to you being in class to support them and are going to ask you for your help. 'Miss, can you tell me what I should do now?' is not what you want to hear when your attention is focused on trying to work out whether or not the pupil being observed is on task or not.

Quite clearly the one thing you cannot do is tell the class that you are not in the lesson today to help them but to keep a close eye on 'little Johnny' to see how well he is working. To be effective, observation must of necessity be 'subversive' or 'covert', i.e. the person being observed must not be aware that he or she *is* being observed as this will change the way they behave.

Two strategies at least need to be in place to avoid distraction. One is that the teacher and you need to agree that, in this lesson, at least for a certain period of time, your focus of attention should be on observation. This might mean that the teacher presents the class with work she knows they can do so that you will not be asked for help or that the teacher herself will intervene and respond to such requests.

The second strategy is that you yourself are very focused and respond to children's requests politely but firmly, stating that you are unable to help them at present but will do so as soon as you can. You are unlikely to cut out distractions altogether, but if you are focused, children quickly pick this up and will stop bothering you.

You could say that you are wanting to see how well the group can work by themselves and so for this session, or for the next ten minutes, you will be making notes about them, during which time they should try and work independently. In this way you have explained your presence with a notebook or clipboard without specifically alerting the 'target' pupil to your real motive.

The basic concepts of reliability, validity and subjectivity of observations

Reliability has to do with different observers coming to the same conclusions about what they see. To be reliable in your observations, you need to observe what others would observe in the same situation.

Validity has to do with observing or measuring what you actually say you are observing or measuring. For instance, if you are asked to observe how often a particular pupil is on task over a specified period of time, that is what you should observe and record. What is meant by being 'on-task' will have to be agreed before the observation begins, for example, the pupil is writing or reading, with looking out of the window counting as being 'off-task'.

Subjectivity calls into question the possibility of any observation being entirely reliable or valid. Observers will see things through their own 'lens', as it were. You will take note of aspects of pupils' behaviours and learning that others may miss entirely or unconsciously dismiss as being irrelevant, and others will place emphasis on aspects you think unimportant. This is what makes observation more complex than it first seems. If you are asked to note down when the pupil is talking inappropriately to other children you may take note of when their conversation is about football and note that as being inappropriate whereas someone else observing might not take any notice of that as they focus on the fact that, although the pupil *is* talking, he is still writing.

The protocols to be observed when observing pupils

Observers can be 'participants', 'semi-participants' or 'non-participants'. It needs to be agreed with the class teacher what your role will be. As the titles suggest, a 'participant observer' is one who joins in a lesson while making observation notes during it. A 'non-participant' is someone who sits in the class but 'outside' the lesson, looking in as detached a way as possible about what is going on. An Ofsted inspector has the role of 'non-participant observer'. A 'semi-participant observer' is somewhere in between these two. Your role as a TA is likely to be either participatory or semi-participatory. It is difficult to keep accurate and complete observation notes if you are totally absorbed in the lesson, but, it is highly unlikely that you will be able to be completely distanced from it either; thus the role of 'semi-participant observer' is likely to be the one you take on as you observe pupils.

Self-assessment activity 9.1

Whether you have been specifically asked to or not, have a practice at closely observing a pupil in a class where you work. You obviously need to agree this with the teacher concerned before you start doing this.

Decide what behaviours or activities you are going to focus on and then decide what form of observational recording you will do.

Before you begin your observation, seek to answer the following questions:

1   What do you expect to see?
2   How do you expect to be able to record what you see?
3   What are you likely to miss out?

4   What difficulties might you encounter when carrying out this observation?

5   How will you handle distractions?

6   How will you seek to ensure that the pupil(s) being observed do not know that their actions or behaviours are being recorded?

After your observations, return to these questions and write down how accurately the actual observation corresponded to your predictions or anticipations:

1   What factors contributed to their being differences between your prediction and what actually happened?

2   What took place much as you thought it would?

3   What have you learned from this process?

4   What would you do in the same way again?

5   What would you do differently next time?

Unit 9.2 Report on pupil performance

How to summarise and present information from observations of pupil performance

Normally speaking you will be observing not for your own benefit, but to provide information to teachers. It is important, therefore, that you record your observations both accurately and legibly so that you can present your findings to others. In all the examples above the name of the TA observing, the name of the pupils and the date/time of the observation are an integral part of the written record. This is important information for the observation, but can easily be omitted. Teachers need to know who has undertaken the observation so that they can talk with you about it afterwards.

The information contained in the observations is called *data* (a plural word). Data do not speak for themselves; they have to be analysed. As a result of your observation, you will have some insight into the behaviours of a pupil or group of pupils within a certain context, but this insight needs to be interpreted. You need to present the data to the teacher in the way agreed beforehand, and it needs to be presented in such a way that your interpretation of the data can be verified. It is no good, for instance, you simply telling the teacher that 'little Johnny' never paid attention to the lesson. Your observation record should enable you to be much more specific than this. You should, for example, be able to say that, from the data you collected, 'little Johnny' was on task in literacy for 60 per cent of the time, but only 40 per cent during maths. This may tell you and the teacher something of how 'little Johnny' approaches these two subjects.

Observations are only useful if they provide data which are presented in accessible ways.

The importance of confidentiality, data protection and sharing information

All records, including the records made of pupil observations, are to some extent sensitive. Only those with genuine reason should have access to such records. You need to find out exactly how your school responds to this. Most schools will, however, employ similar principles:

- Whole school records and pupil files will be kept in the school office in lockable cabinets.
- Class records will be kept safely and placed out of reach of children (in the case of primary schools).
- Individual pupil records kept by **SENCOs** and others with school-wide responsibilities will also be kept in a secure place.
- Any unwanted paper records will be disposed of appropriately – shredded if possible – to ensure that they cannot be read later.

There should be clear procedures in place and you need to be aware of these.

However, it is not records who talk, it is people. All school staff must be aware of their duty of confidentiality. This means that no one, teachers or TAs, should discuss information regarding pupils with any unauthorised person. Trust takes time to build, but can be destroyed very quickly. Schools need to operate in an atmosphere where trust exists between staff and parents.

Checklist

✔ I am aware of some the reasons why I might be asked to observe pupils.
✔ I am familiar with several techniques of observation.
✔ I know how to record observational data and how to feed this back to the relevant people.

Further reading

Hobart, C. and Frankel, J. (2004) *A Practical Guide to Child Observation and Assessment* (3rd edn). Cheltenham: Nelson Thornes.
Riddall-Leech, S. (2005) *How to Observe Children*. Oxford: Heinemann.
Tilstone, C. (ed.) (1998) *Observing Teaching and Learning*. London: David Fulton.

Chapter 10

Unit 11: Contribute to supporting bilingual/multilingual pupils

In this chapter we consider two elements:

*   Support development of the target language.
*   Support bilingual/multilingual pupils during learning activities.

The stages of language acquisition and the factors that promote or hinder language development

Children of all languages learn to speak following similar stages. It is important to remember that when you are working with a pupil who is new to English, they have already gone through the process of learning at least one language, sometimes more.

Age of the child	Language development
0–6 months	Pre-linguistic stage – attract attention by making different sounds and gestures which is reinforced by adults responding to them.
6–18 months	First words – begin to formulate words by repeating sounds and words made to them.
18 months–3 years	Rapid vocabulary development – begin to formulate sentences; begin to respond to rhyme and simple song.
3–8 years	Increasingly complex language – most children fluent in their first language.

At each stage of language development children need to be listened to, responded to and helped to expand and correct their vocabulary. The language development of any child can be hindered or helped by the richness or otherwise of the language environment within which they are brought up. A home environment which uses a wide range of vocabulary and involves a high level of verbal interaction between family members will promote a greater level of language development than one where there is very little verbal communication.

Strategies suitable for supporting pupils in developing their language skills in the target language

Although pupils new to the target language are likely to begin to understand what they hear before they have the confidence to start speaking, they should be given every opportunity and encouragement to speak out, without being pressurised to do so. Remember, they are not only learning a new language, they are learning to learn *in* that language as well.

The use of picture cues is very important. It is hard for anyone to learn a language simply by listening to it. Linking words and phrases with pictures is a great help. You can make pictures up or you can select from the large number of resources available on the market.

Use gestures to help your communication, but be careful, not all gestures mean the same in each culture. If in doubt, check it out. Having said this, smiles and 'thumbs up' usually mean the same to everyone.

When seeking to build a pupil's vocabulary, begin with words and phrases that are going to help them communicate with those around them – hello, good-bye, yes, no, please and thank you are useful places to start. 'Can I go to the toilet?' is also a very useful piece of English!

More information can be found on the government website www.standards.dcfs. gov.uk/newarrivals

The interactive use of speaking/talking, listening, reading and writing to promote language development in pupils

Linking speech and text

Pupils new to English need to be taught to read and write in the target language at the same time as learning to speak it. For pupils learning English as an additional language, the more they link what they hear and say with the written word the better. This will both reinforce their knowledge and give them the skills of communicating in a range

Figure 10.1 'Thumbs up' is usually recognised by everyone

of contexts and in a variety of ways. However, the way they are taught and the resources used to help them develop the full range of interrelated literacy skills may be different to that used with native speakers.

Prediction

Prediction plays an important role in reading fluently. Pupils new to English may find it difficult to predict what is likely to happen in a story due to limited vocabulary or a different cultural background. Talking with the pupils about the story before it is read or quickly scanning through it with them, particularly taking note of any pictures or illustrations, can be a useful way to help develop their skills of prediction. Similarly, reading together stories that are familiar to them although written in English, such as folk tales from their own country, can also help build skills of prediction. Stories with a good deal of repetition also aid this process.

Reading and writing are social activities

Reading and writing are not simply techniques; they are social activities heavily dependent upon often unspoken, shared assumptions of cultural norms. Having said that, many communities place a high regard on literacy and children are exposed to books and to writing from an early age. The skills they have developed in their own language are readily transferable to English.

Assessing levels of reading in a cultural context

Merely listening to children read in English may not give an accurate impression of their reading ability. They may mispronounce words or read in a monotone. They may stumble over phrases and they may not be able to answer questions put to them in English. However, when asked in their community language, they are often able to give a genuine sense to what they have read, gaining their insight from words and phrases they know, the illustrations in the text or the context of the story. Talking in their own language about stories they have read in English can be a real means of promoting reading development and, at the same time, gives teachers and TAs a more accurate picture of their reading abilities.

The cultural content of stories can be illustrated via the following case study.

Case study: assessing a pupil's reading level who has English as an additional language

Mohamed is a Bangladeshi pupil in Year 4. The SENCO in his school wanted to assess his reading levels and used a nationally recognised test to do so. They sat together in a room and the SENCO, Mrs Jenkins, asked him to read from the book and then she asked him some questions to see how much he had understood. The first piece of text presented with no problem, but the next two raised issues of the cultural norms assumed by the stories.

The second story was about someone receiving presents on his birthday. Although Mohamed read totally accurately, it was clear from the way he answered the questions that, although he knew all the answers, he did not really understand the passage. In conversation afterwards Mrs Jenkins discovered that the Bangladeshi community do not give presents for birthdays and celebrate them in a totally different way to that assumed in the story.

The third story was even more problematic. This one was about a lion tamer in the circus ring. Again, Mohamed read all the words accurately, but he could answer none of the questions correctly. When talking with him further, Mrs Jenkins came to realise that Mohamed had never seen, let alone been to, a circus. He had no cultural connection to it. When he had read the word 'ring' he had thought of a piece of jewellery placed on people's fingers. No wonder he could not make any sense of the story.

Mrs Jenkins had used this test many times before, and all the native English speakers she had assessed had been able to relate to the stories, even if they had never been to a circus. She understood that, even if they had, they would never have seen an animal act, yet nevertheless, there was some cultural link between the pupils born into English culture and the story.

How do you think you would go about finding out about the reading levels of pupils with English as an additional language?

Cultural aspects of writing

Children from different community backgrounds bring different skills and experiences to writing as well as to reading. Some will have never formed alphabetic letters before, for instance, pupils from China will have learned to write using characters rather than letters. Others will have learned to read and write from right to left, rather than left to right and still others will have learned to write in columns rather than along lines. Of those who have learned to write in lines and from left to write, many will have learned to write under rather than on the line. When learning to write in English it is important that all this is talked about with the pupils and that what they have previously learned is respected. Remember – there is no 'correct' way to read or write; just different ways.

How to use praise and constructive feedback to promote pupils' learning and the role of self-esteem in developing communication and self-expression

A key aspect of your role is to help boost and maintain self-confidence so that, when they are ready, pupils can experiment with the language and not be held back by fear or apprehension. You should also make it clear that it is absolutely fine not to say anything but to enjoy a period of quiet, taking in what is happening around them.

You can promote self-esteem by praising their efforts in the language, by providing them with basic vocabulary and modelling its correct usage. Simply by getting alongside pupils and making them feel welcome goes a long way to helping them overcome their insecurities. Make sure you pronounce and spell their name properly. If you are unsure, ask the pupils and take advice from them.

As you work with pupils you need to ensure that both you and everyone else treat them with respect. Any form of racial harassment should be dealt with promptly according to the school's policy.

Class and school displays can help promote cultural and language diversity. Signs around the school in a range of languages, welcome displays showing a map of the world with flags pinned on to it of the countries where pupils originate from, or photographs and pictures from different countries are all ways commonly used to show each pupil that they are valued.

Curriculum plans and learning programmes developed by the teachers with whom you work when supporting bilingual/ multilingual pupils

To adequately prepare your support for pupils learning the target language, you need to know what is going to be taught in the lesson. You need to see the teacher's plans for the lessons coming up and need to know the learning objectives for any particular lesson. If you get to see these a day or two before the actual lessons you can be thinking about how you can support the pupils and what resources you could draw upon or even make.

If you are asked to work with pupils learning to speak English in small groups or individually outside of the class using specific programmes, you need to be familiar with those programmes before you start. You need to be given time to read through all relevant literature, such as teaching manuals, and to look through all the materials in the programme. You may need to alter some of it or to focus on particular aspects of it to best support pupils learning the target language.

How to obtain information about a pupil's languages and educational background and skills, individual learning targets and language support needs

Schools will have records regarding the ethnic background of its pupils using the categories given by the government. As well as general information such as dates of birth, gender and any medical issues, these records should also include, where appropriate, the country or countries of origin of the pupil's family, the date of the pupil's entry into the UK, the language(s) spoken at home and any relevant cultural or religious information, such as dietary or clothing requirements.

More detailed information regarding a pupil's educational and cultural background will come through conversation with that pupil or with the pupil's parents or carers, with the support of a translator where appropriate. From such a conversation it is possible to find out about the pupil's previous educational experience, whether any particular abilities or difficulties have been evidenced and to what extent the pupil can read and write fluently in their first language. If they have learned their first language without much difficulty, they are likely to learn English in the same way. Conversely, if they have experienced difficulties in their first language, they may well face learning difficulties when being taught English and extra support is likely to be needed.

Example of form for discussion with parents (adapted from a local authority's form)

Parent conference form for newly arrived families who have English as an additional language

Name of school	
Date of meeting	
People present	
Name of pupil	
Name to be called in school	
Date of birth	
Year group and class in school	
Class teacher	
Place of pupil's birth	
Countries lived in by the pupil (with dates where known)	
Date of arrival in UK	
First/home language	
Previous educational experiences	
Name of father	
Country of origin	
Mother's name	
Country of origin	
Siblings (names, ages, schools)	
Religion	
Dietary requirements	
First language classes attended (either current or past)	
Extended stays (if appropriate)	
Any other relevant information, including medical	
Refugee or asylum seeker background?	

Example of first language assessment (adapted from a local authority's form)

Summary of assessment of first language and EAL

Pupil name	
Date of birth	
Year group	
Initial assessment completed on	

Speaking	**English**	**L1**
Silent period		
Offers and responds to greetings		
Responds to verbal questions with one-word answers		
Responds to verbal questions with two to three word phrases		
Responds to verbal questions with complete sentences		
Answers requests for personal information		
Can name:		
Colours		
School items		
Clothes		
Food		
Body parts		
Household items		
Types of transport		
Animals		
Names items on a picture		
Describes items on a picture		
Talks about what is happening in a picture		
Initiates talk to ask for support with a task		
Initiates talk to tell someone about an event		

Contributes to a group discussion		
Contribute to a class discussion		
Retells a simple story		
Retells a more complex story using a broad range of vocabulary		

Listening/comprehension	English	L1
Listens attentively for short periods		
Listens attentively for extended periods		
Follows class and school routines with support from peers		
Follows class and school routines with support from adults		
Follows class and school routines independently		
Responds to simple instructions with support from peers		
Responds to simple instructions with support from adults		
Responds to simple instructions independently		
Responds to more complex instructions with support from peers		
Responds to more complex instructions with support from adults		
Responds to more complex instructions independently		
Responds to closed questions with nod/shake of head		
Points to items after being described verbally to the pupil		
Can follow a one-to-one conversation		
Can follow a conversation in a small group context		
Can follow a conversation/discussion in a whole class context		

Reading	English	L1
Has no knowledge of a written alphabet (or characters)		
Can read/say the names of some letters of the alphabet (or characters)		
Can read/say the names of most/all letters of the alphabet (or characters)		
Can say the sounds of some letters of the alphabet		

Can say the sounds of most/all letters of the alphabet		
Can read own name		
Can read basic words, e.g. cvc words (in English)		
Can understand basic words		
Can read the high frequency words for Year R		
Can understand the high frequency words for Year R		
Can read the high frequency words for Year 1/2		
Can understand the high frequency words for Year 1/2		
Can read simple stories or other texts		
Can understand simple stories or other texts		
Can read complex stories or other texts		
Can understand complex stories or other texts		

Writing	English	L1
Has no knowledge of a writing system		
Can use marks/emergent writing		
Can copy letters (or simple characters)		
Can copy words (or characters)		
Can write on the line		
Can write left to right on the line		
Can write top to bottom on the page		
Can write initial letter of own name		
Can write own name		
Can write some letters of the alphabet (or characters)		
Can write most/all letters of the alphabet (or characters)		
Can write simple words (or characters)		
Can write harder words (or characters)		
Can write simple sentences with basic punctuation		
Can write complex sentences with accurate punctuation		
Can write a simple narrative or recount		

Following an assessment such as this it is possible to judge where the pupil is functioning in terms of literacy in relation to national standards. Those who are not yet at Level 1 of the **National Curriculum** can be assessed using EAL scales published by **QCA** (2000). Normally speaking, pupils for whom English is their first or only language and who are not yet accessing the National Curriculum at Level 1, even though they are in Year 1 or above, will be assessed using 'P scales' ('performance scales'). These are not appropriate for EAL pupils as they are designed to be used with pupils who have been identified as having some kind of **special educational need**. It is very important that pupils new to English are *not* regarded as having SEN.

The point of giving a level to newly arrived EAL pupils is twofold – one support can be more effectively given; and, two, progress can be monitored over time, as shown by the following table:

Name of pupil: _____				
QCA/EAL Scale levels or N.C. Levels as appropriate				
Date	Speaking	Listening	Reading	Writing
Initial assessment				
Review				
Review				
Review				

Strategies suitable for supporting pupils in developing their language skills through different learning activities and experiences across the curriculum

Positioning in class

Where EAL pupils sit in class is important. It is tempting to place them with pupils of lower ability as there they are likely to have access to extra adult support. However, good practice suggests that this is not as helpful as placing such pupils next to those who can communicate effectively in spoken English. These act as good role models for the pupils new to the target language.

Encourage talk

Encourage lots of talk between pupils so that the pupil learning English has plenty of opportunity both to listen and to speak in the target language in a non-threatening situation.

Dual language resources

For pupils who have some fluency in reading their first language, the use of dual language books or software can also be a help, particularly if the stories are familiar to the pupils. School libraries should have a stock of such books, both fiction and non-fiction, in the major languages which are likely to be encountered in the school. The **local authority's** ethnic minority advisory service is also likely to be able to loan such books to schools. All pupils should be encouraged to continue to learn to read in their first language.

First language use

Provide as many opportunities as possible for pupils to work and converse in their first language. Pupils new to English make progress more rapidly if they also continue to make progress in their first language, so encourage them to keep using it.

Classroom context

Generally speaking, supporting pupils new to English should take place within the classroom or ordinary lesson, whatever the subject or learning focus. Pupils need to learn to listen to the target language and to speak it in the context of real life. In this situation, your role could be to encourage them to 'have a go' at speaking in class or group discussions or to verbally answer questions. However, you need to make sure you do not put pressure on pupils to speak in the target language before they have the confidence to do so. You can also get alongside pupils and quietly explain and, where appropriate, simplify teacher instructions.

Keep a positive attitude

Underlying all these strategies is your own demeanour and attitude. Whatever support you actually provide for pupils for whom English is an additional language, you can:

- encourage all children, including those from different cultures and ethnic groups, to have a sense of pride in who they are;
- encourage friendships between all children;
- challenge negative attitudes and low expectations.

Specific focused teaching

All pupils learning English as an additional language will need to be taught the basic sound structure and **phonic** rules of the language. For younger pupils this is likely to take place within the class, but older pupils may well need to be withdrawn from class to be taught these basic skills. However, not too much emphasis should be placed on learning phonics and the formal structure of the target language at first. Rather, pupils should be given books and texts to read that are both simple yet set in a context to which they can relate. It is important that pupils learn the meaning as well as the mechanics of what they read.

Case study: new pupils with no English

Janet is a TA working in a Year 2 class in an infants school. Over a third of the pupils in the class have English as an additional language. Two pupils have just arrived in the country with no previous experience of English at all; one is from Poland and the other from Kerala, in southern India. He speaks Malayalam. The Polish pupil has never been to school before as children there do not start school until they are 7 years old.

It is an art lesson – the pupils are preparing for Christmas and are drawing, colouring, painting or making decorations. This is an excellent opportunity for Janet to encourage the two new pupils to make relationships with other children and to introduce the two pupils to some English vocabulary.

The class teacher places the two pupils on a table where there are good English speakers and also where there are speakers of their first languages. During the activity Janet picks up various items, shows them to the two pupils and clearly says what they are, nodding to them to repeat what she says. In this way, they begin to learn vocabulary such as 'brush', 'paper', 'glue' and 'paint'. One pupil willingly tries to repeat the English words, the second pupil is far more quiet. Janet does not try to push this pupil into responding, knowing that it takes some pupils a long time to feel secure enough to attempt English words.

The other children talk easily to them, and having pupils who speak their own language helps them feel at home in the class.

Bilingual assistants

Bilingual assistants may be available via the local authority's ethnic minority service. They can support pupils both in class and individually or in small groups outside of the class by explaining to pupils in their own language what is going on in the lesson. They will also be available to relay specific messages or instructions to pupils or to ask them questions which the teacher expressly wishes to communicate with the pupils. They can also express to teachers and TAs any concerns and questions that the pupil may have. It can be a source of frustration and even distress for pupils if they are unable

Self-assessment activity 10.1

1   List as many ways as you can remember or think of to support pupils who are new to the English language.
2   Try and think of a particular situation where pupils learning English as an additional language may be at a disadvantage relative to those for whom English is their first language.
3   What strengths might a pupil learning English as an additional language bring to that process?
4   What differences do you think might be experienced by pupils who are learning English as an additional language between secondary schools and primary schools?

to communicate their needs to those who are trying to support them. Understanding where the pupils are coming from is a major factor in successfully meeting their needs.

Pupils new to English need to be taught to read and write in the target language at the same time as learning to speak it. The more they link what they hear and say with the written word the better. This will both reinforce their knowledge and give them the skills of communicating in a range of contexts and in a variety of ways.

How to feed back information on pupils' participation and progress in learning activities to teachers and contribute to planning for future learning

The need to identify need

Learning can only take place where the teaching connects with the pupils in a way they can understand and relate to. Teaching must also move the pupils on in some way, *i.e.* it cannot be too far ahead of them so that they do not understand what is being taught, but neither can it be something that they already know. To pitch the curriculum at an appropriate level, teachers need to assess their pupils. Assessment can either be formal, such as via tests, or informal, such as through teacher observation. Within schools, a combination of both is undertaken.

As a TA, you can play a vital role in assessing pupils with EAL.

Evaluating pupils' learning

The extent to which you will be responsible for evaluating activities to support development of the target language will be determined by the level and type of support you are asked to provide for pupils learning English as an additional language. If most of the support is to be provided within class, helping pupils access the lesson, you will need to find out what vocabulary the pupil is going to need to know in order to understand and participate in the lesson and organise ways to teach this vocabulary prior to the lesson. The evaluation will therefore be to assess to what extent the pupil was able to access the lesson.

In order to evaluate learning activities you will need to keep records of the sessions showing how well the pupils have responded to what has been planned and how effective the resources you have used have been in promoting learning. Your plans will be altered by your evaluations – what has worked well can be continued and developed, what has not gone so well will need to be changed.

Assessment for learning

The principles of **Assessment for Learning** (AfL) apply just as much when you are supporting pupils with EAL as they do when you are working with English-speaking pupils. The purpose of AfL is to raise pupil achievement, especially those of 'vulnerable groups' such as EAL pupils. In order for this to be effective a number of qualities of AfL need to be applied consistently in the classroom:

- Learning goals (for the individual pupils) and **learning objectives** (of the lesson) need to be shared with pupils in language and terms they understand.

- Pupils must know and understand what they are aiming for in any particular lesson and over a whole unit of work (the 'big picture').
- Feedback from the teacher or yourself as a TA (either oral or in written form) should relate to the learning objectives and help pupils identify how they can improve.
- Teachers (and TAs) must believe that all pupils can improve on past performance (i.e. intelligence is not a fixed entity).
- Both teacher and pupil must be involved in reviewing and reflecting on the learning that has taken place – for EAL pupils this could entail the use of a bilingual assistant.
- Pupils need to learn self-assessment techniques enabling them to see areas for themselves which they need to develop to make progress.
- There must be a recognition that motivation and self-esteem can be facilitated by effective assessment.

Role of TAs

A combination of in-class observation, regular ongoing analysis of work (both in class, homework and **summative assessment**) and diagnostic testing will normally yield a detailed picture of a pupil's needs and abilities. As a teaching assistant, you can play a vital role in this assessment process. You may well be in a position to conduct more detailed observations than the class teacher. You could, for instance, undertake an observational checklist of how much a pupil participated verbally in class or group discussions over a particular period of time. Alternatively, you could conduct a reading or spelling test of high frequency words with the pupil either individually or in a small group when such a test would not be appropriate to give to the class as a whole.

Knowing the needs of the pupils with whom you work

Whatever information is gleaned regarding a pupil, that knowledge must be communicated in some form to those with responsibility for that pupil's teaching. You will need to be familiar with the records kept for the pupils you support so that you are kept informed of the latest analysis of their learning needs. Each school will have its own system and procedures with which you need to become familiar. Some schools employ an 'Individual Language Plan' which is similar to an **IEP** but is used with EAL pupils rather than those experiencing SEN.

Checklist

✔ I am know how to obtain information regarding pupils I support who are learning English as an additional language.

✔ I am familiar with the strategies for supporting such pupils.

✔ I know how to respond to cultural differences between pupils.

✔ I am able to promote cultural diversity within the school.

✔ I am able to provide accurate and useful feedback to teachers regarding the progress of pupils with EAL.

Further reading

Cummins, J. (Foreword) and Gibbons, P. (2002) *Scaffolding Language, Scaffolding Learning: Teaching second language learners in the mainstream classroom.* Portsmouth, NH: Heinemann.

Hall, D., Griffiths, D., Haslam, L. and Wilkin, Y. (2001) *Assessing the Needs of Bilingual Pupils: Living in two languages.* London: David Fulton.

Haslam, L., Wilkin, Y. and Kellet, E. (2004) *English as an Additional Language: Meeting the challenge in the classroom.* London: David Fulton.

Websites

www.naldic.org.uk/
http://nationalstrategies.standards.dcsf.gov.uk/node/96715
www.ofsted.gov.uk/
www.standards.dcsf.gov.uk/newarrivals
www.standards.dcsf.gov.uk/ethnicminorities/
www.teachernet.gov.uk/teachingandlearning/library/EALteaching/

◈ Gathering evidence

✍ *Setting the scene*

Sadie is working with a Year 3 pupil who has newly arrived in the UK from Poland. It is February, part way through the school year. The boy, Lech, has been placed in a class where there is another Polish boy, Jaroslaw, who arrived in the UK in September and has therefore been learning English for five months. Although Sadie's NVQ assessor observed her once supporting Lech, the evidence for this module is best presented via an expert witness (in this case the ethnic minority service teacher attached to her school). This teacher observed Sadie over a period of week and together they kept a log to show how she has met various performance criteria.

**11.1 Support development of the target language
(Performance Indicators in italics)**

6 February
Log entry

1 p.m. I met with the head teacher, the ethnic minority service teacher and the Inclusion Manager to *obtain accurate and up-to-date information about the pupil's first and target language development and use this knowledge in providing appropriate support for the pupil* about Lech. At this meeting I was shown his parents' application form and the notes made by the head teacher at the time of an initial meeting with Lech's parents. We then discussed the best way to support Lech.

3 p.m. I met with Miss Hardcastle (Lech's class teacher) to *clarify and confirm the strategies to be used to support bilingual/multilingual pupils in developing language skills in the target language.* We agreed on the following:

• sit Lech with the other Polish speaker to provide mutual support
• place the two of them at a table with pupils who are good English speakers and good workers to act as role models
• that I will spend ten minutes each day with the two Polish pupils to teach social vocabulary and basic school vocabulary
• that I will show him how to use ICT software held by the school to teach basic English vocabulary and phrases.

Candidate signature: Sadie Brown

Witnessed by Mrs Ruislip
Henrietta Ruislip, specialist teacher with the Ethnic Minority Learning Service

As a team we were appreciative of Sadie's involvement.

Expert witness statement
Mrs Ruislip, specialist teacher with the Ethnic Minority Learning Service
9 February

8.40 a.m. Sadie met with Lech and his parents at the Reception and took him into the class, introducing him to Miss Hardcastle. She showed him the seat next to Jaroslaw and gestured to him to sit down, smiling at him and giving him simple instructions, such as 'sit please'. Jaroslaw was able to speak quietly to Lech, explaining what was happening in class. In this way she *responded to the pupil's use of home language in a manner which values cultural diversity and reinforces positive self-images for the pupil.*

9–10 a.m. Literacy lesson – the focus of the week's lessons is to use the story of Red Riding Hood to identify main themes in traditional stories. Today, the focus for Lech is to make him feel at home, give him space to settle in and to help him learn social vocabulary. As agreed with Miss Hardcastle, Sadie's aim was to *provide opportunities for the pupil to interact with herself and others using their knowledge of the target language.* To this end, during group work, most of the time was spent with Sadie chairing a discussion rather than asking the pupils to write anything. She sought to include Lech as much as possible, asking Jaroslaw to translate where appropriate. Lech was quite keen to make his views felt about good and evil in stories, and he found Jaroslaw translating for him to be most useful.

To *use language and vocabulary which is appropriate to the pupil's age, level of understanding and stage of target language development,* Sadie placed a box of flash cards with pictures, photographs and signs in the middle of the table which all pupils, including Lech, with Jaroslaw translating, could choose from to help make their points. She asked Lech who he thought was good in the story and who he thought was bad. Lech himself chose appropriate picture cards and she modelled the words for him, which he repeated after her. Being aware of the need to *use praise and constructive feedback to maintain the pupils' interest in the learning activities*, she smiled at him, giving him the 'thumbs-up' sign and saying 'good' in response to his efforts.

3–3.15 p.m. At the end of the school day Sadie met with Miss Hardcastle and myself to *provide feedback to relevant people on the progress made by the pupil in developing language skills in the target language.*
For Lech to be fully integrated into the school Sadie's support is essential.
Though it is early days I was very impressed with her support.

Mrs Ruislip (specialist teacher with the Ethnic Minority Learning Service)

---

10 February
Log entry

1–1.20 p.m. The school has bought a box of resources aimed at teaching English social vocabulary and basic language structure to children new to the language. By choosing part of this resource box which taught pupils the vocabulary of ordinary classroom objects, I *provided opportunities for the pupil to practise new language skills.* We began by looking together at the large picture of the classroom in the pack which had various items labelled, such as 'book', 'pencil', 'ruler'. I then pointed to a particular item, then picked up the real thing and said the word. Lech repeated this after me. I used repetitive phrases: 'This is a pencil', 'this is a ruler' and so on. By the end of the session, Lech could say each of the items as I held each one up.

Candidate signature: Sadie Brown

Expert witness comments
Sadie has been a tremendous help in the class helping Lech settle in. She has a good manner with pupils who may be anxious about school and Lech warmed to her at once. The extracts from her log are an accurate account of what happened. Without her involvement, Lech would have found his first week in an English school much more difficult.

Teacher's signature: Mrs Ruislip
Name (printed and role): Henrietta Ruislip, specialist teacher with the Ethnic Minority Learning Service

---

Assessor's comments

This is a very detailed and thorough account. You have clearly grasped what is needed to support a pupil new to English. Almost all the performance indicators are covered explicitly in these log extracts. What is very helpful is that both you and your expert witness have structured your comments under headings relating to the performance indicators. Also, well done for having your expert witness countersign your log entries and adding her comments.

Signed:
Terrie Cole
Terrie Cole, NVQ assessor   16 February

Chapter 11

Unit 12: Support a child with disabilities or special educational needs

Laws and codes of practice affecting provision for disabled children and young people and those with special educational needs

The DDA

The Disability Discrimination Act 2005 (DDA) defines a person with a **disability** as someone who 'has a physical or mental impairment which has a substantial and long-term adverse effect on his/her ability to carry out normal day-to-day activities'. This automatically includes people who have chronic medical conditions which, if left untreated, will result in their death.

Website: www.opsi.gov.uk/Acts/acts2005/ukpga_20050013_en_1.

Reasonable adjustments

All schools have a legal obligation to promote disability equality and to '*take such steps as it is reasonable to take to ensure that disabled pupils are not placed at a substantial disadvantage*' (Disability Discrimination Act [DDA] 2005). This is known as the 'reasonable adjustments' duty.

Schools also have a 'general duty' to take into account the time and effort required by pupils with disabilities to access school life and to ensure that such pupils are not subjected to indignity or discomfort and do not experience loss of opportunity to make progress.

Disability Equality Scheme

Schools must prepare a Disability Equality Scheme. This is a three-year action plan detailing the steps to be taken over time to increase access to the curriculum and to improve the physical environment of the school for disabled pupils. Your support for pupils with disabilities will be given in the context of this scheme. You therefore need to be aware of its content and its impact on the school.

For more information on disability legislation and the *Special Educational Needs Code of Practice*, see Chapters 1 and 17.

Specialist local and national support and information that is available for disabilities and special educational needs

Finding information about particular disabilities or special needs can be difficult. It is often a major issue for families, but can also be one for schools.

Local authorities

Local authorities will have mechanisms in place to support parents and schools ranging from specialist support services, such as teachers for the sensory impaired, to teams of specifically trained advisers and/or teaching assistants, the provision of advice centres or the organisation of forums to provide mutual support and information. The **SENCO** in your school will have information about what exactly is available within your local authority and how to access that.

Non-governmental organisations

Numerous non-governmental organisations are able to give information and offer support on a wide range of special needs and disabilities such as **dyslexia**, cerebral palsy and Down syndrome. Again, your SENCO will be able to provide you with information about organisations relevant to the pupils you are supporting.

Websites are a good source of information, for example:

> www.autism.org.uk
> www.bdadyslexia.org.uk
> www.downsed.org.
> www.downs-syndrome.org.uk
> www.dyslexiaaction.org.uk
> www.scope.org.uk

Single point of contact

Over recent years all services working with children have been brought together within local authorities to enhance sharing of information. One initiative in use across the country is the **Common Assessment Framework (CAF)**, developed as a result of *Every Child Matters* (www.everychildmatters.gov.uk/deliveringservices/caf).

The CAF is essentially a means of gathering information, a process of identifying areas of need and concern, and a place to decide action. Any person working with a child or young person, such as a teacher or a health visitor, can organise a CAF if they have concerns regarding that child. They will first discuss the issue with the child's parents or carers, for their permission must be granted in order for a CAF to take place. Then the parents and all the professionals working with that child meet and use the CAF form which provides a nationally recognised format for discussing a range of possible areas of need. As a result of the conversation held via the CAF a clear description of the concerns should be able to be given and a series of action points agreed upon. A **lead professional** will be identified who has the responsibility of co-ordinating support and provision for the child. In order to be effective, regular reviews of the CAF will need to be held.

Part of the CAF process is the provision of a *single point of contact* within each local authority. This is a place where information is centrally gathered so that enquiries can be made by any interested party. If that point of contact cannot itself supply the information required, they will be able to point enquirers in the right direction. A copy of every completed CAF form should be sent to this single point of contact.

As a TA, you may be supporting a pupil who presents with a range of needs. The SENCO in your school could arrange for a CAF to take place and invite all the professionals involved with that pupil to a meeting to discuss the way forward. The pupil's parents will be an essential part of this process. At the meeting a CAF form will be completed, which looks at every aspect of the pupil's life in school, at home and in the community; and a lead professional will be identified who will be the focal point for future work. The completed CAF form will be forwarded to the single point of contact so that any other agency working with the child can find out what is already being done. The CAF may also result in areas of need being identified that can be followed up.

Case study: attending a CAF

Jasmine is a TA providing a physiotherapy programme to a Year 2 pupil. As she gets to know the pupil she comes to believe that there may be a wider range of underlying difficulties being experienced by this pupil. She discusses this with the teacher and the SENCO, who, after further investigation and discussion, decides to arrange a CAF.

Attending and contributing to the CAF, Jasmine is surprised to see the range of issues discussed, including the pupil's family situation and the condition of his housing. It turns out that the family are due to be evicted and, as yet, they have nowhere else to live. The pupil is very much aware of this and, not surprisingly, this knowledge and uncertainty is adversely affecting his ability to concentrate in school.

As a result of the CAF, the local authority's housing department is contacted by the school and the process of rehousing is set in motion. The CAF did not solve any problems, but it highlighted areas that an ordinary school discussion would more than likely have missed. This meant that the family no longer felt isolated and unsure of what to do.

A recent development nationally is 'ContactPoint'. This is an online directory of all children and young people who live in England, planned to be introduced across the country by the end of 2008. Accessible to staff from education, health and social care, it will give basic information about every child and young person in England, including whether or not a CAF has been completed for that person. The aim is to ensure that children and young people are receiving the services they should and to enable support to be co-ordinated effectively.

The Internet

Another source of information is the Internet. If you are asked to support a pupil with a particular disability or special educational need, the Internet can be a very useful source of advice and knowledge. However, caution needs to be exercised when accessing the Internet. You need to be sure that information given over the net is from a reliable source.

Partnership with parents and families at the heart of provision

All parents need to have confidence in the school that they will meet the needs of their children. This is especially so for pupils with disabilities or special needs. Effective communication between the two should help allay fears and boost confidence for parents. Where there is regular and frequent contact between home and school there is little room for misunderstanding and confusion.

In many instances the parents of particular pupils will be the experts. They will often know a good deal more than the school, at least to start off with, if their child has an uncommon disability or special need. For instance, by the time a child with Down syndrome starts full-time education, the parents will have had four to five years of experience with that child. By that time they will have found out a great deal about the condition, will have consulted with a range of professionals and will be very aware of how their child responds to situations. All this information is vital to the school. One useful way of tapping into this knowledge is to keep a home–school liaison book, which parents and teachers both fill in on a daily basis keeping track of what is happening and suggesting further ideas for support.

Parents often form mutual support groups and these, too, can be a source of support and information not only for the parents themselves, but for the schools where their children attend.

School can also be a place of security for parents. Where there is good communication between school and home, and confidence has been built up and maintained between the two, then parents can find school a place they feel 'at home' and are comfortable being in.

How integration/inclusion works in your setting and local area and the reasons for its benefit or otherwise

Every school and local authority has, by law, to have an **inclusion** policy and should be committed to the principle of inclusive education. How this will be achieved or 'outworked' will be different in each locality, although the same basic principles will be being followed.

School environment

The school can make a great deal of difference to a pupil with disabilities. Much will depend upon how the school as a whole views disability and the provision they need to make for pupils with disabilities. It is said that although people may have a *disability*, the extent to which this is, in practice, an *impairment* is largely determined by the physical environment in which they find themselves and the psychological and emotional response of those around them.

There are a number of different models held regarding disabilities:

- *Medical deficit model* – there is something 'wrong' with the pupil that must, to the best of the school's ability, be 'remedied'.
- *Charity model* – 'disabled pupils' must be pitied, all sympathy shown to them and their courage esteemed. School provision is there to 'support' them and make them as comfortable as possible.
- *Social model* – disability is seen as difference rather than something of less value, often as much the result of the physical and cultural environment as something stemming from the person themselves. Provision in this model seeks to adapt the environment to make the person with disabilities be as included and independent as possible.

- *Bio-psycho-social model* – social factors and 'within' impairment both contribute to the disability.

Pupils are likely to experience less of a negative impact of a disability where schools adopt a social or bio-social model of disability, *i.e.* their disability will exist, but the level of their impairment may diminish.

Self-assessment activity 11.1

- Read your school's inclusion policy, discuss the issue of inclusion with colleagues, and observe what is happening in your school.
- Which of the above models of response to disability do you think best describes your school?
- What is the evidence for this?
- What are the implications of this for your practice and for the experience of pupils in your school?

Provision

Access to appropriate provision, both within school and outside of it will have an important effect on the impact of the disability on the pupil. Counselling can help raise self-esteem. It may help in the transition to recognising and accepting deteriorating sight, hearing or muscle tone.

The role of teaching assistants

Teaching assistants play a crucial part in inclusion, but this is one area where differences in practice are likely to be evidenced. One school or local authority may deploy TAs in a different way to another. They may well have differing roles and responsibilities between local authorities, between schools and even within schools. You will need to be clear as to exactly what your role is. This can be clarified through discussion with the SENCO and/or the teachers you are working with.

Stephanie Lorenz (2002) identifies three types of teaching assistant practice – the 'velcro'd' TA who is constantly pinned to the side of a pupil; the 'helicopter' TA who hovers permanently by the pupil ready to swoop down and help at the slightest sign of difficulty; and the 'bridge-builder' who acts as a link between the pupil and the curriculum, the lesson and, where needed, the school at large. It is the last type of teaching assistant that is conducive to the process of inclusion – the other two may simply serve to promote a sense of 'learned helplessness' on the part of the pupil.

Question

What sort of TA are you?

For more information on inclusion see Chapter 1.

Details about particular disabilities or special educational needs affecting the children or young people in your care

General statements are not possible

It is impossible to generalise about disabilities or special educational needs. A child may have a disability that does not impinge on their learning but does require some level of physical assistance; for instance, a pupil may have cerebral palsy which requires the wearing of a leg support. The role of the TA in this case may be to ensure that the leg support is correctly in place all through the day and especially after changing for PE or games. If that pupil has no other issue this is likely to be the extent of the support given by the TA.

On the other hand, pupils with severe and profound learning and physical disabilities will require a high level of constant TA support, both in terms of learning and physical support such as help with eating or toileting.

Pupil records and information

Before you begin support for any pupil you will need to gain as much information about them as possible. Much of this information should be contained in their **IEPs** (**Individual Education Plans**) – see pages 13–14. Other information will be found in pupils' records held in the school office. It is important for you to be made aware of relevant and current information from professionals such as **educational psychologists**, **occupational therapists** and **speech and language therapists**.

Definitions of disability

Under the Disability Discrimination Act, 2005 (DDA), the definition of 'disability' is very broad and includes those with 'hidden' disabilities such as **autism** or **ADHD** and **dyslexia** as well as those with **physical, sensory or mental impairments**. The essential factors are that, for the child to be disabled, the impairment must be *substantial and long-term* (i.e. lasting longer than 12 months). Chronic illnesses such as diabetes or epilepsy may also be considered a disability.

Visual impairment

'Visual impairment' refers to a range of loss of sight up to and including blindness. It does not include difficulties with sight that can be corrected with the use of spectacles or contact lenses.

Hearing impairment

'Hearing impairment' refers to a continuum of hearing difficulties up to and including total deafness. Common forms of impaired hearing in children are *otitis media* (middle ear infection) and *otitis media* with effusion, sometimes called glue ear, in which sticky fluid collects in the middle ear. Most commonly this is treated by inserting grommets (ventilation tubes) into the tympanic membrane (ear drum) to keep the middle ear ventilated. More serious conditions may require the fitting of hearing aids.

Physical disabilities

Physical disabilities may be the result of accident, illness or congenital factors. These include disabilities affecting the use of limbs, the absence of limbs themselves or damage to the brain controlling nerves and muscles. Under the umbrella of physical disability are conditions such as cystic fibrosis, epilepsy, diabetes, asthma, cerebral palsy, motor neurone disease, muscular dystrophy, spina bifida, Battens disease (a degenerative disease affecting the brain and muscles), Down syndrome and Sotos syndrome (what used to be known as cerebral gigantism). Any chronic condition such as cancer or HIV is defined as a disability, even if the effect has yet to be felt by the person concerned. Facial disfigurement is also defined as a disability.

Medication

Some pupils may require medication to be taken in school. Part of your role may be to administer these medicines. If this is the case:

- it should be written into your job description;
- you should receive appropriate and sufficient training from medical professionals such as the school nurse;
- you should be aware that staff can volunteer to administer medicines, but cannot be required to do so;
- you should understand that, if schools do not allow members of staff to volunteer to administer medicines, they are liable to be practising discrimination (The Disability Rights Commission Code of Practice, 2002).

Categories or types of learning need (SEN)

Global development delay

Children who experience difficulties in every aspect of learning are said to have a 'global developmental delay.' This is subdivided into three areas – moderate learning difficulty (MLD), severe learning difficulty (SLD) and profound and multiple learning difficulty (PMLD):

- *Moderate learning difficulty* – pupils are only able to work at a level significantly below age expectations.
- *Severe learning difficulty* – pupils experience more serious difficulties in all aspects of the curriculum and require a high level of adult support in school and possibly also in life-skills.
- *Profound and multiple learning difficulty* – these pupils' needs are even more severe and complex. They also experience physical or sensory impairments and are likely to have significant communication needs as well. A high level of individual support and personal care will need to be provided for these pupils.

Specific learning difficulties

This term is used to indicate difficulties in learning that are limited in scope rather than general 'across the board' problems. Specific learning difficulties (SpLD) can relate to aspects of literacy, to numeracy or to issues of motor control; they include dyslexia, **dyspraxia** and **dyscalculia**. The common factor between them is that children experiencing them may be functioning at age-appropriate levels or even above age-appropriate levels in aspects of the curriculum not affected by these specific difficulties. However, some children with global delays may also experience specific learning difficulties as well.

The implications of needs for supporting different types of learning activities

The type of support provided for pupils with learning needs will not only be determined by the nature of their difficulty, but also by the learning activities in which they are engaged. In one way or another, all pupils with cognition and learning needs are likely to require support in lessons involving literacy and/or numeracy (see Chapter 7). However, pupils experiencing differing needs are likely to require different provision in other parts of the curriculum.

A pupil with dyspraxia, for instance, may need support and encouragement in aspects of the curriculum such as PE and games or where there is a high level of physical dexterity required such as ICT, art, music or food technology; whereas a pupil with a global developmental delay may actually shine in these subjects and require no support whatsoever. Conversely, the pupil with dyspraxia may be able to contribute extremely effectively in the more aesthetic aspects of the curriculum which focus on emotional literacy such as SEAL (Social and Emotional Aspects of Learning, see page 56), RE (Religious Education) or PSHE (Personal, Social and Health Education) with Citizenship. In these subjects a high proportion of lesson content could well be discussion and verbal interaction. In the same subjects, however, the pupil with global developmental delay may need a lot of support from a TA in order to understand what is being said in the lesson.

Figure 11.1 It is important to remember that all pupils have that 'X Factor'

The 'informal curriculum'

Within school, however, pupils do not just learn through what is presented as the formal curriculum. What could be termed the 'informal curriculum' takes place on the playground, through clubs, social events and as friendships develop or break up and what pupils experience here can have a profound effect on their learning. Many pupils with learning needs require support in these activities. Some need help learning to make and maintain friendships; others need to be taught how to play appropriately with their peers and how to develop an effective response when relationships falter. As a result of their needs, some may experience bullying and this needs to be responded to appropriately. Your role as a TA may therefore involve a lot more than helping pupils read and write in class lessons.

Case study: an unhappy child

Richard is a Year 4 pupil at a large junior school. He is big for his age and can be quite clumsy – although he does not have an official diagnosis of dyspraxia, he shows many of the traits, such as finding it hard to write and to co-ordinate his movements. He cannot yet, for instance, tie shoelaces and he usually buttons his shirt up wrongly when changing back from PE.

In the playground he tries to join in other children's games, but does not really know how to play properly. He usually simply barges in and often knocks into other pupils. They, naturally, get annoyed with him and often tell him to go away. Richard does not really know how to respond to this. Sometimes he will get angry back, but usually he will go into a corner of the playground and simply wander about by himself. He rarely actually cries, but he is obviously unhappy. It is clear he does not understand how to make and maintain friendships or how to react when they go wrong.

How could you as a TA help him?

How to use alternative and augmented communication systems

Alternative and augmented communication systems are strategies and materials designed to minimise the adverse effects of a disability. Whatever actual materials are being used, the teacher or TA should position themselves in such a way that the pupil with sensory or physical impairments can see and hear them without interruption; and they should speak clearly, remembering the visual clues from their body language may not be available to a pupil with a visual impairment. When speaking to the pupil directly the teacher or TA should use the pupil's name first so that he knows he is the one being addressed. Many pupils will benefit from being able to touch and handle concrete materials or artifacts rather than simply see pictures or be told about them.

Visual impairment

Teaching and learning materials for those with visual impairments include:

* enlarged or embossed print – the majority of pupils with visual impairment use print;
* line markers;

- bold, well-contrasted print;
- non-serif fonts of an appropriate size – often N18 or larger: **This is N18 in a non-serif font**;
- 'tactile' resources;
- braille – used by about 4 per cent of pupils with visual impairment (Farrell 2006);
- moon resources;
- PECS (Picture Exchange Communication System);
- audio recordings (tapes or CDs).

The actual resources used will be dependent on the specific needs and circumstances of the pupil. Specialist advice may be needed to decide which would be the most appropriate methods to use:

- *Tactile* resources mean those that involve the sense of touch. When supporting pupils using such resources it is important to remember that, unlike visual information, tactile information is processed in sequence where the pupil gains information about each part and then uses that information to build up a picture of the whole. This means it can take a lot longer for a visually impaired person to gain the knowledge required in a lesson or activity.
- *Moon* is a tactile resource that uses a raised line adaptation of the normal alphabet. While it is not as comprehensive as Braille it is easier to learn and to use and is therefore helpful for pupils with visual impairments who are unable to learn Braille.
- *Braille* uses a 'cell' of six raised dots, combined in different ways to make up letters, punctuation and words. When supporting pupils using Braille it is important to remember that an average Braille reader takes two or three times longer than the average print reader.

Hearing impairments

A range of teaching and learning methods and resources are available to support pupils with hearing impairments:

- lip reading;
- Makaton;
- British Sign Language (BSL) (a language in its own right with its own vocabulary, syntax and grammar but no written form);
- sign-supported English (SSE) (a modified form of BSL that supports the use of spoken English – to that extent it is similar to Makaton, which seeks to support verbal skills with recognised signs and gestures).

Whatever communication method is used with pupils who have hearing impairments, using visual cues is vitally important. This can include using symbols such as those produced by Widgit. Worksheets and texts need to be illustrated where possible.

Television, video or DVDs can be particularly hard for pupils reliant on lip-reading as much of the information may be conveyed through voiceovers, speakers who are not visible or by people speaking quickly. Where this is the case, the availability and use of sub-titles is important.

If the pupils you are supporting use these sorts of communication methods you must become familiar with them yourself. This may necessitate you receiving formal training.

Where specialist equipment, such as hearing aids or radio microphones are used, part of your role will be to train the pupil to take care of them and be increasingly responsible for their use.

Case study: independent use of hearing aids

Theodore is a Year 5 pupil requiring the use of two hearing aids. These are linked to a radio microphone that his teacher wears on a loop around her neck. The hearing aids are tuned in specifically to the radio microphone, which means he is able to hear what the teacher is saying without having any noise around him accentuated as well. The only difficulty is that the hearing aids are very small and they require regular cleaning as he has a discharge in his ears which frequently bungs them up.

Erica is supporting Theodore in class. Part of her role is to show him how to clean his hearing aids and to make sure that he does so on a regular basis. At the start of each day she meets him and the first thing she asks is, 'Have you cleaned your hearing aids?' Theodore does not want to clean them himself and would actually like Erica to do it for him. Erica is very firm and refuses to do for him what he can and should do for himself!

Erica's aim is for Theodore to automatically clean his hearing aids each day without her having to nag him – but this is still some way off.

Whatever the type of specialist communication system used, both you and the pupil are almost certainly going to need the support of advisory services provided by the local authority or local health authority.

Planning for each child/young person's individual requirements in partnership with other colleagues

Some planning will simply be a matter of establishing a routine, for instance, what the response should be for a pupil with diabetes who experiences hypoglycaemia. Other plans involve the deployment of adapted resources to ensure the effective inclusion of pupils, such as enlarged texts and a sloping board for a pupil with a visual impairment.

However, much planning will be more complex, seeking to ensure that educational, medical and social support is co-ordinated effectively. A pupil who requires intensive physiotherapy, for instance, needs to receive this at a time of day when they are most receptive, when privacy can be ensured and when they are not due to receive extra tuition in reading or speaking and listening.

The exact nature of the planning will differ according to age and need. The younger the pupil, the more likelihood there is of the need for detailed planning. For the majority of pupils, as they grow in years, so they are able to grow in independence.

Whenever you are asked to support pupils with significant SEN or disabilities, you must be involved in the planning process for that child or young person. Initially the planning will be a means of support and structure to you. If done well it should give you a framework to enable your support to begin with confidence. As you become more expert in supporting that pupil, so your input to the planning will increase until, in some instances, you become the chief planner.

Case study: planning for a pupil with Down syndrome

Cyril is a pupil with Down syndrome who is entering junior school in two months time. Samantha is going to be the TA providing the main support for him. As part of her preparation she meets with his current teachers, his parents and a specialist support teacher to plan his transition. Three key areas are considered – what Cyril is capable of doing independently, what he can do with some support and what he will need a lot of support with. As a result of this, Samantha knows that Cyril can feed himself, but she may well have to help him get changed for PE and when he has gone to the toilet – for this an Intimate Care Policy will be required as well.

How to make sure what you do is suitable for all the children/young people you work with

As a TA you are likely to be involved with delivering some kind of intervention programme for pupils with SEN and/or disabilities. These are teaching initiatives different from or additional to those that are normally delivered in class.

The types and frequency of interventions provided for pupils will depend upon a number of factors – their type of need, the severity of that need, and the resources and expertise available either within or at the school. Not all interventions require additional adult support, but many do, and it is these we consider here.

Interventions to promote literacy or numeracy skills are likely to share the following characteristics. They will be:

- **Multisensory** – teaching involving the auditory and visual senses and the sense of touch (kinaesthetic); equipment can also relate to a sense of smell or taste, for instance a pupil whose sight is deteriorating may be given different smelling gel pens (strawberry smelling red pens, apple smelling green pens and so on).
- Systematic – teaching following a definite structure and routine.
- Sequential – teaching where one thing follows after another, i.e. the teaching must be given in a certain order.
- Cumulative – teaching in one session builds upon what has been learned in previous sessions; this means that new learning cannot take place until current learning has been mastered.

The steps from one level to another are likely to be small and there is going to be lots of repetition to ensure understanding is gained.

Most intervention programmes are designed with a specific purpose in mind and you must become familiar with it before you start to use it. You need to know what the intervention is designed to do both in order to delivery it properly and to measure its effectiveness; it will be no use delivering a sight–vocabulary programme to pupils and then complaining that their phonic skills have not developed.

Interventions are to be for a specific period of time and must not be allowed to continue indefinitely. If they are achieving their purpose, then the pupils on them will be making progress, possibly catching up on their peers. If progress is not happening, then consideration must be given to changing the programme.

Consistency of delivery is key. The best programme in the world will be ineffective if it is only conducted occasionally. Most programmes are designed to be delivered for short periods of time, three or four times a week. This must be timetabled in and planned for and the planning kept to if pupils are to benefit from the intervention.

It is also important to remember that interventions are not a substitute for good quality class teaching.

Self-assessment activity 11.2: intervention programmes

In the table below make a list of five intervention programmes available in your school. Try to find out enough information to complete each column – you may need to ask your SENCO or other TAs to help you!

Name of intervention programme	Aim of programme	Individual or group programme?	How often should it be delivered?	In what way, if any, it is multisensory?

What specialist aids and equipment are available for the children/young people you work with and how to use these safely

If you are using specialist equipment you must receive thorough training in its use, its storage and its maintenance before you begin to support a pupil. Local authority specialists, health professionals or non-governmental organisations, will often give such training. It is not enough to 'have a go' and try to learn on the job.

The possible impact of having a child or young person with a disability or special educational need within a family

The impact of having a child with a disability or a special educational need upon the family is likely to be variable. Some parents and children will welcome a 'diagnosis' that explains why difficulties are being experienced in school; others will resist it. All will, however, have to cope with the educational and, possibly, the health system, which at times can appear intensely bureaucratic and unwieldy.

Quality of life

It is stating the obvious to say that a long-standing or progressive disability is going to have a profound effect on a child. However, the actual effect is conditional upon a number of factors and will vary from child to child. When supporting a pupil with disabilities you need to take account of these factors and the influence they have on the child's response to the disability.

The child themselves

A child's character and personality will be a large factor in influencing the effect of the condition. Two children with the same disability may respond in very different ways – one resenting it, becoming depressed and giving up on life; the other embracing it as the 'way things are' and living life to the full, making the most of what opportunities there are.

Family support

Where the child is surrounded by a close-knit, supportive and well-informed family, the effect of a disability may be less than where that disability is a source of conflict and tension within the family. The emotional and psychological support provided by loving parents and siblings cannot be overemphasised.

Checklist

✔ I know where to go to get information on special needs and disabilities.

✔ I understand the importance of partnership with parents and families.

✔ I am aware of how inclusion operates in my school.

✔ I am familiar with my role within the inclusive process.

✔ I am familiar with my role with the process of recording used by my school and make use of it.

✔ I understand the need to negotiate support with the pupils themselves.

Further reading

Addy, L. (2003) *How to Understand and Support Children with Dyspraxia*. London: LDA.

Birkett, V. (2003) *How to Support and Teach Children with Special Educational Needs*. London: LDA.

Farrell, M. (2006) *The Effective Teacher's Guide to Autism and Communication Difficulties*. Oxford: Routledge.

Farrell, M. (2006) *The Effective Teacher's Guide to Sensory Impairment and Physical Disability.* Oxford: Routledge.
Lorenz, S. (1998) *Children with Down's Syndrome.* London: David Fulton.
Neanon, C. (2002) *How to Identify and Support Children with Dyslexia.* London: LDA.
O'Regan, F. (2002) *How to Teach and Manage Children with ADHD.* London: LDA.
Portwood, M. (1999) *Developmental Dyspraxia: Identification and intervention: a manual for parents and professionals.* London: David Fulton.
Sherratt, D. (2005) *How to Support and Teach Children on the Autism Spectrum.* London: LDA.
Spooner, W. (2006) *The SEN Handbook for Trainee Teachers, NQTs and Teaching Assistants.* London: David Fulton.

Websites

www.autism.org.uk
www.bdadyslexia.org.uk
www.downsed.org
www.downs-syndrome.org.uk
www.dyslexiaaction.org.uk
www.everychildmatters.gov.uk/deliveringservices/caf
www.nasen.org.uk/
www.opsi.gov.uk/Acts/acts2005/ukpga_20050013_en_1
http://publications.everychildmatters.gov.uk/default.aspx?PageFunction=productdetails&PageMode=publications&ProductId=DfES+0558+2001& (SEN Tool Kit)
www.scope.org.uk
www.teachernet.gov.uk/wholeschool/sen/
www.thechildrenstrust.org.uk/
http://sites.childrenssociety.org.uk/disabilitytoolkit/

◈ Gathering evidence

ᷱ Setting the scene

During the afternoons, Nazreen supports a Year 5 pupil with Down syndrome, Percy. He is registered disabled and has a **statement of special educational need**. His posture is poor due to weak muscle control. He experiences difficulties speaking more than a few words or simple phrases at a time. He speaks at a fast rate as well which at times makes it hard to understand what he is trying to say. He also finds it hard to listen to what others are saying to him without making noises or butting in after a few sentences. Nazreen's NVQ assessor observed her supporting Percy in a history lesson where the focus was finding out about the wives of Henry VIII.

NVQ assessor's observation

Name of NVQ candidate: Nazreen Begum

Name of NVQ assessor: Terrie Cole

12.2 Provide support to help the child to participate in activities and experiences

Date: 18 May

12.2 P1 observe the child in everyday activities, identifying any barriers to participation in activities and experiences

Throughout the lesson I observed Nazreen taking note of the fact that Percy experienced difficulties both in physically participating in some of the activities and in verbally communicating his ideas and comments. In particular I observed the following:
- Nazreen being aware of Percy's difficulties with *physical* aspects of the learning – cutting out pictures and pasting them onto a large display.
- And his *cognitive* aspects – sequencing the wives in order and identifying how each of them was disposed of!

12.2 P2 offer alternative activities if applicable

Although Nazreen supported Percy within the class for the majority of the lesson, on one occasion he was becoming frustrated and started calling out. Nazreen, in agreement with the class teacher, took him out of the class for ten minutes to use the computers in the ICT suite, giving Percy a 'time-out' opportunity to relax and gather his thoughts. At the end of this time they re-entered the classroom and continued with the lesson.

12.2 P3 adapt activities and experiences to enable to child to take part

During the lesson Nazreen provided a number of adaptations for Percy to aid both his understanding and his communication (both written and verbal):
- Using cards with visual signs/symbols on to reinforce instructions such as 'listen' or 'write'.
- Lined paper to help him write.
- Enlarged and simplified worksheets.
- Books containing larger print, simpler vocabulary and more pictures than those used by most of the rest of the class.

12.2 P4 use any specialist aids and equipment as required

Nazreen ensured that Percy was using the specialist equipment provided for him in an appropriate manner:
- Sitting properly on specially constructed chair provided by the occupational therapy service.
- Using a sloping board when he read, wrote or drew.

4.1 P2 Use a considerate and sympathetic approach while paying attention and listening to children and young people
4.1 P3 Allow children/young people to express themselves in their own time, using their own words or alternative communication

Nazreen was very gentle and warm in her approach to Percy and gave Percy her undivided attention. Percy tends to rush his words and consequently other pupils find him difficult to understand. Though Percy had difficulties in making himself understood Nazreen praised him for his efforts.

12.2 P5 adapt the environment, including layout of furniture and accessibility of equipment

Nazreen has adapted the classroom environment so as to give Percy the physical space he needs. In consultation with the class teacher, she placed his seat at the end of one group at a greater distance to other pupils than is usual in the class and near the door so they could make an exit if need be without disrupting the other pupils. Nearby there is a shelf with all his adapted equipment such as communication cards and sloping board. Nazreen can reach this without needing to move far away from Percy.

12.2 P6 encourage children's positive behaviour
(3.4 P5, P6)

Nazreen told me previously that this area is especially important as, at times, Percy's behaviour can be challenging. Experience has shown that his behaviour tends to deteriorate if he is 'sickening' for something such as a cold. During my observation I saw that, as well as quietly taking him out of the class for the ten minutes, she responded to his propensity for calling out throughout the lesson in the following ways:

• Sitting next to him and encouraging him to listen to the teacher and to other pupils by pointing to them and placing her finger on her lips if he was going to call out.
• Refocusing his attention on the speakers whenever it began to wander by pointing to them and using the symbol card for 'listen'.
• Repeating or rephrasing the teacher's questions and asking him to give her his own answers as the rest of the class were thinking.
• Encouraging him to put his hand up and give an answer when he had one, making sure he waited to be asked rather than calling out.
• Encouraging him to speak slowly rather than rush at it so that he can be better understood.
• Encouraging him to ask other pupils to pass the scissors or the glue and not just snatch them.

Question

4 K4 Why is it important to give children sufficient time to express themselves in their own words?

Answer

Percy finds self-expression difficult. You can see he knows what he wants to say but he has problems with getting the sounds out and when he gets excited he speaks too fast. I tell him to go slow so he is understood. Being understood helps him in his social friendships. The worst thing for Percy is for people not to be able to understand what he is saying. He gets so frustrated when that happens.

Terrie Cole
NVQ assessor
18 May

Chapter 12

Unit 14: Support individuals during therapy sessions

This unit contains three elements:

- Prepare and maintain environments, equipment and materials prior to, during and after therapy sessions.
- Support individuals prior to and within therapy sessions.
- Observe and provide feedback on therapy sessions.

Introduction

This chapter relates to supporting individuals during therapy sessions within mainstream schools. TAs supporting individuals in more specialised settings or supporting individuals with complex needs within mainstream schools will need to access more detailed training.

The development of **inclusion** has meant that TAs in mainstream schools are likely to be involved in supporting individual pupils with some form of therapy programme. This can range from providing daily speech and language therapy seeking to help children correctly pronounce sounds and words, through occupational or physiotherapy programmes to strengthen joints and muscles, to leading on behaviour programmes teaching strategies for managing anger.

Whatever the nature of the therapy being provided, you will probably be working directly or indirectly with a professional external to the school such as a **speech and language therapist** or **occupational therapist**. This will necessitate you becoming familiar with their reports, their roles and the terminology they use – all of which can be confusing! However, it is likely that the lead person in your school overseeing and managing these sessions will be the **SENCO** and you can turn to this person for advice and support for yourself. Time will need to be set aside for discussing both the needs of the pupil(s) you are being asked to support and for planning what support is to be delivered, how, when and where.

You should never be asked to conduct therapy sessions of any sort without adequate training – this includes being made aware of the needs of the pupil, the nature and purpose of the therapy, signs to look out for regarding progress and/or lack of progress and even distress, and the means of recording and feeding back information regarding the sessions. The following sections provide an introduction to this sort of training, but, of necessity, do so in a very general way.

Values – legal and organisational requirements on equality, diversity, discrimination and rights

The right to be heard

Providing therapy to children and young people takes place within the context of what is variously termed 'pupil voice', 'student voice' and 'Hear by Right'. Taking account of and valuing the views of the pupils' themselves is a crucial aspect of providing therapy.

'Children should be seen and not heard.' It's been a long time since this was the accepted mantra within society in general and education in particular. But even now it is not necessarily clear as to how children's voices are to be heard. The actual practice varies from school to school. This can be particularly the case for pupils who have **special educational needs** or **disabilities**. How, for instance, should pupils with significant communication difficulties be enabled to make their views and opinions known?

Legislation

The rights of all children and young people are encapsulated in law – internationally through the United Nations Convention on the Rights of the Child (particularly Articles 12 and 19), and in national law and procedure, such as *Every Child Matters* and the Children Act, 2004.

Pupil participation is one of the key principles underlying the **SEN Code of Practice** (DfEE 2001). One of the success factors of SEN provision set out in the Code of Practice relates to children and young people being heard: *those responsible for special educational provision take into account the wishes of the child concerned, in the light of their age and understanding* Paragraph 1:6 (bold type in the original).

The Code of Practice exemplifies areas where pupils' views should be taken into consideration. These include setting targets, contributing to **IEPs**, assessing their needs and discussions about their choice of schools. In practice, it should also include how and when therapy sessions are delivered.

In order to participate effectively, pupils need to be trained and encouraged to say what they really feel. Teachers and parents need to learn how to promote this level of involvement, not least by giving pupils time to talk and **actively listening** to them when they do.

Hear by Right

'Hear by Right' has been developed by The National Youth Agency as a framework to assess how well public and voluntary bodies involve children and young people. It is a means of measuring the levels of pupil participation and serves to indicate ways in which this participation can be increased. The framework is based on what the agency calls the 'Seven S' model:

- shared values
- strategy
- structures
- systems
- staff

Figure 12.1 Pupils need to be listened to

- skills and knowledge
- style of leadership.

Each one of the Seven S's has practical applications that schools can measure themselves against. For instance, under 'shared values', children and young people's participation is seen to be most effective when it is properly resourced, is valued and all have an equal opportunity to get involved.

For more information visit the National Youth Agency website: www.nya.org.uk

Practical outworking

Pupils being supported via therapy sessions will have opinions and views both about their needs and about their therapy. While they should not dictate what happens to them, their views should be listened to. Part of your role as a TA may be to ask them questions about their views and encourage them to speak honestly. Some pupils find therapy sessions either physically painful or emotionally and psychologically embarrassing, but never say anything. In order to support them most effectively these experiences need to be appreciated and understood by those providing the therapy.

The conditions and impairments that the therapy is addressing

Whenever you are asked to provide therapy sessions for individuals or groups of pupils, you will need to be made aware of the specific conditions and impairments being experienced by those pupils. Probably most commonly in mainstream schools these will relate in one way or another to speech and communication difficulties.

Speech and language issues

By the time they start school most children are able to understand 2,500–2,800 words and use 1,800–2,000 words (see Unit 4). They can listen to stories and talk about events in the past and future using organised thoughts. They can use intelligible speech and are beginning to connect ideas together. However, not all children develop in this way.

The reasons why pupils experience difficulties with communication and interaction are many and varied, including:

- speech and language delay;
- language impairments or disorders such as **pragmatic language disorder;**
- specific learning difficulties such as **dyslexia** and **dyspraxia;**
- autistic spectrum condition, including **Asperger's Syndrome;**
- **sensory or physical impairment** including deaf/blindness, deafness and visual impairment;
- moderate, severe or profound learning difficulties.

If you are asked to support pupils experiencing difficulties in communication and interaction, you need to receive appropriate training from speech therapists, specialist teachers coming into school or through courses. 'On the job' training is not sufficient.

Below are some of the more common terminologies used by speech therapists when describing the language development of children.

Expressive language

How the child communicates their own ideas, thoughts, views, etc.

Receptive language

What the child understands from what is spoken to them.

Language delay

Normal speech and language development, but at a slower pace than would be expected.

Language disorder

Uneven speech and language development profile – some aspects may be OK, others not.

Specific language difficulty

Difficulties with only one or two aspects of speech and language development.

Word-finding difficulties

The child finds it hard or even impossible to retrieve words from their memory.

Autistic Spectrum Condition (ASC)

Although by no means all pupils experiencing difficulties with communication and interaction will be on the autistic spectrum or have a pragmatic language disorder, the characteristics of the difficulties experienced by these pupils serve well to illustrate the needs of many pupils.

Those on the autistic spectrum experience what has been called the 'Triad of Impairment' – impairment of social interaction, impairment of communication and impairment of flexibility of thought (imagination).

In social settings problems experienced by these pupils are likely to include:

- not understanding or misunderstanding rules of conversation;
- not knowing how to join a conversation or initiate one;
- difficulties with expressive and receptive language;
- not understanding rhetorical questions;
- talking without making room for anyone else to speak;
- talking to themselves without regard for those around them;
- inappropriate vocabulary and/or accent;
- limited understanding of gesture;
- limited understanding of non-verbal cues, e.g. not realising when someone is angry;
- limited understanding of literal terms;
- rigidity of thought;
- lack of understanding of formal/non-formal situations.

Pupils experiencing these sorts of difficulties will need a totally different approach to someone who knows *how* to communicate effectively but finds it hard to actually do so due to physical or sensory impairment.

Difficulties can result in:

- a vulnerability to suggestions from peers (e.g. getting in with the 'wrong crowd');
- bullying;
- poor peer relationships;
- low self-esteem;
- lack of confidence;
- difficulties in coping with change;
- frequent checking with an adult about what they need to do;
- inappropriate emotional responses.

Difficulties with communication and interaction should not in themselves be seen as evidence of all round learning difficulty. Adults working with children experiencing communication and interaction difficulties can easily have too low an expectation of them. It may be helpful for such pupils to undertake non-verbal assessments to establish their level of academic functioning where language is not an issue.

When you are supporting pupils with communication and interaction difficulties, you need to read their records and discuss their exact needs with the SENCO. It may also help to talk with teachers and TAs who have previously supported the pupils. You need to know the specific difficulties experienced by the pupils as your response will differ according to their needs. A pupil, for instance, who experiences communication difficulties because of a cleft palette, but who is otherwise age-appropriate in his skills, will need a very different type of support to a pupil who is on the autistic spectrum and who communicates with others only by standing right in front of them and shouting.

Self-assessment activity 12.1

See if you can link the terms below with the correct brief descriptions. Be careful – one description does not relate to any of them:

Speech and language delay	difficulties with social communication
	difficulty with all aspects of learning
Language disorder	difficulty with fine or gross motor skills
Dyslexia	normal language development, but slower than most children of a similar age
Dyspraxia	inability to hear within the range of most children which impacts on learning and communication
Autistic Spectrum Condition	
Visual impairment	specific difficulty learning to read and/or spell despite being taught well
	sight problems correctable with glasses
Hearing impairment	development of language patchy, some within normal limits, others below what would be expected for the child's age
Moderate learning difficulty	

Case study: speech and language therapy sessions

Samantha provides a ten-minute speech and language therapy programme to Jonathan, three times a week. He has particular difficulty pronouncing 's', 'sh' and 'f'. For all of these he automatically says 'th'. Each session she chooses from a range of resources, seeking to vary the input so that Jonathan receives a range of support and does not either get bored or discouraged at trying to do the same thing each time. The resources she uses are her own mouth, demonstrating and modelling how to shape the lips and tongue to correctly pronounce the target sounds; a small plastic mirror so Jonathan can view his own mouth shape and compare it with Samantha's; cards with photographs of a correctly shaped mouth for each letter sound; a telephone receiver type instrument that goes from the ear to the mouth of the speaker so they can hear what they actually say; and a pack of photocopied sheets of picture exercises to give practice in pronouncing the target words.

Physical issues

Therapy sessions will not be addressing the causes of any impairment. Your support in these contexts is likely to be more in the line of helping pupils to learn strategies for independent working and of adapting resources. You will be involved in therapy sessions with pupils who would be expected to benefit from their participation in the sessions.

In terms of physical issues this could relate to children with dyspraxia who find it difficult to write, or children with weak posture or muscle control who need to do regular exercise to build their strength.

Case study: physiotherapy sessions to develop fine motor control

Each week Miranda takes a group of four pupils from Year 3 for twenty minutes to help them improve their fine motor control. They all find it hard to hold a pencil properly and consequently their handwriting is very poor. She begins with gross motor movement such as rotating each arm in turn and then trying to rotate one arm clockwise while simultaneously rotating the other anticlockwise. This is to loosen arm muscles, to help the children consciously focus on moving part of their body, and to have fun!

The next part of the session involves a range of exercises such as squeezing open plastic clothes pegs of various sizes and resistance using different fingers with their thumb and then having them roll up a strip of bandage placed on the table with one end under the ball of their hand using each finger at a time. These are examples of 'hand-gym' exercises and are designed to strengthen hand and finger muscles, develop flexibility of finger movement and, again, focus children's concentration on what their bodies are actually doing.

Social, emotional or behavioural issues

Within schools it is quite common for some form of social skills training to be given in the form of group therapy, often led by a TA working under the guidance of a specialist teacher. Children experience a range of challenging emotions and behaviours – some are excessively withdrawn or fearful, others struggle to maintain a sense of worth or self-identify, and yet others strive to maintain external calmness when inside they are angry or resentful. There are a huge number of reasons for such experiences, most of which school cannot alleviate – but therapy sessions within school can help to give children strategies to cope with issues which face them in life.

The benefits and problems that might occur prior to, during and after therapy sessions

The overriding benefit of therapy sessions is the ability to give targeted, specific, individual support to pupils on a regular basis tailored to exactly meet their needs. While much of this may be able to be done at home, undertaking it also in school gives pupils the added benefit of further practice and of knowing that home and school are working together to provide support.

Problems that can occur relating to therapy sessions are sometimes practical – for instance, taking the pupil away from lessons or trying to find a quiet place where the sessions can be done which, at the same time, provides privacy for the pupil but is not overly secluded. Other problems are more psychological, in that the pupil may feel 'singled out' by doing the sessions. Children should participate in the planning and organisation of their therapy sessions in order for these sorts of issues to be minimised.

Self-assessment activity 12.2

1   Outline problems you think a TA might encounter when being asked to provide therapy sessions for a pupil on a regular basis.
2   What types of therapy sessions are provided within your school?
3   What type of therapy sessions are you yourself helping deliver?

The outcomes that therapy sessions aim to achieve for individuals

Therapy sessions are set in place to help children improve in specific ways, for example, to strengthen arm, hand and finger muscles so that they do not become tired when they write for extended periods of time. There should always be an agreed benefit set in place for any therapy session. These benefits could be recorded as targets or as teaching points as in the following example:

Example of a social skills group in Year 5 – teaching conversation skills

A series of six weekly sessions teaching children the following strategies:

• turn-taking;
• listening to others;
• disagreeing with others in a constructive way;
• sharing opinions;
• coping with personal views being disagreed with;
• resolving disagreements.

Part of your role in providing therapy sessions is to monitor pupil progress so that it can be readily seen to what extent these targets are being reached. There is little point continuing with weekly or even daily sessions if no benefit is accruing; however, it can be very difficult to judge progress on a day-to-day basis. You could also have the situation where therapy is being provided not so much to improve a condition, but to prevent it getting any worse or, at any rate, to slow the process of decline down.

An essential aspect of your role is to liaise with other professionals within school and with the experts from outside of school. You should never be left to make your own judgements about how effective a particular therapy is proving to be, but you should be able to accurately report back to these people with evidence of your observations.

The best ways of supporting individuals through therapy sessions

There are two sides to this coin – one is practical, the other is psychological or emotional.

Practical support

Practically speaking, the best way to provide support is to follow the programme set by expert professionals. As a TA your role is to deliver the programme, not to devise it in the first place. This does not mean you mechanically and rigidly keep to a script in an unthinking way. To provide effective support you yourself need to understand what the purpose of the therapy is and to be familiar and secure with how you are to deliver it. You need to be adaptable and resourceful, without being inventive.

Adapting adult language

If you are providing therapy sessions for pupils with communication or interaction difficulties, then you are quite likely to need to adapt the way you would normally speak and converse with children. The following is a list of suggestions which may be of use:

- Ask questions at an appropriate level – responding to 'What's this?' requires fewer language skills than replying to 'The bucket is leaking; how are we going to collect water now?'
- Keep it simple.
- Keep the order of mention the same as the order of action, e.g. 'Go to the shelf and take out the book' rather than 'Take out the book when you get to the shelf'.
- Repeat and/or rephrase.
- Use gesture or sign.
- Chunk information.
- Demonstrate/model.
- Give instructions step by step.
- Use the child's name at the beginning of the spoken language.
- Monitor your own use of language.

Psychological support

Psychologically, a vital aspect of supporting pupils during any kind of therapy is to boost their confidence, **self-image** and sense of well-being, to be a listening ear to them, to create an environment where they feel secure and needed. Therapy can easily degenerate into something which is 'done to' a child, over which they have little say. One aspect of 'best ways' of supporting pupils is to do everything you can to make sure this does not happen. This includes seeking to maintain the pupil's independence, dignity and agency (the ability to make choices and to take responsibility).

Many children experience communication and interaction difficulties as a result of slow processing of information. Their speech is laborious and drawn out. As they seek to verbalise a response to the teacher in class, many of their peers begin to snigger and make comments because it is taking such a long time. Faced with this, the child is going to withdraw into themselves and not want to talk at all. Within a therapy session, an important way to minimise the effect of any such difficulty is to give the child time to speak and to think. All adults working with that child need to be familiar with their difficulties and understand the effort they are putting into speaking.

Conversation skills

Pupils with a visual or hearing impairment may, for different reasons, find it difficult participating in everyday conversations or discussion groups. This will restrict both their social and their emotional development. The pupil with a visual impairment may not be able to pick up on the visual cues given off through the body language of those with whom they are talking. On the other hand, while pupils with a hearing impairment can see what is going on, they may very well only be able to 'tune in' to part of the conversation. Within an individual therapy session, you can help address these specific issues by, for instance, practising strategies to participate in conversations.

Learning difficulties

Some disabilities may lead to moderate or severe learning difficulties. Degenerative conditions are likely to be marked by progressively more complex learning difficulties. Needing to acquire new skills reinforces the fact of the inexorable degeneration which in turn can lead to a reduction in self-esteem and a sense of hopelessness. Therapy sessions can go some way towards alleviating this, for instance by teaching pupils Braille or to use other augmented communication systems (see Chapter 11 for more details).

Handwriting can be a particular issue for pupils with disabilities, even when that disability is not necessarily pronounced. For pupils with low vision, handwriting is likely to be difficult because the pupil cannot easily see what they are writing. Pupils with hearing impairments may find aspects of literacy particularly frustrating, such as learning phonics and decoding skills. All these can be addressed during therapy sessions by, for instance, the use of hand-gym activities which seek to develop the muscles of the arm and hands.

Checklist

✔ I understand the importance of taking the pupils' views into account when delivering therapy sessions.

✔ I am familiar with the reasons why pupils might need therapy.

✔ I appreciate how various disabilities and special needs can impact on pupils' emotional and psychological well-being.

✔ I understand the aims of any therapy sessions I am being asked to provide.

✔ I have been trained to a sufficient level to deliver any required therapy sessions.

✔ I can adapt my support to meet the needs of individual pupils.

Further reading

Speake, J. (2003) *How to Identify and Support Children with Speech and Language Difficulties.* London: LDA.

Websites

www.dcsf.gov.uk/slcnaction/
www.everychildmatters.gov.uk/
http://hbr.nya.org.uk/
www.nas.org.uk/
www.nhs.uk/conditions/physiotherapy/
www.standards.dfes.gov.uk/research/themes/pupil_voice/
www.thechildrenstrust.org.uk/page.asp?section=00010001000300100003&itemTitle=Speech+and +Language+Therapy

Chapter 13

Unit 15: Support children and young people's play

This unit contains four elements:

- Create a range of environments for children and young people's play.
- Offer a range of play opportunities to children and young people.
- Support children and young people's rights and choices in play.
- End play sessions.

This chapter is one of the 'mini-chapters' focusing on key aspects of the unit.

The importance of play in children's and young people's learning and development

The word 'play' means different things in different contexts. We speak of children's 'playtime', of going to the theatre to see 'a play', of 'playing' a musical instrument and of children 'playing up'. In the context of this module, 'play' refers to the activities of children and young people that they willingly and voluntarily engage in as a means of recreation, leisure and pleasure. During play children are in control of their own learning. In terms of theories of learning, play relates to Vygotsky's concept of the 'Zone of Proximal Development' (see pages 33–4) in that children are extending their thinking and activities in keeping with their capacity to develop.

Within mainstream school play could be unsupervised activities such as playing football or skipping during breaks, or supervised activities such as chess or jigsaw clubs at lunchtimes. Play involves some kind of interaction between children and an activity; it is not the same as being entertained through watching television or playing video games.

As a TA in a mainstream school you may be asked to support children in structured or unstructured play. Consider the following scenario. What role do you think a TA could have in helping James develop play skills?

Scenario

It is December. James has just joined a Year 3 class from another part of the country. His home background has been disrupted and he is finding it hard to settle in school. Previous records show that he struggles with the very basics of reading. You have been asked to help him learn the alphabet and you decide that it would help engage him if you used an alphabet jigsaw. However, when you show him the jigsaw it is clear he has never seen one before and does not know what to do with it.

The scope and benefits of play

Play is not a luxury. For children and young people to develop into fully rounded human beings they need to have opportunity to play in a safe and secure, but not restricting, environment. Piaget argues that play is an essential element in developing children's social and language skills (see pages 29–33).

Play helps children develop in a number of ways:

- Emotionally: play engages with the emotions of the child giving them a sense of satisfaction and pleasure, boosting a sense of self-worth and self-identity (see pages 55–6).
- Socially: children learn to agree, share, disagree and resolve disagreements through play.
- Imaginatively: much play involves using and developing the imagination, whether it is using a piece of wood as a sword or creating an imaginary world out of a sheet and some cardboard boxes.
- Communication: play can also promote language development and skills of listening to others and expressing personal viewpoints and preferences.
- Intellectually: play helps children develop flexibility of thought by trying out new ideas and putting ideas together.

But having said this, play, by definition, is something of worth in its own right.

The types of play environment that stimulate children and young people's play and the role that you can play in helping to provide that environment

Clearly play is, or should be, an essential part of the Early Years experience of children. The role-play area, the sand pit and the water trays, the construction toys and the tricycles are part-and-parcel of life for the 4 year old. Some of this will continue into Year 1 and possibly even Year 2, but then it all too often dries up. In the busy life of school, the demands of the curriculum can easily push out a time for play except in the playground.

The following table begins to outline areas where children could be given opportunities to play in school. Some of it has been filled in. Have a go yourself at completing the rest of it, or adding to or changing what is already there.

Year groups	Possible occasion for play	Type of play
1–2 (Key Stage 1)	Wet playtimes Golden time	Free choice using classroom resources
3–6 (Key Stage 2)	Lunchtime clubs After-school activities	
7–9 (Key Stage 3)		Board games Using clay and other art materials
10–11 (Key Stage 4)	Drama Lunchtime activities	Imaginative role-play

Why it is necessary for children's imaginative play to flow freely with minimal adult intervention, while recognising that sometimes sensitive intervention may be necessary to move play along

Possibly the first and overriding issue is to do with choice. To play, children need to be able to choose. They need to be able to direct their own play and to negotiate with others the rules of their games. Exploration is a key aspect of imaginative and social play and if this is stifled due to over-controlling adults, something essential is lost.

However, it is often not possible simply to let children 'get on with it' and you as a TA might be called upon to support play at whatever age the children are, with older ones being given the opportunity to play board games or make up plays for themselves. How might you go about supporting a group of children, say in Year 5 or 6, to organise their own play?

Think about this under the following subheadings and jot down some of your thoughts:

- asking children about their desires and preferences;
- establishing ground rules;
- ensuring safety;
- ensuring all children are included;
- adapting the environment;
- dealing with conflicts.

What problems might you encounter as you seek to support children in their play?

The benefits to children of physical play and exercise and the need for sensitivity in dealing with those who find it more difficult to participate

There is something therapeutic about play. Why is it that children, young people, and even adults if they allowed themselves to do it, derive such pleasure from simply messing around with sand, mud, sticks, wooden bricks, construction kits and so on? What is it about a plastic sphere that makes you want to kick it or throw it?

Figure 13.1 Not all incidents are conducive to play

Consider the following case study and try to work out what is happening for the children involved. Then seek to identify what your role as a TA could have been in this.

Case study: Sam and David

Sam is in Year 3, David is in Year 6. Both get into trouble regularly. Neither can be trusted to be in the playground unsupervised without getting into fights. They are spending lunchtimes in a classroom with a TA. In the classroom are a range of toys and resources. Sam and David decide to play with a construction kit and some magnets. They happily talk together while they are constructing spaceships, tanks, submarines and the like. At the end of the lunchtime they ask if they can come back again tomorrow as they enjoyed it so much.

---

1   What benefits have Sam and David gained from this play activity?
2   What would have turned this from a play activity into an adult-organised activity?
3   What, if anything, would have been gained or lost by turning it into an adult-organised activity?
4   Can you see any lessons here for supporting pupils in general through play?

'Golden time'

Many schools (infant and junior) employ the idea of 'golden time', usually at the end of the school week. This is a period when the children get to choose their activities from a range of options. Activities could include watching DVDs, drawing, listening to music; but they could also include playing games, either inside or out. Sometimes children are allowed to bring in their own games to play; in other schools a bank of resources is available for them to choose from:

1   What benefits do you think this sort of approach brings to the children and to the school?
2   Can you see any dangers or pitfalls?
3   If the school views the golden time merely as a means of rewarding good behaviour and controlling bad behaviour (if pupils misbehave during the week they miss their golden time), can the golden time continue to be seen as 'play'?

How to bring a play session to an end in a way that respects the children and young people's needs and involvement but meets the requirements of your play setting

Almost by definition, play cannot continue forever. Within a school the timetable must be adhered to, lessons must be attended, subjects must be taught, knowledge must be gained and play must end. In reality most children know this and are prepared for it, but younger children and older ones who may have some aspect of learning or social and communication interaction disorder may find it difficult to stop their play. These pupils may become so focused on their activity that it almost becomes an obsession. This requires quite a specialist approach. In general, though, ending play sessions should be straightforward and become part of the learning process for the pupils.

Again, by definition, play is enjoyable – and who wants to stop doing what is enjoyable? Pupils are unlikely to stop by themselves. Your role may include bringing play activities to an end and returning the pupils to ordinary school lessons.

As a TA you can stop the play activity in a number of ways. 'Oi, you lot – stop what you are doing and clear up NOW!' may not be the best way to go about it.

For play to be effective it must be brought to a close in a calm and peaceful manner, not in a way which cuts across the whole concept of the activity and destroys the enjoyment and gain experienced by the pupils. The obvious way to bring it to a close is to have agreed with or stated to the children beforehand how long the play session was to last so that they are prepared for the ending. Children have no problem with the end of playtime; many indeed welcome it, especially if it is cold outside!

Even when ending times have been agreed it is useful to give a warning, such as, 'Guys, in five minutes we are going to need to pack away.' This both prepares the pupils for clearing away and also, particularly for younger children, teaches them concepts of time – they begin to learn what five minutes 'feels' like. It may be necessary to speak to specific children by name to ensure they have heard you and are preparing to respond.

Part of learning to play is to take responsibility for clearing up and storing equipment in a safe and secure way. You can assist children in doing this, insisting that they do all this within the timeframe allowed for the play activity. You do not want to be left at the end of the session with a whole load of sand to sweep up or water to mop up.

Checklist

✔ I understand the importance of play in children's development and learning.

✔ I am aware of the environments in my school which stimulate children's play.

✔ I understand the need to intervene as little as possible in children's play.

✔ I know how to help children who find play difficult.

✔ I am familiar with how to bring play sessions to an end in a way which does not destroy the benefits of the session.

Further reading

Lindon, J. (2001) *Understanding Children's Play*. London: Nelson Thornes.
Moyles, J. (2005) *The Excellence of Play*. London: Open University Press.
Pound, L. (2005) *How Children Learn: From Montessori to Vygotsky – educational theories and approaches made easy*. Salisbury: Step Forward.

Websites

www.literacytrust.org.uk/
www.ncb.org.uk/
www.playscotland.org/pdfs/charter-for-childrens-play.pdf
www.standards.dfes.gov.uk/eyfs/

Chapter 14

Unit 16: Provide displays

This unit contains two elements:

- Set up displays.
- Maintain and dismantle displays.

This chapter is one of the 'mini-chapters' focusing on key aspects of the unit.

Introduction

Display can take many forms – most commonly it is the term used to describe what is put up on classroom or corridor walls, but it could equally refer to a display of historical artefacts or religious symbols 'displayed' on a table. 'Display' refers to any mechanism whereby information is conveyed to members of the school community on a semi-permanent basis.

Display is more than just decoration. It is not something simply in the background of the classroom or school corridor designed to make the building more attractive – wallpaper would do this and with considerable less time and effort. Display is an integral part of teaching and learning in school – or at least it should be. If display is to be this and if you are to be effective in setting up displays, a number of factors need to be considered.

What the purpose and theme of the display is

All displays must have a purpose, and that purpose will determine both the content of the display and the materials used in the display. Some displays are used to convey information, others are there to provide examples or stimulus for pupil work and still others to show pupils' work.

Information can be conveyed via pictures, diagrams, photographs and written comments. Such displays might include pictures of characters and places relating to a particular subject theme.

The following pictures are of displays provided to stimulate pupil learning by giving reminders of what has already been taught in class and which should be taken note of in all writing activities.

The next picture is a work in progress where pupils and teacher each contribute aspects to the display as the lessons progress. This is sometimes referred to as a 'Working Wall'.

Figure 14.1 This display reinforces class and school values, focusing on roles pupils are to take in a project developing collaborative learning

Figure 14.2 Display showing different ways of constructing sentences, reminding pupils of the need to use different connectives

Figure 14.3 Display showing phonic blends and digraphs to aid pupils in their spelling

Figure 14.4 A 'Working Wall' showing initial stimulus for learning

If you are asked to set up a display, you will need to know what the purpose of that display is.

What the organisation's policy is for the display of different material

Whether or not the school in which you work has a written policy for display, it is likely that there will be procedures regarding how displays should be constructed and you will need to comply with these. It may be, for instance, that all pupil work should be 'double mounted', i.e. placed on two sets of coloured card or backing paper to provide an attractive frame for the work. Alternatively, schools may have a policy that pupils' work should be as 'natural' as possible and not want any additional mounting at all.

The important aspect of any display is that it engages with the pupils and that they have some form of ownership over it. If a school is extremely rigid in the type of displays it wants, this could actually stifle children's imaginations and creativity.

Ideally children themselves need to be taught how to cut, mount and display work and other materials. They should be given choices as to what goes on displays and how the display is constructed. School policies or procedures are likely to be encouraging this sort of ownership and learning. Your role could well be to support children who find this sort of fine motor control or creative thinking difficult. In this situation, you will not so much be working on the display yourself as helping pupils with their own displays.

Self-assessment activity 14.1

1   In your school/class – who decides whose work should go up on displays?
2   How would you respond to a pupil who says, 'My work is never put up'?

Where to locate displays for optimum impact and accessibility

There is no point in putting displays where no one can see them. Displays need to be easily visible to every member of the school community. One place where displays are especially effective is in school entrance halls. The first impressions gained of a school are often through their displays. People can tell a lot simply by the visual atmosphere created by displays in the entrance lobby. For instance, if all there are countless sporting cups and medals, you might get the impression the school is highly competitive and focused on winning. Alternatively an entrance hall with a map of the world displayed and small national flags pinned onto the countries where pupils come from may give an indication of the cultural inclusiveness of the school.

Within the classroom, displays need to be at a low enough level to be able to be read and seen by the children. When you are putting up displays you are likely to be restricted to the use of notice boards, but you should still try to place them at an appropriate height.

Figure 14.5 This school is geared to win

How to evaluate the display for its usefulness and attractiveness

Displays should be attractive, but this does not mean sterile. Scruffy displays with bits of curled up paper falling off the end of one drawing pin do not present a particularly helpful picture of the value placed by the school or teacher on pupils' work or engagement with activities. However, displays which show only the very best of work and are kept in pristine condition may not reflect an inclusive and accepting mentality. Similarly, if the same displays are kept up month in, month out, this could say something about the lack of value placed on interacting with pupils through creative art.

Any evaluation of displays must be linked to the purpose of the display, which in turn relates back to the overall ethos of the school.

Whatever the purpose of the display, however, care taken with the backdrop is likely to enhance both the attractiveness and the value of a display. Pieces of work pinned straight onto cork board will not carry the same impact as if the notice board was first backed with coloured paper or fabric and the edges of the board trimmed with matching or contrasting colours. All this takes time, but it is worth it.

What health and safety implications there may be for the display

Putting up displays can be a risky business. They are usually on walls which require standing on tables, ladders or chairs. They entail the use of drawing pins or staple guns. They may involve the movement of large and cumbersome items. All of this is potentially hazardous. When putting up displays you need to be very conscious of this dimension. Before engaging in any such activity you need to check with your school's Health and Safety Officer regarding school policies and procedures. It may be, for instance, that you are not insured if you climb onto tables or chairs in order to reach to the top of a display board.

Sometimes displays become dangerous in that objects mounted on them start to fall off. If this is the case and the display becomes unsafe, you need to know how to respond. Either the display needs to be made safe or it needs to be dismantled.

Whether putting up or dismantling displays, it is important to work on this at times when classrooms and corridors are not busy with moving children and staff. You do not want to be halfway up a ladder and find someone bumping into it.

Figure 14.6
TAs are not
tightrope walkers

How to safely remove the display

Taking a display down can be more hazardous than putting it up in the first place. It can also be done so quickly that pupils' or teachers' work is damaged. Care needs to be taken when removing displays that all work is protected and stored appropriately once down and that all potentially hazardous items such as drawing pins are accounted for and put away safely.

It may well be that you need someone to help you when dismantling displays. Do not be afraid to ask for help or to say that you cannot do it by yourself. You are a TA not a tightrope walker.

Checklist

✔ I understand the purpose and themes of any displays I am asked to work on.
✔ I understand the importance of producing attractive and durable displays.
✔ I appreciate how children value displays that are effective.
✔ I know where displays should be located in the school and classroom.
✔ I know how to safely remove a display.

Further reading

Hodgson, N. (1988) *Classroom Display: Improving the visual environment in schools*. Diss, Norfolk: Tarquin Publications.
Makoff, J. and Duncan, L. (1989) *A World of Display*. London: Belair Publications.
Whiteford, R. and Fitzsimmons, J. (1996) *Hands on Display*. London: Belair Publications.

Websites

www.teachernet.gov.uk/teachingandlearning/library/classroomdisplays/

Chapter 15

Unit 17: Invigilate tests and examinations

This unit contains two elements:

* Prepare to run tests and examinations.
* Implement and maintain invigilation requirements.

This chapter is one of the 'mini-chapters' focusing on key aspects of the unit.

The centre's tests and examinations policy

If you work in a primary school, you are unlikely to have a policy explicitly setting out the procedures for tests and examinations; however, in a large secondary school you will need to familiarise yourself with this policy, or at least with the procedures followed. Policies and procedures are likely to have the same expressed or assumed aims – ensuring fairness of access to tests, making sure no pupil is at an advantage over another, that the rules of any tests are followed, e.g. by allowing only the set time for the test and not giving more or less time than is stipulated, and that cheating is not allowed.

Another aspect of procedure should be to ensure that the manuals of tests and examinations are read and understood. Commercially produced tests and national examinations have been, or should have been, developed to high standards of reliability and validity so that the statistical tables of scores connected with those tests are accurate. Within schools, assessments such as formal tests should only be used in the way they were intended and for the purpose with which they were devised.

Tests and examinations are examples of **summative assessment**. Summative assessment is as its name suggests, a summation of what pupils have learned. It usually takes the form of more formal testing at the end of a topic or unit of work. The most obvious summative assessments experienced by pupils in schools in England over recent years have been the Standard Attainment Tasks (SATs) given at the end of each of Key Stages 1, 2 and 3 and the GCSEs sat at the end of Key Stage 4. These forms of assessment measure pupils against national standards rather than against their own past performance. Summative assessment does not in itself inform planning or further teaching as it takes place once the teaching has come to an end.

An alternative to summative assessment is **formative assessment**. Essentially formative assessment is an ongoing process of finding out how well pupils are learning what is being taught while it is still in the process of being taught. This type of assessment is able to inform the teacher's planning for future lessons. It also provides the opportunity for pupils themselves to see how they are doing and to agree targets for their next steps in learning. Much of formative assessment is likely to be informal, although more formal test results can be used in a formative way. Formative assessment can be used to measure pupil progress against their past performance.

To put it succinctly, summative assessment is assessment *of* learning, whereas formative assessment is **assessment for learning**.

Your role in the test and examination process and how this relates to the role of others

There are two main aspects to invigilation – invigilating internal school tests or examinations, including National Curriculum tests such as SATs, and invigilating national external examinations such as GCSEs. While the former will take place in all schools, the latter applies only to secondary schools.

As a TA, your role may be more supportive in the case of national external examinations than might be the case for internal school tests. Those responsible for invigilating national external examinations will have a job description specific to that role and should have received relevant training. A typical training programme for such invigilators is provided by the National Assessment Agency (www.naa.org.uk).

Whatever type of examination you are helping invigilate, your role may include any or all of the following:

- collecting and distributing examination papers;
- ensuring all papers remain sealed and secure until the appropriate time;
- ensuring that the correct examination papers have been delivered to the venue;
- ensuring that the right candidates have turned up to the right examination, which may require the taking of a register;
- reinforcing the rules of behaviour in the exam situation;
- collecting test papers at the end of the examination in line with the requirements of the setting, e.g. in alphabetical order of pupil surname or related to examination numbering;
- taking the collected papers to the appropriate place or person in a secure way.

Figure 15.1 TAs may be responsible for the secure delivery of test papers

If there is a problem with any of the above you should have been told exactly who to contact and how. In primary schools this is likely to be a teacher or the head teacher, but in secondary schools this could well be the exams officer. If part of the procedure in your setting is contacting the appropriate person by mobile phone, before the examination starts you need to ensure that you have a fully charged phone that is in credit.

What sorts of access arrangements may be required and the implications for invigilation of tests and examinations

It is quite likely that, as a TA, your role may be to invigilate for pupils who have been identified as needing access arrangements such as extra time, having a reader or requiring a scribe. If this is the case you need to be clear about what is and what is not allowed under those arrangements. You can seek the advice of the SENCO or other special needs staff if need be. It may also be useful for you to read for yourself the access arrangements published by the respective examination boards. For instance, for Key Stage 2 SATs, each junior school has a booklet sent to it produced by the National Assessment Agency (NAA) entitled Assessment and Reporting Arrangements for Key Stage 2. If you are working in this context it would be useful to get hold of a copy of this publication.

Most access arrangements can be organised within the school, but some need to be referred to the NAA for prior approval, such as the granting of additional time. If you are invigilating an examination where access arrangements have been agreed, it is vital that you follow those arrangements exactly. The following give an indication of what such arrangements might be:

- A *reader*: this is a person reading large parts of a paper, or indeed an entire paper, to a pupil in a one-to-one situation. A reader should not be reading a paper to a whole class. Readers need to be familiar with the test style of the paper and be aware of what is required by the examination. They should not be related to the pupil they are supporting. An invigilator helping a candidate read the odd word here or there does not constitute a reader. Readers are only to be used for pupils whose reading ability is sufficiently low that this will impair their ability to access the examination. Readers must not be used where the examination is actually a test of reading.

- A *prompter*: this is a person who, following a procedure agreed with the candidate before the examination, seeks to ensure that he or she sustains their concentration and focus. Such prompts could be tapping on the desk in front of the pupil if it is felt they are 'drifting'. Such a support must be normal classroom practice and can only be applied to those pupils who have a clear difficulty in sustaining concentration.

- A *scribe*: this is a person who writes out all or part of a candidate's answer at their dictation. Such support is available to pupils whose writing speed or style impedes their ability to record their knowledge on paper. Scribes may also be used if a pupil has sustained a physical injury that prevents them from writing. The use of a scribe must be documented normal classroom practice.

- *An amanuensis*: if the examination is actually a test of writing, then an amanuensis rather than a scribe must be used. The difference between the two is that an amanuensis can write only exactly what the pupil dictates, so that all punctuation marks, capital letters, paragraph breaks, etc. must be specifically spoken by the candidate. This type of access support is used only rarely.

All access arrangements should be part of the normal classroom experience of the pupil in receipt of such arrangements, which will be evidenced by such documents as IEPs. It is very important that you do not make any decision yourself about granting access arrangements. If there is uncertainty over access arrangements you must contact the person in charge of the examination immediately.

Case study: invigilating using rest breaks

Sadie is invigilating a pupil for Key Stage 2 SATs who requires a rest break part way through. This is normal classroom practice and has been agreed beforehand. The paper requires a time of forty-five minutes. Sadie and the pupil are in a room by themselves, apart from the rest of the year group. She brings the paper, unopened, to the room, gives it to the pupil, reads out the instructions to this pupil, sets the clock and asks him to begin. Twenty-five minutes into the paper, she asks him to stop and take a five minute break. She stops the clock, places the paper in her bag, and she and the pupil walk around the playground for a few minutes, arriving back in the room in time to start up again. She gives the paper back to the pupil, then resets the clock, giving the pupil a further twenty minutes before collecting in his paper. He has finished five minutes after everyone else, but has had no extra time. Sadie's job has been to ensure that the pupil gets the physical break he needs, but does not gain an unfair advantage over his peers. She also has the responsibility of ensuring that this pupil's paper is safely and securely delivered to the head teacher who is collating all the papers of the year group.

The correct procedures for setting up an examination room

If you have a responsibility in this area you may need to do any or all of the following:

- Ensure the seating plan (if needed) is correct and is clearly displayed.
- Where appropriate, ensure the clear display of warning notices, e.g. no talking, no use of calculators, no mobile phones.
- Check all classroom walls are free from displays which may give hints or information to pupils taking the test, taking down or covering up any displays that may aid candidates.
- Ensure the clock is accurate, in working order and visible to all students.
- Check all the required equipment is readily available and in good working order, e.g. calculators, pens.

What stationery and equipment is authorised for use during tests and examinations and your responsibility for arranging supplies

Your setting may have specific regulations regarding equipment that pupils may bring into the examination room, such as transparent pencil cases. You will need to be familiar with what is and what is not authorised and be prepared to enforce those regulations with pupils. If this presents any difficulty, you need to know who to turn to for support and help.

Self-assessment points to consider

1   You are invigilating a Key Stage 3 SATs paper for maths and a pupil puts her hand up part way through. You go to her and she says, 'Miss, I don't understand what this question means?' What should your response be?
2   In a long examination, there is a tendency for invigilators to lose focus themselves. List as many ways as you can think of to prevent this happening to you.
3   During the course of an examination a pupils raises his hand and asks you if he can go to the toilet. How should you respond?
4   You observe a pupil looking furtively at their sleeve and think they may be cheating. What should you do?
5   What should you do if a mobile phone goes off part way through an exam?
6   How would you respond to a candidate who was tapping his pen on the desk and distracting others? You feel he is not aware that he is doing it and it may well be helping him to think.
7   What would you do if the fire alarm went off in the middle of an exam?

Checklist

✔   I understand the procedures for administering tests and examinations in my school.
✔   I appreciate the difference between summative and formative assessment.
✔   I am confident in the role I have in invigilating examinations and tests.
✔   I am familiar with the access arrangements for tests and examinations in my school.
✔   I know how to set up an examination room.
✔   I know what equipment pupils should bring with them into an examination and what equipment they should not and I know how to respond to pupils who seek to breech the rules.

Chapter 16

Putting it all together!

It is amazing how quickly time goes. All the students had almost finished the course and were looking ahead to the summer holidays.

Terrie was having her last tutorial with Nicki Smith who was presenting her evidence for Unit 5, Element 5.2. For this unit she had compiled:

- A self-appraisal.
- An appraisal with her SENCO.
- A Personal Development Plan.
- A diary of training events that she had participated in.

The *self-appraisal and appraisal* covered **P2**, 'Reflect on your practice to identify achievements, strengths and weaknesses.'

On the basis of her self-appraisal and appraisal Nicki wrote her *personal development plan* which covered:

P3 seek and take account of constructive feedback on your performance from competent others;

P4 take an active part in identifying and agreeing personal development objectives; and

P5 undertake agreed development actions conscientiously and within the required time scale.

The diary of training events will provide evidence for **P6** 'Make effective use of the development opportunities available to you'.

The rest of this chapter shows the material Nicki collected.

Self-appraisal form for TAs

Name: Nicki Smith

Position: TA, Secondary School

What I feel have been the key tasks/responsibilities of my job in relation to:

• supporting the school
• supporting the pupils
• supporting my colleagues
• supporting the curriculum.

My key task within the school is to assist the teacher and to support the pupils as required. As I work in a secondary school, I am assigned to a department, in my case, the English Department. I am responsible for students who are on the SEN Register. Most of my time is taken up with students who have statements or who are on School Action Plus. My job is to support these students and to assist them in doing their work. This is not as easy as it sounds as some of the students would like you to do the work for them. However, my role is to encourage them to be involved in their learning and to participate in the learning process as much as they can.

Aspects of my work I'm most pleased with and why

I find working with the pupils most rewarding. It is great when they experience that 'light bulb' moment.

Aspects of my work I would like to improve and why

I know that several pupils who are to begin school (Year 7) next year have been diagnosed with ASC. As I will be supporting these pupils I would benefit from further training.

Things preventing me from working as effectively as I would like

Most of my support is given by the SENCO and the Senior HLTA. Though I talk to individual teachers briefly about their lessons plans and pupil progress, I feel that I would benefit from having more time to discuss such issues with teachers.

Changes I feel would improve my effectiveness

Finishing my NVQ 2 course will help me understand the relevant knowledge and skills that I need to have to be a TA.

My key aims for next year

Attend specialist training on Autistic Spectrum Condition (ASC) and more training on behaviour management.

Training I would like to have

Training on ASC and behaviour management. Perhaps further training on interactive whiteboards would be useful.

How I would like my career to develop

Next year I would like to continue with my NVQ 3 and who knows in time work towards an HLTA.

Signed: N. Smith (TA)   Date 10 June

Appraisal with teaching assistants

Name of TA: Nicki Smith

Name of appraiser: Jamie O'Brien (SENCO)

Date of current appraisal: 10 June

Date of previous appraisal: Not applicable as Nicki began her employment at the beginning of this academic year.

Achievements over the past year with regard to (i.e. what has gone well, what the TA is most pleased with):

Support for the pupil

Nicki relates well to all pupils. Nicki has coped well with students who present with challenging behaviour and has high expectations for all pupils.

Support for the teacher(s)

Nicki is very good at using her initiative. If something needs to be done, Nicki gets on with the task. Nicki's comments on pupil progress are considered and reflective.

Support for the school

Nicki was very involved in preparation for the sixth form school's Christmas pantomime.

Type of training received (with dates)	Summary of what was learned
Sept.: Healthy Eating Session Oct.: Understanding the English Framework	Advice on healthy diets and indicators of eating disorders Knowledge of English Curriculum for Key Stage 3 and 4 (run for TAs by Head of English Department)

Impact on what the TA does

As we have started a Healthy School Initiative the information on healthy diets has been important. Unfortunately, there are a number of students in the school who have eating disorders and it is important that all staff become aware of early indicators.

Areas for development (i.e. what may not have gone so well or what needs to be learned/taken on board):

Support for pupils

It would be advantageous for Nicki to attend training on ASC. There are some sessions on Social Stories coming up that might be very useful.

Support for the teacher(s)

Nicki has expressed an interest in furthering her knowledge regarding behaviour management strategies and the use of Interactive whiteboards

Career aspirations and possibilities

Finish NVQ 2

Targets for the next year

1 Training in autism
2 Training in aspects of behaviour management
3 Training in the use of IWBs

Action to be taken

What action?	By whom?	By when?
Training in autism	SENCO to arrange	ASAP
Training on aspects of behaviour management	SENCO to arrange	
Advanced training on the use of IWBs	SENCO to arrange	

Date for next appraisal   June 2010

Signed: J. O'Brien (appraiser)

TA: N. Smith

Diary of training events (compiled by Nicki Smith)

Date	Event	Witness signature	Witness position
27 Sept.	Healthy eating	J. Harris	County adviser
30 Oct.	English Curriculum	G. Talbot	Head of department
24 Nov	County training day for teaching assistants at professional development centre. On the day we had a chance to meet 60 other TAs from across the county. We had specific workshops on negotiating roles and responsibilities	G. Taylor	County adviser
10 Jan.	Training afternoon with TAs from neighbouring schools.	G. Taylor	County adviser
26 Feb.	Input at college on Assessment for Learning.	D. Wills	College lecturer
17 Mar.	First Steps: training on interactive whiteboards at college.	D. Smith	Trainer

> **Assessor's comments**
>
> Nicki, your self-appraisal and appraisal provide very good evidence for this unit. Your diary of training events clearly shows how you have made effective use of developmental opportunities and support available to you.
>
> What you need to do next is to write up your personal goals for next year. Remember they need to be written in such a way that they can be seen as realistic, achievable, specific, measurable and time-related.
>
> Terrie Cole
> NVQ assessor

My personal development plan: Nicki Smith

After re-reading my self-appraisal and appraisal and reflecting on the comments made, I set myself personal goals to improve my practice as a TA. These goals are specific, measurable, achievable, realistic and time-related.

Goals	What I need to do to meet my goal . . .	I will know that I have reached my goal when . . .	I hope to achieve this goal by . . .
To be more knowledgeable about autism	Attend further training Research topic online	When I begin to feel competent at supporting pupils with autism	May 2010
To develop skills relating to behaviour management	Attend training Go to local library	By feedback from pupils and teachers regarding how I manage episodes of challenging behaviour	May 2010
To finish the NVQ 2 course	Continue to put together my portfolio	I have finished and been awarded an NVQ 2	July hopefully!

The last class – making a difference

Terrie: As this is our last lesson it is time to reflect on how things have gone.

Miranda: Some of the words were really hard: CAF, assimilation, accommodation and Zone of Proximal Development.

Sadie: What about phonological processing, Well I get a headache just thinking about that.

Terrie: These terms are challenging – but has it made a difference knowing what these terms mean?

Nazreen: Now I find I understand what the teachers are saying in the staff room.

Miranda: I used the term Vygotsky Zone of Proximal Development to my teacher the other day and you should have seen how she looked at me. She was really looking at me with new eyes.

Nicki: Knowing these terms has given me a language to talk to the teacher in.

Terrie:	So has this course empowered you?
Miranda:	Finding things out like Piaget's discovery learning and that mistakes are an important part of the learning process – I remember Piaget said that cognitive disequilibrium was unpleasant.
Nicki:	How many times have you practised saying that word?
Miranda:	Anyway – being confused or in a state of cognitive disequilibrium is a motivating force to learn new information. In a sense to learn new information you first have to realise that there is something you don't understand. Well – I have believed in that all my life but now I have a theory to connect my thoughts to.
Sadie:	Talking about cognitive disequilibrium – well I have certainly been confused at times during this course, but it has made me think and I have learned so much.
Nazreen:	My mate says that I don't really need to know all these terms and all this knowledge but I work with students a lot by myself, out in the corridor, in the resource centre and in the learning support unit. So I think that the knowledge that I now have means that I am able to do what I do – better – that I am better able to support teaching and learning.
Terrie:	Now, we are almost finished, but I want to leave you with one last thought. I remember at the beginning of this year we were talking about collecting evidence and what evidence was. Now what did you say Nicki?
Nicki:	Evidence was just writing a good story.
Terrie:	Ok but what do you think now? What I would like to think is that this course is not about writing stories but about changing your story, that is changing your personal story. Have a think about that!

The end!

After much hard work, Miranda, Nicki, Sadie and Nazreen finally finish the course. As they look at each other's portfolios they realise that although there are similar features in their portfolios there are also differences.

As Terrie Cole, their assessor, comments, there is no one right way to put together the evidence for an NVQ 2 in supporting teaching and learning in schools.

When their certificates finally arrived, Miranda, Nicki, Sadie and Nazreen could be seen doing a victory dance.

Figure 16.1
Doing the victory
dance

Chapter 17

Legislation relating to SEN and inclusion in England and Wales

Major education acts

1981 Education Act

- 'Medical model' of need (i.e. there is something 'wrong' with the child) replaced by a more 'social model' (i.e. need is created by inappropriate environments).
- Enshrined the term *special educational need* within educational legislation – covers pupils who would previously have been in special schools and those who would have been in special or 'remedial' classes within mainstream schools.
- Defined 'special educational need' up to the present day. Children have a learning difficulty if they:
  - have a significantly greater difficulty in learning than the majority of children of the same age; or
  - have a disability which prevents or hinders them from making use of educational facilities of a kind generally provided for children of the same age in schools within the area of the local education authority.
- Parents given new rights.

Education policy from this Act on has been to encourage schools to include those pupils who previously would have attended special schools. The implementation of this Act led to a rapid rise in the number of support staff being employed in schools.

1988 Education Reform Act

This Act introduced far-reaching and long-lasting changes for education:

- The National Curriculum – all pupils share the same statutory entitlement to a 'broad balanced curriculum'.
- Local management of schools (LMS) – schools rather than LEAs are responsible for managing funding and for the quality of education for all their pupils.

For the first time it was laid down in law that schools were to provide a common curriculum for all children.

1993 Education Act

Children with special educational needs should – where this is what the parents want – normally be educated at mainstream schools. The act enshrined this principle in law for the first time. However, pupils and their families had to satisfy a series of conditions. The act also set up the SEN tribunal system under which parents could appeal against certain decisions made by the LEA in the statementing process.

1996 Education Act

- Consolidated the Education Act, 1993.
- LEAs have a general duty to educate children who have special educational needs in a mainstream school if that is what parents want.
- The governing body of every maintained school must ensure that:
  - teachers are aware of children's SEN;
  - the necessary provision is made for any pupil who has SEN;
  - children with SEN join in the activities of the school with their peers as far as is 'reasonably practicable'.
- Schools should appoint a SEN governor; however, the responsibility for SEN provision remains with the full governing body as a 'whole-school issue'.
- Governors, with the head teacher, are required under the act to:
  - develop a whole-school policy for SEN;
  - publish it in the school prospectus;
  - inform parents about the success of the policy in the governor's annual report.

2002 Education Act

Schools are required to offer extended services to their local communities. The aim is that, by 2010 all children should have access to a variety of extended services in or through their school in line with the *Every Child Matters* agenda. Children with disabilities and/or special educational needs must be able to access all extended services.

The act also sets out the circumstances in which aspects of teaching roles can be performed by staff other than teachers in line with Workforce Remodelling. This relates to all staff other than teachers and not simply HLTAs.

2005 Education Act

Changes were made to Ofsted – from now on short notice of inspections would be given to schools of an inspection; schools are required to complete a 'Self-Evaluation Form' (SEF) on an ongoing basis as a basis for inspection; and inspections themselves would be shorter (two or three days).

Changes were made to the Teacher Training Agency (TTA) – this now becomes the Training Development Agency (TDA) and is responsible both for the continuing professional development of teachers and of all support staff, including teaching assistants. The syllabus to which this book relates has been developed by the TDA as a direct consequence of this legislation.

School governors are no longer required to produce an annual report for parents nor to hold annual parents' meetings; instead they are to publish an annual 'school profile'.

2006 Education and Inspections Act

This Act enables all schools to become Trust schools. It clarified the role of local authorities, in some areas strengthening this role. It aimed to tighten admissions arrangements so that all pupils get a fair chance to apply to schools. It also put in place new measures to support excluded pupils; established Diplomas for young people in secondary schools; established new standards for nutrition for food being provided in maintained schools; and established a single inspectorate to cover all services provided for children and for life-long learning.

2008 The Education (Special Educational Needs Co-ordinators) (England) Regulations

Governing bodies must ensure that SENCOs meet the following requirements:

- They should be a qualified teacher and working as such in the school.
- An induction period should be completed.
- The governors have a legal responsibility to ensure that the SENCO carries out a range of responsibilities relating to SEN.

Other legislation (in chronological order)

Health and Safety at Work Act (1974)

This is the overarching legislation covering health and safety policies, and all school polices must relate to it. Every school must produce a plan for health and safety to ensure that hazards are assessed and the necessary arrangements are made to avoid or control risks.

Under the Act, it is illegal for a member of staff to take no action if they spot a potential danger. All staff are required by law to ensure that their actions do not put others at risk. This includes tidying up materials and putting things away after use.

The Children Act (1989)

- Enshrines in law the principle that the interest of the child must always be put first.
- Children should be involved in all that happens to them – their views must be ascertained and taken into account by those working with them.
- All staff are required to protect children against risk and danger.
- Regulates child protection matters, particularly how disclosures should be responded to. Members of staff have a legal duty to report any concerns and suspicions.

The Disability Discrimination Act (1995)

- Duty 'not to discriminate against disabled pupils and prospective pupils in the provision of education and associated services in schools, and in respect of admissions and exclusions'.
- Duty to plan for increased accessibility – 'wherever possible disabled people should have the same opportunities as non-disabled people in their access to education'.

- Based upon a social model of disability:

    - recognises difference and diversity within the community;
    - sees the potential problems as within the environment *not* within the person;
    - need to identify *barriers* to be overcome;
    - a disability is only a handicap if the environment makes it so.

Data Protection Act (1998)

The aim of the Data Protection Act is to protect the rights of the individual by ensuring that any information kept is accurate and is protected. This legislation applies to records kept on pupils in schools.

There are eight basic principles to the act:

1   Information must be obtained and processed legally.
2   Data should only be held for specific purposes.
3   Personal data held for a purpose must not be disclosed in a manner incompatible with that purpose.
4   Personal data held should be accurate and not excessive.
5   Personal data should be accurate and up to date.
6   Personal data should not be kept longer than necessary.
7   An individual should have access to their records.
8   Appropriate security measures should protect the data.

Schools need to make individual records available to the appropriate parents as well as pupils; keep attendance and academic records only as long as they are relevant; and ensure that all records are stored securely, whether they be paper records or computerised.

Paper records must be stored in a secure cabinet or area; they must not be left lying around anywhere. Disposal of records must be undertaken with care – shredding is recommended. They must not simply be placed in waste paper baskets.

The Race Relations (Amendment) Act (2000)

Having its origins in the report following the murder of Stephen Lawrence, this act built on the regulations laid down by the Race Relations Act, 1976. It made it incumbent upon all public bodies, including schools, not only to work against racial discrimination and address racial harassment, but to actively promote racial equality and good race relations. This applies to staff, parents and pupils alike.

The Special Educational Needs and Disability Act (SENDA) (2001)

This act states that public bodies (including schools) need to take account of the Disability Discrimination Act (DDA), 1995. In so doing it gave legal 'teeth' to some of the provisions in the revised SEN Code of Practice (2001):

- Schools have a legal obligation not to discriminate against pupils who have disabilities and to make all possible provision for their needs.
- The right to a mainstream education for children with special educational needs is strengthened both for pupils with statements and those without.

- Where parents want a mainstream education for their child everything possible should be done to provide it. Equally where the parents of pupils who have statements want a special school place their wishes should be listened to and taken into account.
- Mainstream education cannot be refused on the grounds that the child's needs cannot be provided for within the mainstream sector.

The Children Act (2004)

This Act provides the legal underpinning for the government's initiative 'Every Child Matters: Change for children' with its 'five outcomes':

- be healthy
- stay safe
- enjoy and achieve
- make a positive contribution
- achieve economic well-being.

Every school must be working towards these five outcomes.

Local authorities are required to ensure the delivery of extended services in or through schools. They are required to create children's services directorates, publish children and young people's plans and to identify a lead member for children's services. They must also take measures to ensure that 'swift and easy referral' to specialist services for those pupils who require such provision is available through all schools by 2010.

The Disability Discrimination Act (2005)

- Adds to DDA 1995 and SENDA 2001, does not supersede them.
- Duty to promote disability equality – the 'general duty' on public bodies.
- Duty on the 'responsible body' (for schools this is the governors) to 'take such steps as it is reasonable to take to ensure that disabled pupils are not placed at a substantial disadvantage'.
- Duty to prepare a Disability Equality Scheme – an action plan detailing the steps that the 'responsible body' will take to fulfil its obligations.

The Equality Act (2006)

This act established the Commission for Equality and Human Rights (CEHR) which replaced the Equal Opportunities Commission, the Commission for Racial Equality and the Disability Rights Commission. Any discrimination by public bodies, including schools, on the grounds of religion or belief or sexual orientation was made unlawful except for certain exemptions. All public authorities have a duty to actively promote equality of opportunity between men and women and to ensure sexual discrimination does not take place.

Chapter 18

National documents and strategies relating to SEN and inclusion

Government documents for England and Wales (in chronological order)

Special Educational Needs: Report of the Committee of Enquiry into the Education of Handicapped Children and Young People (The Warnock Report, Department of Education and Science (DES), 1978)

The Warnock Report is the bedrock upon which all subsequent SEN strategy and legislation has been based. The Report coined the phrase *'special educational need'* (SEN) and established the understanding of a *'continuum of need'*, which required a corresponding *'continuum of provision'*.

At the heart of the Warnock Report was the belief that fundamental distinctions between children in the way they are educated are wrong: *'The purpose of education for all children is the same; the goals are the same'* (DES, 1978, p. 5).

Code of Practice on the Identification and Assessment of Special Educational Needs (Department for Education (DfE), 1994)

This document set the tone for special educational needs provision throughout the country. It was based upon the findings of the Warnock Report and every school had to 'have regard' to it. However, it only related to identification and assessment, it did not say *how* pupils with learning difficulties should be taught or *what* they should be taught, neither did it detail what the learning difficulties might be.

Excellence for All Children: Meeting Special Educational Needs (Department for Education and Employment (DfEE), 1997)

This consultative document was produced by the newly elected Labour government to establish its commitment to inclusion: 'By inclusion we mean not only that pupils with SEN should wherever possible receive their education in mainstream school, but also that they should join fully with their peers in the curriculum and life of the school.'

A Programme for Action: Meeting Special Educational Needs (Department for Education and Employment (DfEE), 1998)

This followed the consultation document *'Excellence for All Children'* and looked at ways of fostering inclusion by considering a range of issues in SEN practice. It led directly to the publication of the revised Code of Practice, which was first issued in draft form in July 2000 and was implemented in January 2001.

Social Inclusion: Pupil Support (DfEE, 1999, Circular 10/99)

This document identified groups of pupils at particular risk of disaffection and social exclusion. For pupils at risk of permanent exclusion, pastoral support programmes (PSPs) are to be set up by the school and relevant agencies, which could include social services, housing, careers services, community and voluntary groups. Educational psychologists and behavioural support teams are likely to be involved.

The National Curriculum (Curriculum 2000) Inclusion Statement (Qualifications and Curriculum Authority (QCA)/Department for Education and Employment (DfEE), 2000)

Curriculum 2000 aimed to provide a more inclusive framework than previous versions of the National Curriculum. In planning and teaching the National Curriculum, teachers are required to have 'due regard' to the following principles:

- Setting appropriate challenges.
- Providing for the diversity of pupils' needs.
- Providing for pupils with SEN.
- Providing support for pupils for whom English is an additional language.

Working with Teaching Assistants: A Good Practice Guide (Department for Education and Employment (DfEE), 2000)

This document was distributed to all schools in the form of a ring binder. Provided mainly for head teachers and managers, it was part of the government's strategy to improve the lot of teaching assistants in schools across the country. However, it also provides valuable information for teaching assistants as it looks at their role in school and gives guidance on how they may best be deployed and managed. It does not, however, deal with issues of pay and grading, explicitly stating that the government believes this is best left for negotiation at the local level. This document fixed the use of the term 'Teaching Assistant' to cover roles that had previously been described by a variety of terms.

Special Educational Needs Code of Practice (Department for Education and Employment (DfEE), 2001)

All schools 'must have regard to' this Code of Practice, which supersedes the Code of Practice of 1994.

For more details see Chapter 1.

Supporting the Target Setting Process (Qualifications and Curriculum Authority/Department for Education and Employment (QCA/DfEE), 2001)

This provides guidance on target-setting for pupils with special educational needs who are working towards Level 1 in the National Curriculum by setting out for English, laths and science finely graded attainments known as the 'P scales' ('performance scales').

Removing Barriers to Achievement: The Government's Strategy for SEN (Department for Education and Skills (DfES), 2004)

This sets out the government's strategy for the education of children with special needs and disabilities. The key areas are early intervention, removing barriers to learning, raising expectations and achievements, and delivering improvements in partnerships.

This document identifies three levels of intervention in terms of 'waves':

- Wave One is normal high-quality teaching.
- Wave Two is additional adult support in small groups which could be in class or outside of class.
- Wave Three is more intensive, often individual, extra adult support to pupils, normally in a withdrawal situation outside of class.

Every Child Matters: Change for Children (Department for Education and Skills (DfES), 2004)

The consultative Green Paper 'Every Child Matters' was published by the government in 2003 alongside the report into the death of Victoria Climbie, seeking to strengthen services preventing the abuse of children. It focused on four themes:

- Supporting families and carers.
- Ensuring appropriate intervention takes place so that vulnerable children do not 'fall through the net'.
- Improving the accountability of all children's services and seeking to promote their inter-working.
- Ensuring that people working with children are valued, rewarded and trained.

Following the consultation, Parliament passed the Children Act, 2004 and published Every Child Matters: Change for children in November 2004.

Every organisation involved with providing services for children is to work together, share information and develop networks so that every child, whatever their background or their circumstances benefits from the Government's stated 'five outcomes':

- be healthy
- stay safe
- enjoy and achieve
- make a positive contribution
- achieve economic well-being.

As part of their strategy to meet these objectives, the government established a Children's Commissioner for England and created Children's Trusts throughout the country. Extended schools and the 'Common Assessment Framework' (CAF) also form part of this strategy. A further expression of ECM came in June 2007 when government reorganisation designed to integrate all services related to children led to the creation of the new Department for Children, Schools and Families (DCSF).

Workforce Reform/The National Agreement (2003)
(www.remodelling.org/remodelling/nationalagreement.aspx)

In order to reduce teacher workload (and thereby improve 'work-life balance') and to raise standards in schools a 'National Agreement' was signed by government, employers and trades unions in January 2003. Under this, routine administration tasks have been removed from teachers and given to support staff and guaranteed professional time for planning, preparation and assessment (PPA) has been introduced.

The National Agreement recognises that support staff have a crucial role to play in Workforce Remodelling and led directly to the establishment of 'Higher Level Teaching Assistants' (HLTA). The government also developed nationwide strategies to improve training and career possibilities for all support staff. The Teacher Training Agency (TTA) became the Training and Development Agency for Schools (TDA) and for the first time included training for support staff as well as teachers. This body oversees the work previously undertaken by the National Remodelling Team.

Working Together to Safeguard Children (Department for Education and Skills (DfES) 2006)

This document is a combination of statutory legislation and guidance. It updates the previous child protection publication of 1999, taking into account new legislation and developments in practice. Essentially, it sets out how organisations such as schools should work together with all children's services to both safeguard children from harm and promote the welfare of all children. It identifies particular vulnerable groups of children, such as asylum seekers and those looked after by local authorities, but its remit is for all children. It is published under the umbrella of *Every Child Matters*.

The National Strategies Inclusion Development Programme (IDP) 2008–2012

In 2008 the government distributed DVDs to all schools relating to the *Inclusion Development Programme (IDP)*. This was the first of a planned series of materials to aid schools in their continuing professional development. The aim is to ensure that all school staff, both teachers and TAs, have a 'Foundation Knowledge' of the major aspects of inclusion. The 2008 DVD dealt with dyslexia and social, communication and interaction difficulties. Following DVDs will consider behavioural needs, autism, moderate learning difficulties and the like.

Appendix

Photocopiable resources

ROLES AND RESPONSIBILITIES RELATING TO BEHAVIOUR

Routine	School and class rules:	Role and responsibility of yourselves and others			
	Pupils are expected to	I (the TA) will intervene when	I (the TA) can use these strategies	I (the TA) will inform the teacher if	The teacher will
In the playground					
Standing outside in the corridor waiting to come into class					
Beginning of the day					
Where to sit					
When wishing to participate in class					
When requesting help					
Going into assembly					
Walking in corridors					
Using ICT equipment					

ROLES AND RESPONSIBILITIES RELATING TO BEHAVIOUR (continued)

The sorts of problems that might occur when supporting learning activities and how to deal with these	Possible explanations and strategies that can be used to support learning
Pupils may find the task too difficult.	
Pupils say that they are bored and they don't want to do the task.	
Pupils who always ask me to do the work for them.	
Pupils who find it difficult to pay attention.	
Pupils who always want to have things their way.	
Pupils who feel they are not as good as other pupils.	
Pupils who make fun of other pupils that are struggling with their work.	
Pupils who refuse to do what I ask them.	
When working with groups one pupil may not want to join in.	
Even when the group is set by abilities there still may be a range of abilities within the group. How do I meet every pupil's needs?	
When working with groups one pupil always wants to dominate the group!	
When playing a game there is one pupil who always wants to go first.	
When playing a game there is always one pupil who finds it hard to lose.	

ANYWHERE PRIMARY SCHOOL INDIVIDUAL EDUCATION PLAN

Name:	Date of birth:
Class/year:	IEP no:
Male/female:	Stage:
EAL: Y/N	First drawn up:

Summary of concern:	
Medical condition:	External agencies:
Review dates:	Present:
Comments:	Actions:

Targets	Success criteria	Possible resources	Possible strategies	Outcomes
Start date:				Date:
1				
2				
3				

ANYWHERE PRIMARY SCHOOL INDIVIDUAL EDUCATION PLAN (continued)

ASSESSMENT RESULTS, PROVISION AND EXTERNAL AGENCY COMMENTS	NOTES/PARENTAL CONTACT
Screening tests (name of assessment):	
Reading (name and date of test):	
Spelling (name and date of test):	
Maths (name and date of test):	
Provision	
External agencies	

A Teaching Assistant's Guide to Completing NVQ Level 2, 2nd edn, Routledge
© Susan Bentham and Roger Hutchins 2010

EXAMPLE OF IEP TARGETS

Targets Start date:	Success criteria	Possible resources	Possible strategies	Outcomes Date:
1 To read and spell words with the long vowel phonemes *ai/ ee/ ea/ oo*	Pupil reads and spells a selection of these word accurately on five occasions	Plastic letters, worksheets, phonic books and CDs, phonic cards	Play games such as pairs, complete worksheets, listen to pupil read and focus on these phonic patterns	
2 To use the above spelling rules in own writing	Pupil uses spelling rules being worked on in five pieces of independent writing	Spelling banks, prompt cards	Make sure pupil understands the spelling rules, talk through written work with pupil focusing on the rule	
3 To listen to and follow instructions that have been given by an adult to the whole class	Over a period of one week 75% of instructions are followed within one minute of them being given	Target sheet, behaviour star chart, reward stickers	Make sure expectations of this behaviour are clearly understood and that pupil is aware of this target. Praise when achieved. Remind when missed	

ANYWHERE PRIMARY SCHOOL INDIVIDUAL BEHAVIOUR PLAN

SECTION I

Name of pupil: _____   D.O.B.: _____

Class teacher: _____   NC year: _____

Name of Parent(s)/Carer(s): _____

Nominated person responsible for operating the plan: _____

Start date of plan, as agreed with parents and pupil: _____

Review dates:

• mid point: _____

• end: _____

External agencies (where applicable): _____

Persons contributing to the plan:

Name	Contact no./address

ANYWHERE PRIMARY SCHOOL INDIVIDUAL BEHAVIOUR PLAN (continued)
SECTION 2

Approaches/behaviour causing concern

1

2

3

Pupil's strengths

Desirable alternative behaviours (long-term goals)

1

2

3

Short-term targets	Success criteria
1	1
2	2
3	3

ANYWHERE PRIMARY SCHOOL INDIVIDUAL BEHAVIOUR PLAN (continued)

SECTION 3

Strategies to support pupil

-
-
-

Special arrangements to be made

-
-
-

Support to be offered to help the pupil

Home:

Other agencies:

Rewards:

Home:

School:

Agreed consequences

-
-
-

ANYWHERE PRIMARY SCHOOL INDIVIDUAL BEHAVIOUR PLAN *(continued)*
SECTION 4

Review arrangements

Distribution list

_____

_____

_____

Form completed by

Name: _____

Designation: _____

Signature: _____

CONFIDENTIAL: for monitoring purposes only

Number of fixed term exclusions this academic year and total days: _____

Is the child on the Child Protection Register? YES/NO

Is the child in public care? YES/NO

If YES:

Accommodated by Local Authority? YES/NO

Subject of an interim or full care order? YES/NO

Subject of a supervision order? YES/NO

Ethnic origin: _____

First language: _____

ANYWHERE PRIMARY SCHOOL INDIVIDUAL BEHAVIOUR PLAN REVIEW MEETING

Name of pupil: _____ DOB: _____

Class: _____ NC year: _____

Name of parent(s)/carer(s): _____

Date of initial behaviour plan: _____ Review no: _____

Date of review meeting: _____ Time: _____

Venue:

Attended by:

Apologies from:

Summary of progress since the last meeting:

Agreed action:

1

2

3

Arrangements for next review meeting: _____ at _____ in school

Agreed circulation for this review form: _____

TEMPLATE FOR SELF-APPRAISAL FOR TEACHING ASSISTANTS

Name: _____

Position: _____

What I feel have been the key tasks/ responsibilities of my job in relation to: • supporting the school • supporting the pupils • supporting my colleagues • supporting the curriculum.	
Aspects of my work I'm most pleased with and why	
Aspects of my work I would like to improve and why	
Things preventing me working as effectively as I would like	
Changes I feel would improve my effectiveness	
My key aims for next year	
Training I would like to have	
How I would like my career to develop	

Signed _____ Date _____

TEMPLATE FOR APPRAISAL WITH TEACHING ASSISTANTS

Name of TA: _____

Name of appraiser: _____

Date of current appraisal: _____

Date of previous appraisal (where applicable): _____

Targets set at last appraisal (where applicable)	Outcomes
1	1
2	2
3	3

Achievements over the past year with regard to:
(i.e. what has gone well, what the TA is most pleased with)

• Support for pupils

• Support for the teacher(s)

• Support for the school

Training received by the TA over the past year

• Type of training received (with dates)	• Summary of what was learned
• Impact on what the TA does	• Further considerations

TEMPLATE FOR APPRAISAL WITH TEACHING ASSISTANTS (continued)

Areas for development:
(i.e. what may not have gone so well or what needs to be learned/taken on board)

- Support for pupils

- Support for the school

- Support for the teacher(s)

- Career aspirations and possibilities

Targets for the next year

1

2

3

Action to be taken

What action?	By whom?	By when?
1		
2		
3		

Date for next appraisal

Signed:

TA: _____

Appraiser: _____

RISK ASSESSMENT AND RISK MANAGEMENT FORM – EDUCATIONAL VISITS

Location of the visit:	Purpose of visit:
Group on the visit:	Leader:
Other accompanying adults:	
Group size:	Adult–pupil ratio:

Identifying and assessing risks	*What to do to reduce the risk*
Location of visit	
Risk rating	Reduced risk level
Risk rating	Reduced risk level
Risk to group as a whole	
Risk rating	Reduced risk level
Risk to individual pupils	
Risk level	Reduced risk level

 **PHOTOCOPIABLE RESOURCE**

SCHOOL ACCIDENT/INCIDENT LOG

Date of accident/incident: Time of accident/incident:

Location of accident/incident:

Nature of accident/incident:

Name and title of person dealing with the accident/incident:

Name and title of person completing this log:

Other person(s) involved including their roles/responsibilities:

Any follow up required:

Description of the accident/incident

Response to the accident/incident

Signature of person completing this form: _____

Date signed: _____

Reasons for any delay in completing this form: _____

_____

ANYWHERE PRIMARY SCHOOL SAFEGUARDING CHILDREN REPORT

NAME OF ADULT REFERRING:

NAME OF PUPIL:

DATE OF BIRTH OF PUPIL:

DATE: LOCATION:

NATURE OF CONCERN:

REASONS FOR CONCERN (give details of why you are referring to the DOSC, where possible use the actual words spoken by the pupil):

RECORDS COMPLETED (date and time):

SKIN MAP COMPLETED: Y/N

REPORTED TO DESIGNATED SENIOR PERSON (date and time):

REASON FOR ANY DELAY:

Signed: _____

SKIN MAP

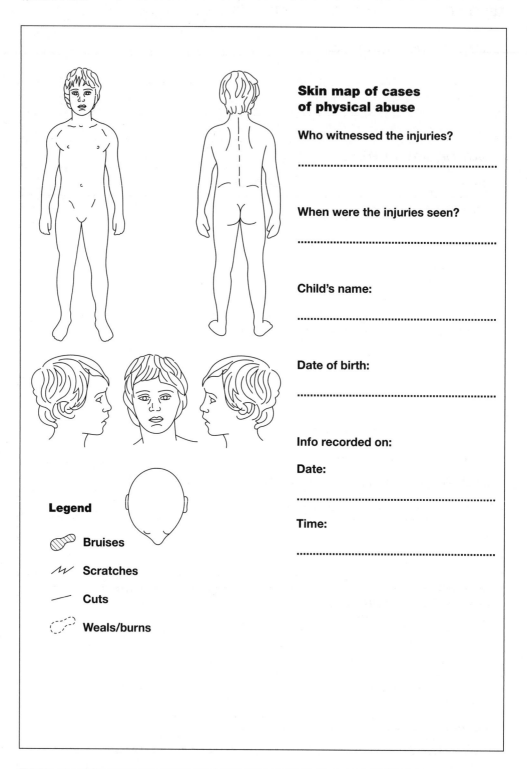

**Skin map of cases
of physical abuse**

Who witnessed the injuries?

....

When were the injuries seen?

....

Child's name:

....

Date of birth:

....

Info recorded on:

Date:

....

Time:

....

Legend

Bruises

Scratches

Cuts

Weals/burns

PARENT CONFERENCE FORM FOR NEWLY ARRIVED FAMILIES WHO HAVE ENGLISH AS AN ADDITIONAL LANGUAGE

Name of school	
Date of meeting	
People present	
Name of pupil	
Name to be called in school	
Date of birth	
Year group and class in school	
Class teacher	
Place of pupil's birth	
Countries lived in by the pupil (with dates where known)	
Date of arrival in UK	
First/home language	
Previous educational experiences	
Name of father	
Country of origin	
Mother's name	
Country of origin	
Siblings (names, ages, schools)	
Religion	
Dietary requirements	
First language classes attended (either current or past)	
Extended stays (if appropriate)	
Any other relevant information, including medical	
Refugee or asylum seeker background?	

EXAMPLE OF FIRST LANGUAGE ASSESSMENT AND EAL
(adapted from a local authority's form)

Pupil name	
Date of birth	
Year group	
Initial assessment completed on	

Speaking	English	L1
Silent period		
Offers and responds to greetings		
Responds to verbal questions with one-word answers		
Responds to verbal questions with two to three word phrases		
Responds to verbal questions with complete sentences		
Answers requests for personal information		
Can name:		
Colours		
School items		
Clothes		
Food		
Body parts		
Household items		
Types of transport		
Animals		
Names items on a picture		
Describes items on a picture		
Talks about what is happening in a picture		
Initiates talk to ask for support with a task		
Initiates talk to tell someone about an event		

Contributes to a group discussion		
Contribute to a class discussion		
Retells a simple story		
Retells a more complex story using a broad range of vocabulary		

Listening/comprehension	English	L1
Listens attentively for short periods		
Listens attentively for extended periods		
Follows class and school routines with support from peers		
Follows class and school routines with support from adults		
Follows class and school routines independently		
Responds to simple instructions with support from peers		
Responds to simple instructions with support from adults		
Responds to simple instructions independently		
Responds to more complex instructions with support from peers		
Responds to more complex instructions with support from adults		
Responds to more complex instructions independently		
Responds to closed questions with nod/shake of head		
Points to items after being described verbally to the pupil		
Can follow a one-to-one conversation		
Can follow a conversation in a small group context		
Can follow a conversation/discussion in a whole class context		

Reading	English	L1
Has no knowledge of a written alphabet (or characters)		
Can read/say the names of some letters of the alphabet (or characters)		
Can read/say the names of most/all letters of the alphabet (or characters)		
Can say the sounds of some letters of the alphabet		

Can say the sounds of most/all letters of the alphabet		
Can read own name		
Can read basic words, e.g. cvc words (in English)		
Can understand basic words		
Can read the high frequency words for Year R		
Can understand the high frequency words for Year R		
Can read the high frequency words for Year 1/2		
Can understand the high frequency words for Year 1/2		
Can read simple stories or other texts		
Can understand simple stories or other texts		
Can read complex stories or other texts		
Can understand complex stories or other texts		

Writing	English	L1
Has no knowledge of a writing system		
Can use marks/emergent writing		
Can copy letters (or simple characters)		
Can copy words (or characters)		
Can write on the line		
Can write left to right on the line		
Can write top to bottom on the page		
Can write initial letter of own name		
Can write own name		
Can write some letters of the alphabet (or characters)		
Can write most/all letters of the alphabet (or characters)		
Can write simple words (or characters)		
Can write harder words (or characters)		
Can write simple sentences with basic punctuation		
Can write complex sentences with accurate punctuation		
Can write a simple narrative or recount		

Bibliography

All-Party Parliamentary Group on Scientific Research in Learning and Education (APPG) (2007) *Well-being in the Classroom*. Oxford: The Institute for the Future of the Mind.

Aronson, E. and Patnoe, S. (1997) *The Jigsaw Classroom: Building cooperation in the classroom* (2nd edn). New York: Addison Wesley Longman.

Assessment Reform Group (2002) *Assessment for Learning: 10 principles*. Obtainable from the ARG website: www.assessment-reform-group.org and from the CPA office of the Institute of Education, University of London.

Bandura, A. (1977) *Social Learning Theory*. Morristown, NJ: General Learning Press.

—— (1986) *Social Foundations of Thought and Action: A social cognitive theory*. Englewood Cliffs, NJ: Prentice-Hall.

Child Development (2005) (online) available from www.cdc.gov/ncbddd/child/middlechildhood. htm (accessed 16 December 2008).

—— (2009) (online) available from www.allthedaze.com (accessed 10 October 2008).

Children and Young People's Unit (2002) *Learning to Listen: Core principles for the involvement of children and young people*. London: DfES.

Chivers, J. (1995) *Team-building with Teachers*. London: Kogan Page.

Cole, M. and Cole, S. (2001) *The Development of Children*. New York: Worth.

Communication and Your Child (2008) AMA Medical Library (online) available from www. medem.com/medlib (accessed 5 January 2009).

Cremin, H., Thomas, G. and Vincent, K. (2005) 'Working with teaching assistants: three models evaluated', *Research Papers in Education*, 20(4): 413–32.

Dennison, B. and Kirk, R. (1990) *Do, Review, Learn, Apply: A simple guide to experimental learning*. London: Blackwell.

Department for Education (DfE) (1994) *Code of Practice on the Identification and Assessment of Special Educational Needs*. London: HMSO.

Department for Education and Employment (DfEE) (1997) *Excellence for All Children: Meeting special educational needs*. London: HMSO.

—— (1998) *A Programme for Action: Meeting special educational needs*. London: HMSO.

—— (1999, Circular 10/99) *Social Inclusion: Pupil support*. London: HMSO.

—— (2000) *The National Curriculum*. London: HMSO.

(DfEE) (2000) *Working with Teaching Assistants: A good practice guide*. London, DfEE Publications.

—— (DfEE) (2001) *Special Educational Needs Code of Practice*. London: HMSO.

Department for Education and Science (DES) (1978) *Special Educational Needs: Report of the committee of enquiry into the education of handicapped children and young people (The Warnock Report)*. London: HMSO.

Department for Education and Skills (DfES) (2003) *Data Collection by Type of Special Educational Needs*. London: HMSO.

—— (2004a) *Every Child Matters: Change for children*. Nottingham: DfES Publications, www. everychildmatters.gov.uk.

—— (2004b) *Removing Barriers to Achievement: The government's strategy for SEN*. Nottingham: DfES Publications.

—— (2005) *Excellence and Enjoyment: Social and emotional aspects of learning (SEAL)*. London: HMSO.

—— (2006) *Independent Review of the Teaching of Early Reading (The Rose Report)*. London: HMSO.

Edwards, C. P. and Springate, K. W. (1995) *Encouraging Creativity in Early Childhood Classrooms* (ERIC Digest). Urbana, IL: ERIC Clearinghouse on Elementary and Early Childhood Education (ED389474).

Gardner, H. (1993) *Frames of Mind*. New York: Basic Books.

Jolivette, K., Stichter, J., Sibilsky, S., Scott, T. M. and Ridgley, R. (2002) 'Naturally occurring opportunities for preschool children with or without disabilities to make choices', *Education and Treatment of Children*, 25(9): 396–414.

Liron, P. (2003) *NVQ Assessment to the A1 Standards*. Camberley: Piers Liron.

Lorenz, S. (2002) *First Steps in Inclusion*. London: David Fulton.

Mellou, E. (1996) 'Can creativity be nurtured in young children?', *Early Child Development and Care*, 119: 119–30.

McCormick, S. (1999) *Instructing Students who have Literacy Problems* (3rd edn). Englewood Cliffs, NJ: Merrill.

National Curriculum (2008) (online) available from: www.nc.uk.net (accessed 29 January 2008).

National Curriculum in Action (2008) (online) available from: www.ncaction.or.uk/subjects/science/levels.htm (accessed 22 January 2008).

National Joint Council for Local Government Services (2003) *School Support Staff: The way forward*. London: The Employers Organisation, www.lge.gov.uk.

National Remodelling Team (2003) *Raising Standards and Tackling Workload: A national agreement*. London: HMSO.

Piaget, J. (1970) *The Science Of Education and the Psychology of the Child*. New York: Viking Press.

Qualifications and Curriculum Authority (QCA) (2000) *A Language in Common*. Sudbury: QCA Publications.

—— (2006) *NVQ Code of Practice*. London: QCA Publications.

Qualifications and Curriculum Authority/Department for Education and Employment (QCA/DfEE) (2000) *The National Curriculum (Curriculum 2000) Inclusion Statement*. London: HMSO.

—— (2001) *Supporting the Target Setting Process*. London: HMSO.

Rogers, B. (1995) *Behaviour Management: A whole-school approach*. London: Paul Chapman.

—— (1998) *You Know the Fair Rule and Much More: Strategies for making the hard job of discipline and behaviour management in school easier*. London: Pitman Press.

Santrock, J. W. (2008) *Educational Psychology*. New York: McGraw-Hill Education.

Sanacore, J. (1999) 'Encouraging children to make choices about their literacy learning', *Intervention in School & Clinic*, 35(1): 38–43.

Sharp, C. (2004) 'Developing young children's creativity: what can we learn from research?', *Topic*, 32: 5–12.

Sigelman, C. K. and Shaffer, D. F. (1991) *Life-span Human Development*. Belmont, CA: Brooks/Cole.

Smith, R. (2002) *Creating the Effective Primary School*. London: Kogan Page.

Training Development Agency (TDA) (2006) *Developing People to Support Learning: A skills strategy for the wider school workforce 2006–2009*. Online. Available from: www.tda.gov.uk/about/publicationslisting/TDA0160.aspx (accessed August 2009).

Training and Development Agency for Schools (2006) *Primary Induction for Teaching Assistant Trainers: Inclusion*. London: TDA.

—— (2007) *National Occupational Standards in Supporting Teaching and Learning in Schools*.

Tuckman, B. and Jensen, N. (1977) 'Stages of small group development revisited'. *Group and Organizational Studies*, 2: 419–27.

Vygotsky, L. S. (1986) *Thought and Language* (new edn), ed. A. Kozulin. Cambridge, MA: MIT Press.

Zimmerman, B.J. (2000) 'Self-efficacy: An essential motive to learn', *Contemporary Educational Psychology*, 25: 82–91.

Index